IMAGES
of America

ROCHESTER

IMAGES
of America

ROCHESTER

Florence Horne Smith

ARCADIA
PUBLISHING

ISBN 978-0-7385-8976-3

Published by Arcadia Publishing
Charleston, South Carolina

Printed in the United States of America

For all general information contact Arcadia Publishing at:
Telephone 843-853-2070
Fax 843-853-0044
E-mail sales@arcadiapublishing.com
For customer service and orders:
Toll-Free 1-888-313-2665

Visit us on the Internet at www.arcadiapublishing.com

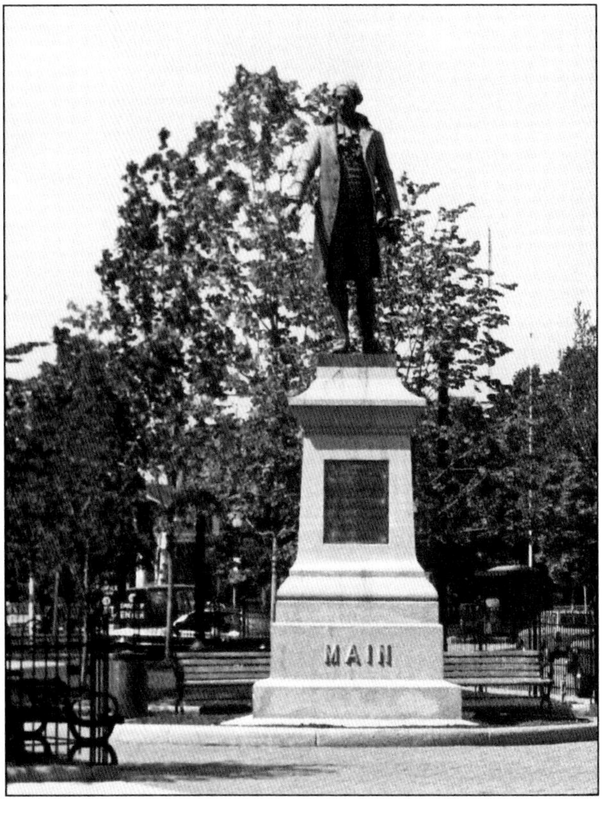

THE PARSON MAIN MONUMENT. The monument on Central Square was erected in honor of Parson Amos Main, the first settled minister of Rochester. The statue was designed by local artist Wilbur Duntley and financed by voluntary donations. On July 3, 1896, most of the eight thousand residents of Rochester, joined by visitors from neighboring towns and cities, assembled in Central Square for the dedication.

Contents

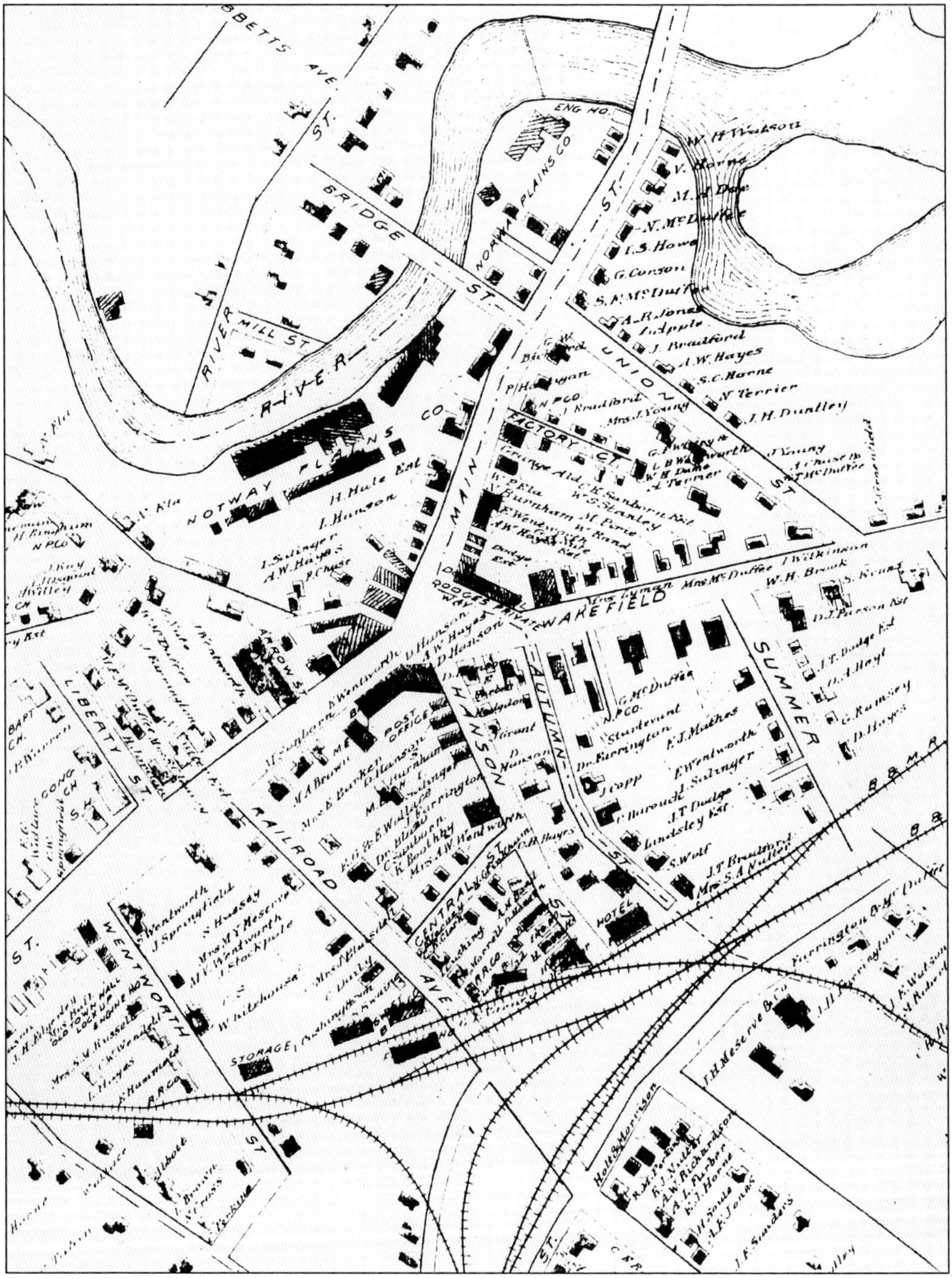

AN 1892 MAP OF ROCHESTER

Introduction

During the latter part of the nineteenth century, Rochester, New Hampshire, was changing from a farming community to an industrial town. The coming of rail travel to the area in 1849 accelerated this change by expanding markets for local goods as well as making raw materials more accessible. People left the farms and moved to town to work in the factories that sprang up all around the railroad center. It isn't surprising that the area around Union Station became known as "Mechanic's Square."

The earliest images in this book coincide with the development of early photography after the Civil War. Some of the old buildings can only be remembered through photographs, with many structures lost to all too common fires and still others sacrificed in the name of progress.

Railroad use declined after World War II, when the automobile became decidedly more popular. Manufacturing and retail industries in the area prospered due to a newfound sense of individualism and mobility. The number of automobiles registered in Rochester in 1930 was 3,090; in 1995 nearly 40,000 motor vehicles were registered.

These images of our past are presented to give residents an opportunity to envision times gone by. Some will remember how it was and others will learn how it used to be, but we hope that all will enjoy.

Acknowledgments

We appreciate the contribution of those who over the years assembled the photographs in the collection of the Rochester Historical Society and wish to thank those who loaned us pictures to use in this book.

Thanks go to the staff of volunteers at the Rochester Historical Museum: Gloria Pelletier, Edward and Shirley Leslie, Mary Harding, and Roger Tremblay, for all their help.

Special thanks to Florence Chasse, who spent hours assisting with the layout of photographs.

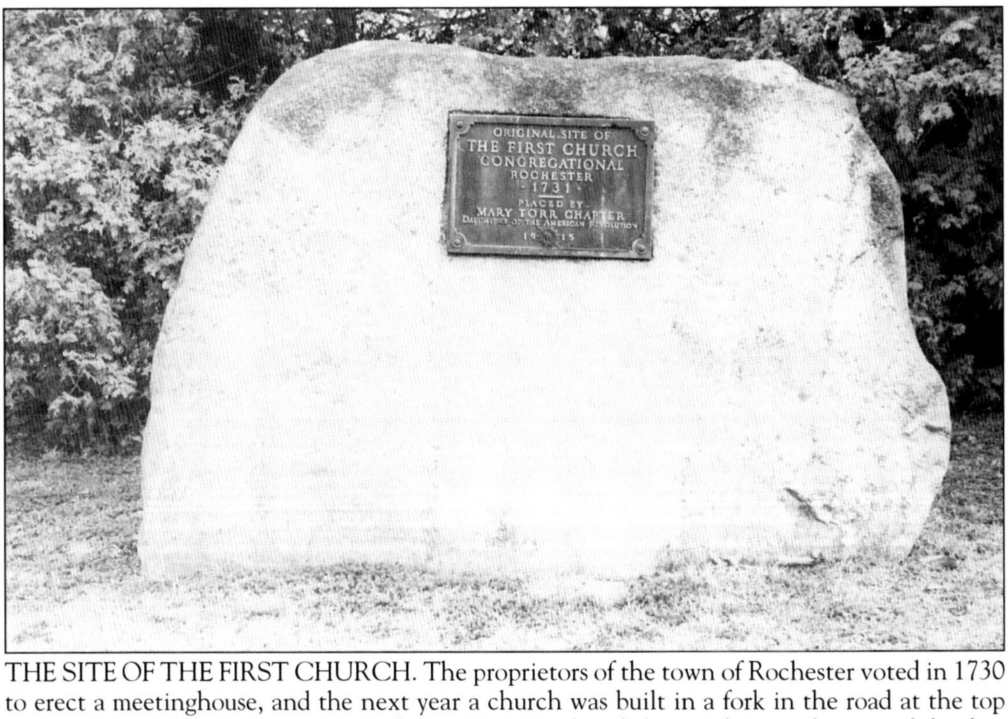

THE SITE OF THE FIRST CHURCH. The proprietors of the town of Rochester voted in 1730 to erect a meetinghouse, and the next year a church was built in a fork in the road at the top of Rochester Hill. The Mary Torr Chapter D.A.R. placed this marker on the site of the first church in 1915.

One

Around Central Square

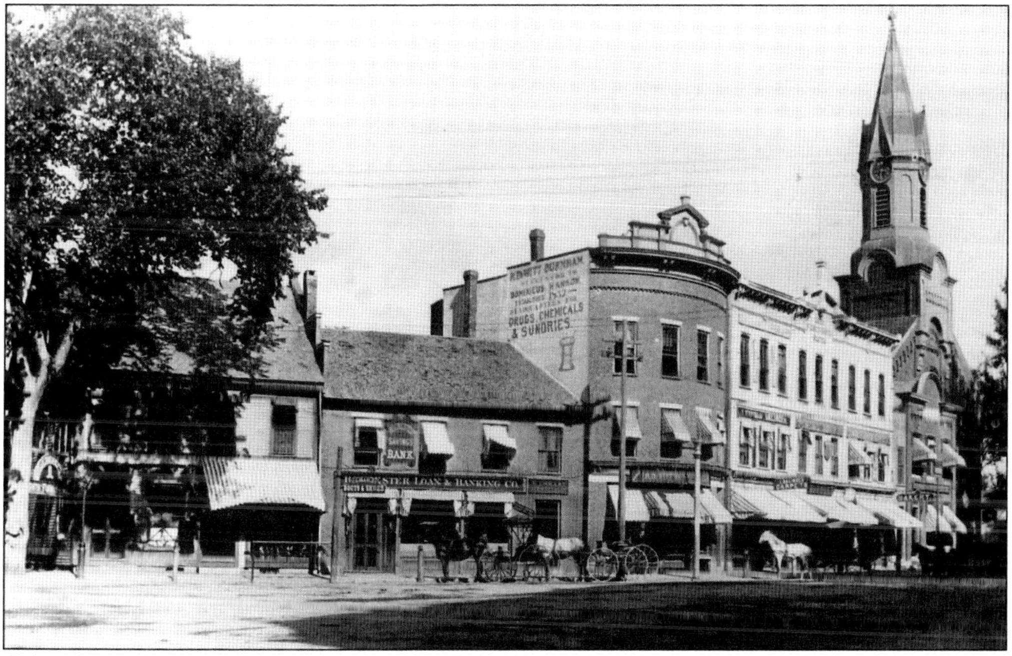

CENTRAL SQUARE IN 1903. Some of the businesses on Main Street near the corner of Hanson Street included Fred Chesley's Hat Store; Rochester Courier; Bradley Boots & Shoes; the Rochester Savings Bank; E.J. Smart, Atty.; and Burnham Drug.

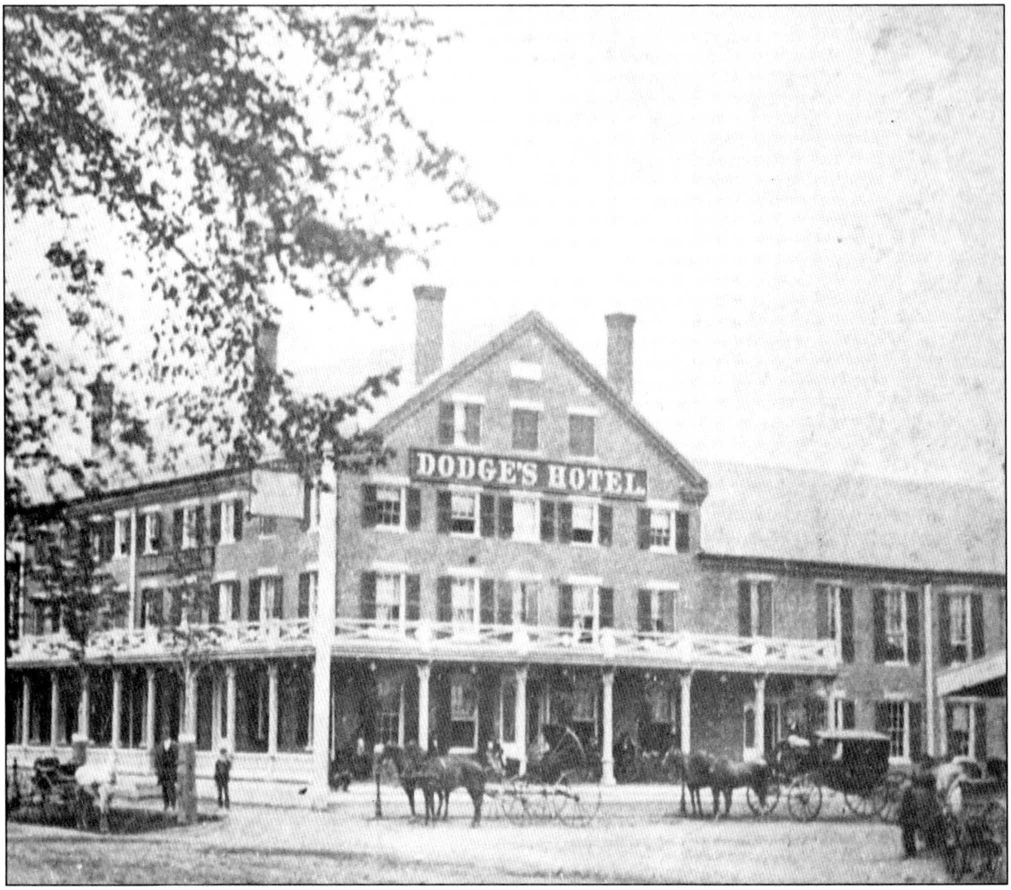

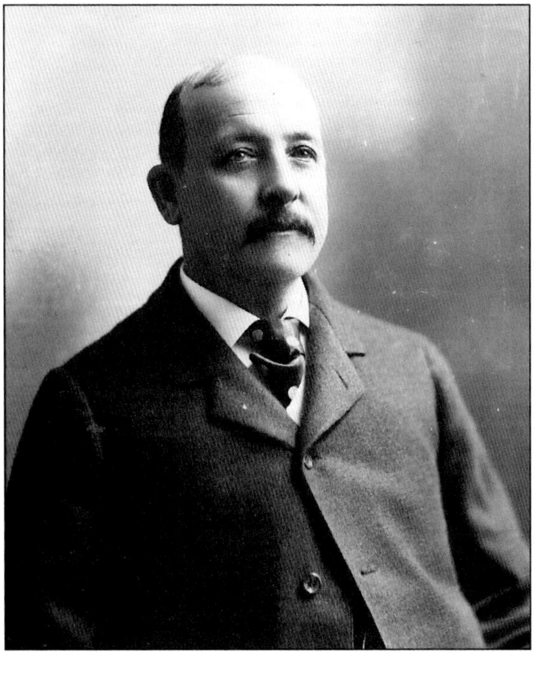

DODGE'S HOTEL. Dodge's Hotel, located on Central Square, was built in 1851 by Jonathan T. Dodge. He had a large stable on the Wakefield Street side of the hotel, with up to ninety horses, and ran several stage lines from there. For nineteen years he carried the mail between Dover and Conway. Jonathan Dodge died in 1871 and his widow Sarah, with the help of her son, J. Thorne Dodge (left, 1844–1901), continued the business. Sarah died in 1889 and J. Thorne ran the hotel with his sister, Martha Jones, until his death in 1901.

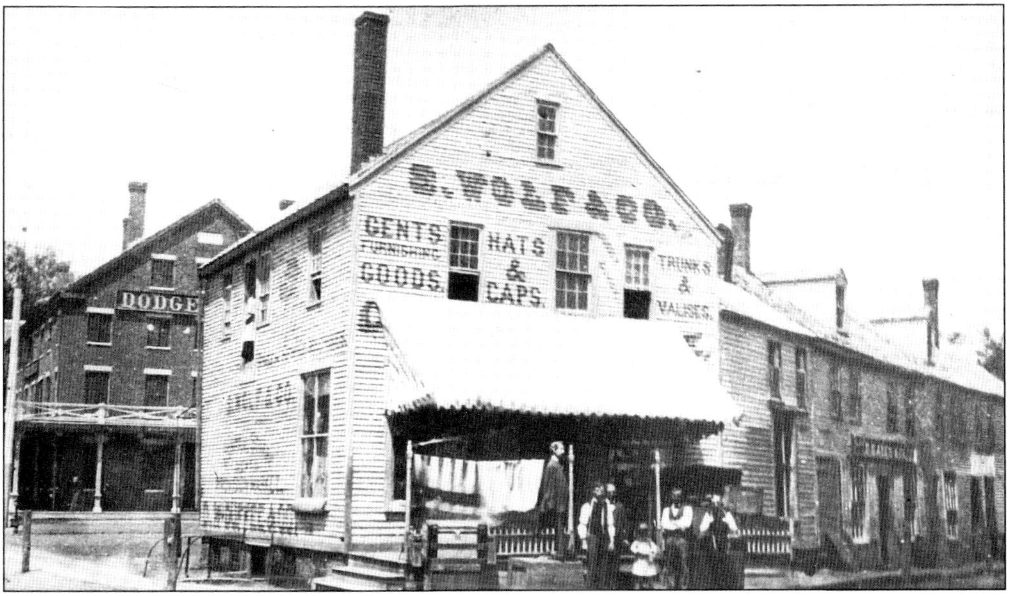

AN OLD STAND OF BUILDINGS ON CENTRAL SQUARE. This ramshackle group of buildings belonging to the Dodge family was purchased by the city in 1891. The square was cleared of buildings and the occupants of the old stores had to find new locations for their businesses.

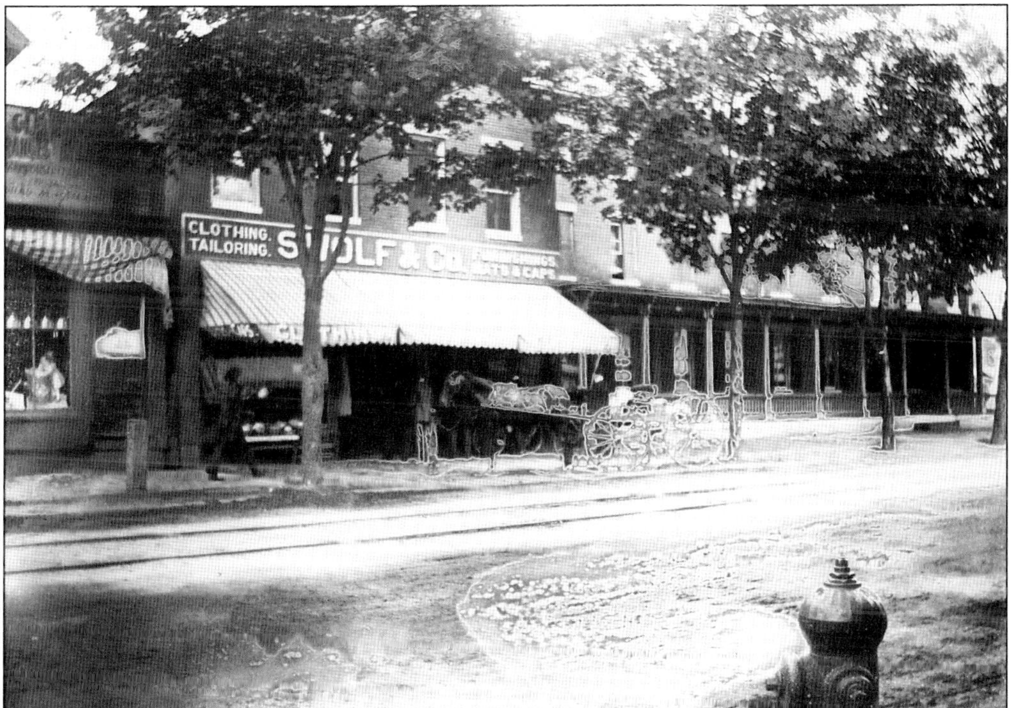

SIMON WOLF'S CLOTHING STORE. Simon Wolf moved his clothing business from the old store on the square to Dodge's brick building on Market Street, around the corner, next to the hotel.

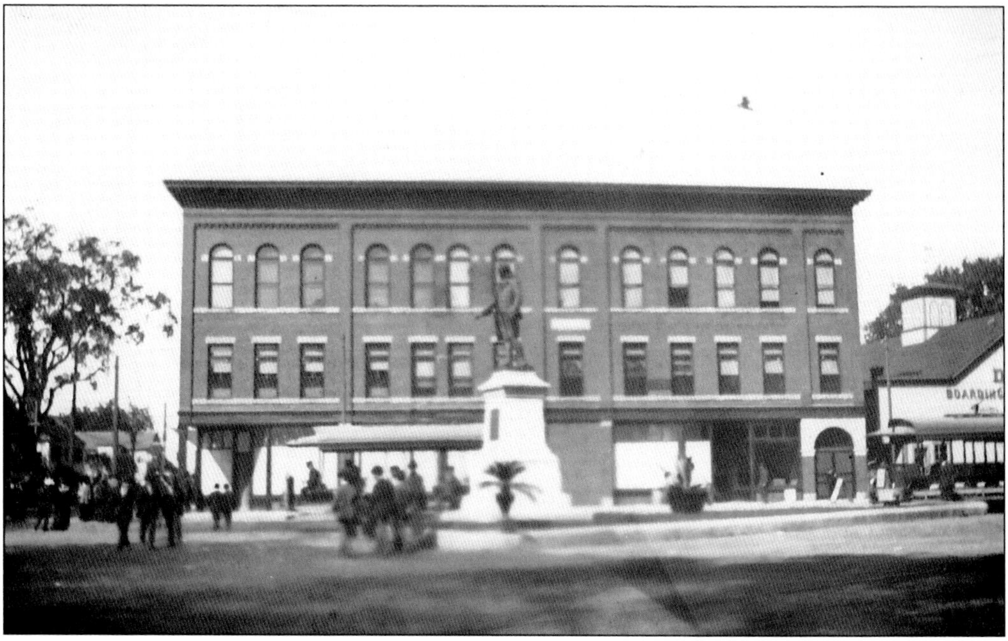

THE DODGE BLOCK, 1902. The three sisters and heirs of J. Thorne Dodge had no desire to continue the hotel business. They had the old hotel buildings torn down and replaced in 1902 with this three-story brick building called the Dodge Block.

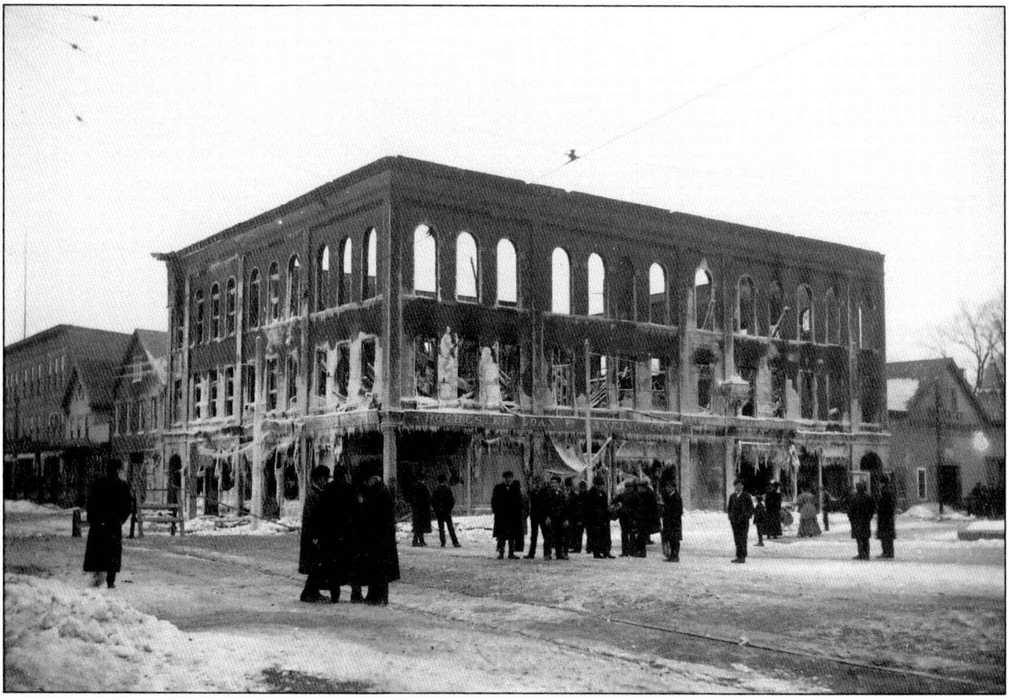

THE DODGE BLOCK FIRE. On the night of March 10, 1908, the six-year-old Dodge Block was badly damaged by fire. The walls were left standing and engineers brought in from Boston assured the owners that the building could be reconstructed using the old walls. In a high wind a few weeks later, the walls collapsed.

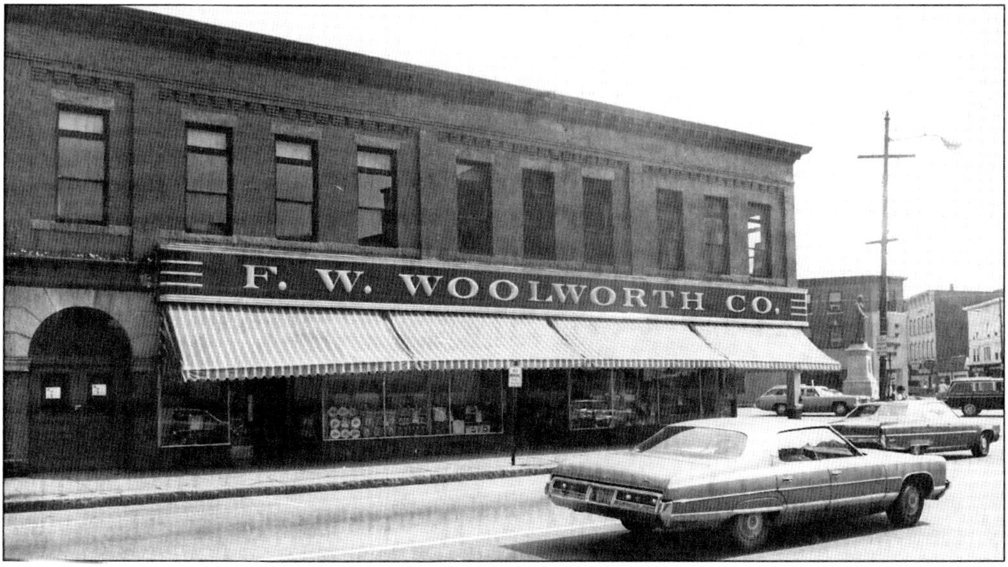

THE NEW DODGE BLOCK. The Dodge Block was rebuilt in 1908 with two stories. Lothrop-Farnum Co. was on the first floor from the time the block was completed until 1912, when the business was evicted to make room for F.W. Woolworth Co. Woolworth's store was in the building from 1912 until it closed on December 31, 1981.

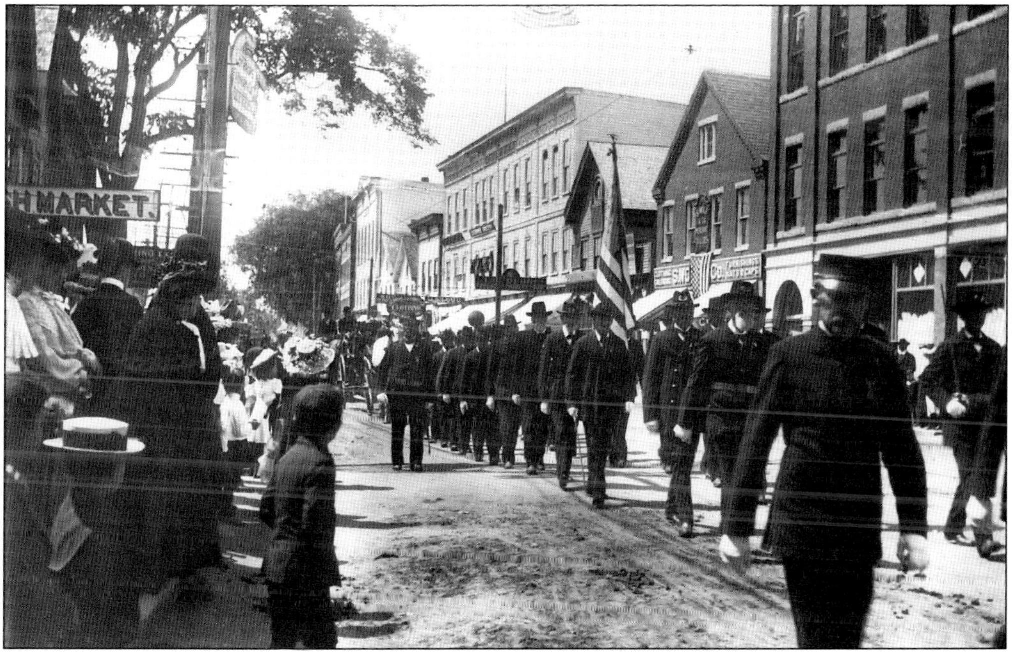

A PARADE ON MARKET STREET AFTER 1902. On the right, readers can see the three-story Dodge Block; S. Wolf & Co. Clothing-Tailors; the Globe Store; Enterprise Grocery; and Lothrop, Farnum & Co., Clothing, Hats & Furnishings.

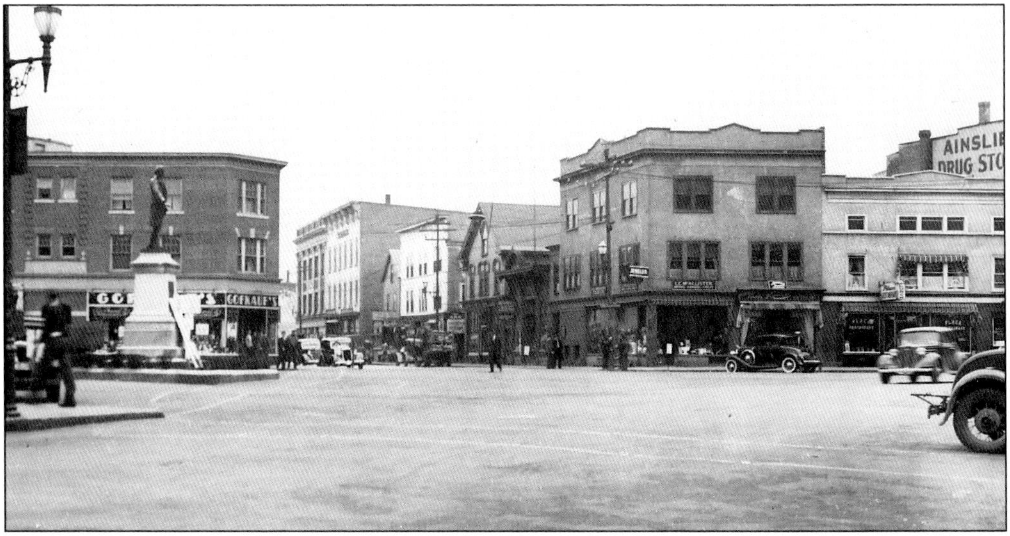

CENTRAL SQUARE IN 1940. The Realty Block was built in 1926 on the former site of Dominicus Hanson's house. Dominicus was born in 1813 in the house built by his father. His son Charles, also born in the house, lived there until his death in 1923. The house was moved in two parts to Autumn Street where it became the Hansonia Apartments.

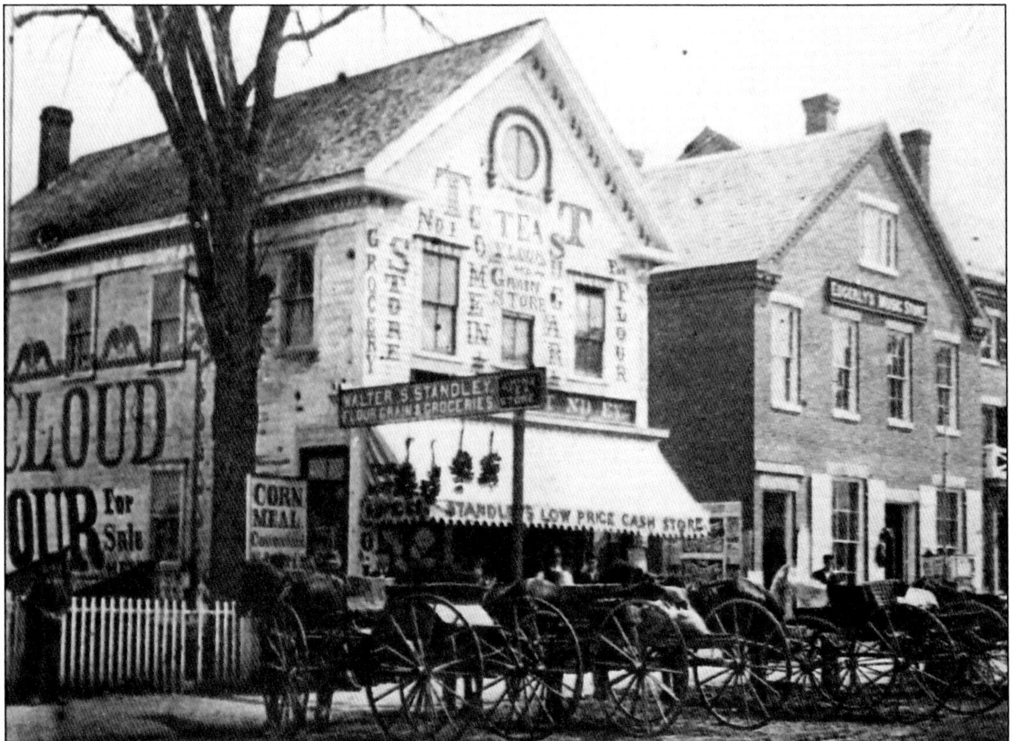

MARKET STREET BEFORE 1880. Edgerly's Music Store was in Dodge's brick building, built in 1856 for the Farmers and Mechanics Bank. In 1860, N.V. Whitehouse and some of his friends purchased a majority of the stock and moved the bank to Gonic, where it became the First National Bank of Gonic.

DOMINICUS HANSON. A wealthy and prominent citizen of Rochester, Hanson died in 1907 at the age of ninety-three. According to his late father's wishes, his son Charles deeded the Dominicus Hanson Park to the city in 1917. Popularly called "Hanson's Pines," it is protected by deed to remain without buildings or highways.

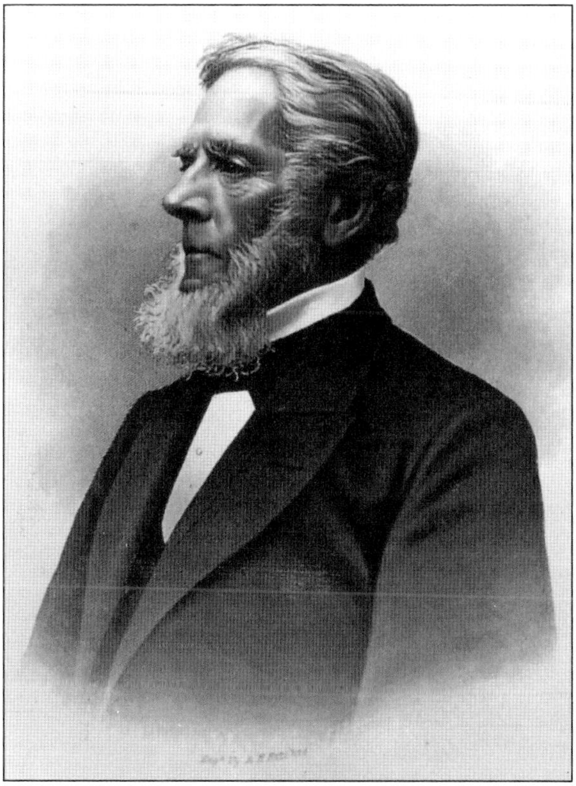

HANSON'S STREET WAS A BUSY PLACE. Dominicus Hanson built this street through his garden in 1849 at the request of the Great Falls and Conway Railroad. It remained a private street which he kept in good repair, and he leased the land and buildings to merchants. Hanson had the street paved in 1901 at his own expense with 56,000 granite blocks. The blocks were covered with asphalt in 1949.

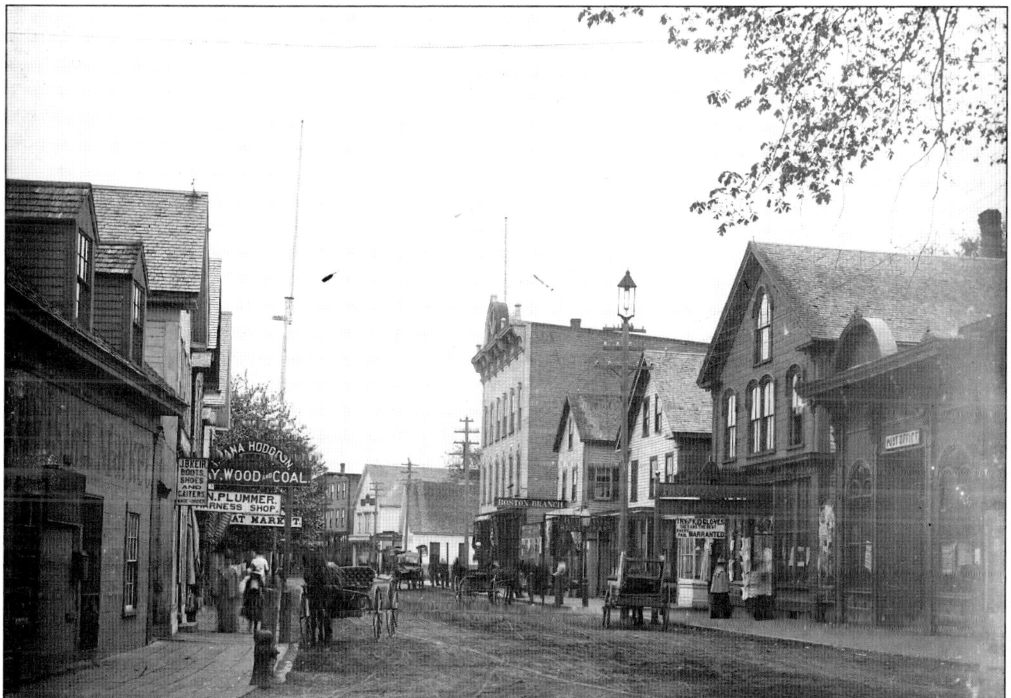

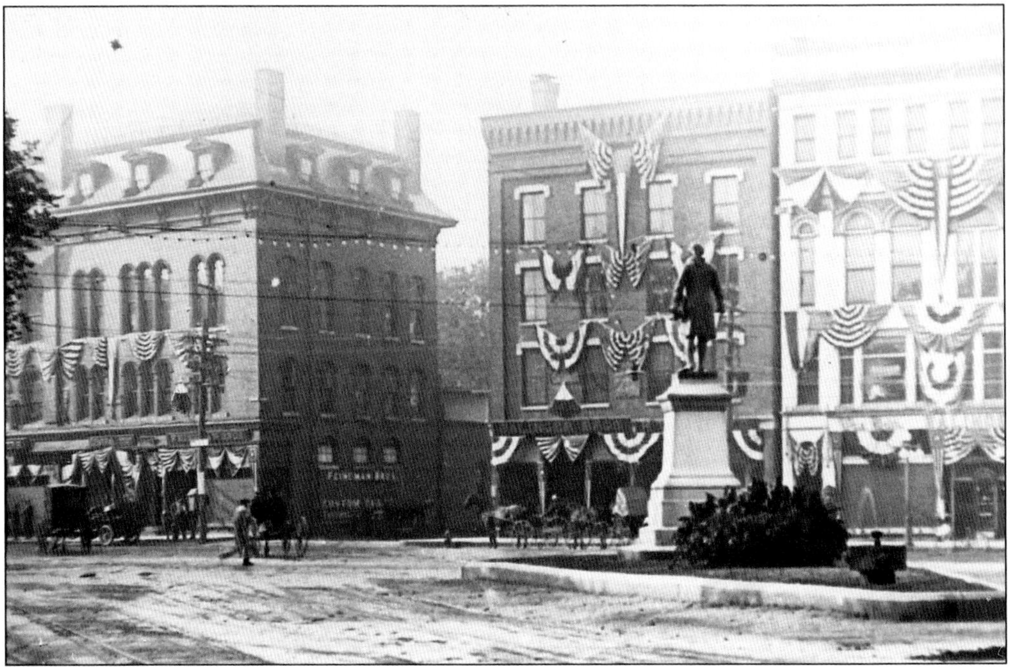

DECORATED FOR THE ROCHESTER FAIR. Each September professional decorators came to Rochester and adorned buildings with bunting for the festive week ahead. This photograph shows the Feineman, Hayes, and Salinger stores dressed to welcome visitors to the fair.

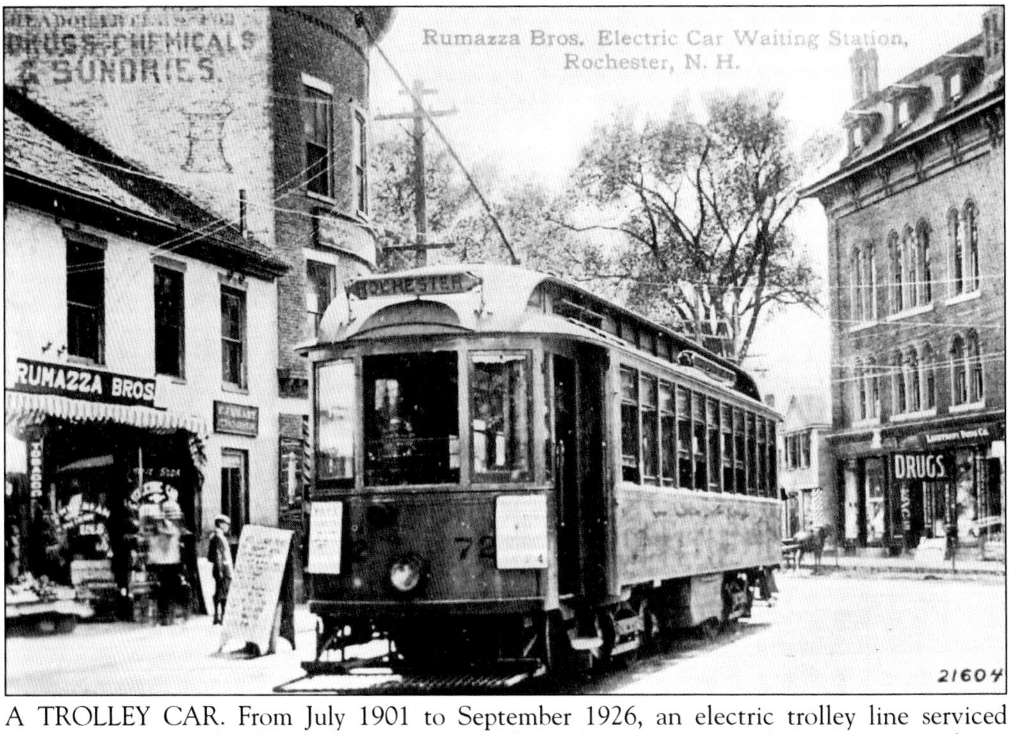

A TROLLEY CAR. From July 1901 to September 1926, an electric trolley line serviced Rochester. A branch of the Dover-Somersworth-Rochester Street Railway ran cars at forty-minute intervals. A waiting station was in Ramazza's Store in the Henderson Block.

THE FIRST ROCHESTER BANK. John McDuffee founded the first Rochester bank on this site in 1835. In 1890 the Rochester National Bank occupied the first floor, while the law offices of J.H. Worcester, L.P. Snow, and Charles B. Gafney were on the second floor. There was a bank at this location from 1835 to 1992.

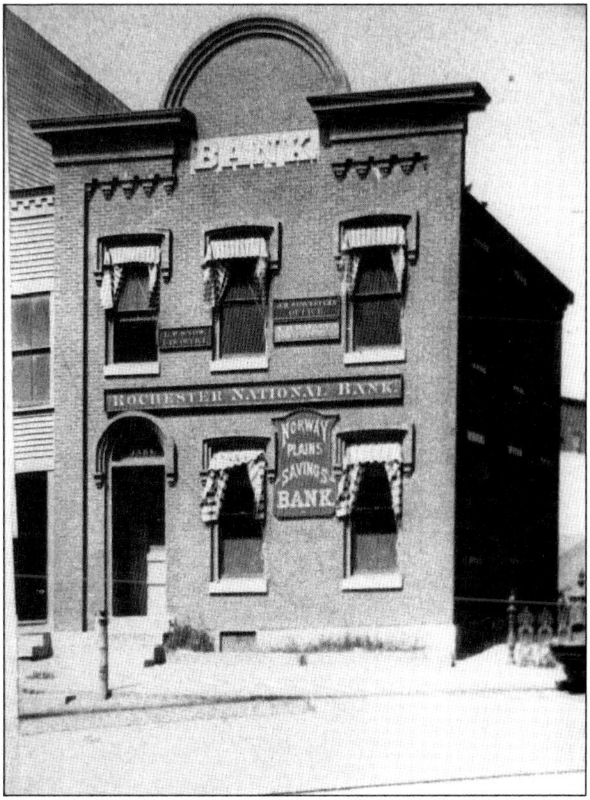

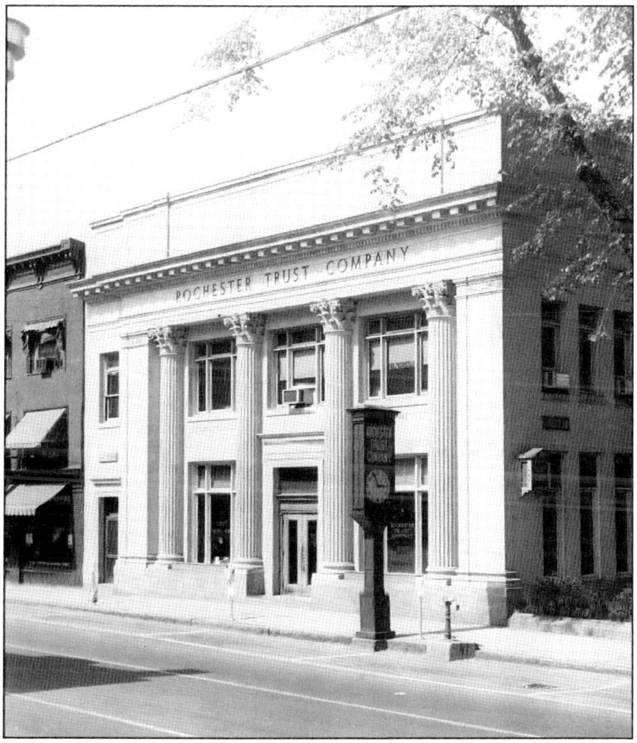

A LATER BANK AT THE SAME SITE. This is the Rochester Trust Company in the same location, 22 South Main Street, after several face lifts and name changes. It was converted into a beautiful brownstone building in 1903.

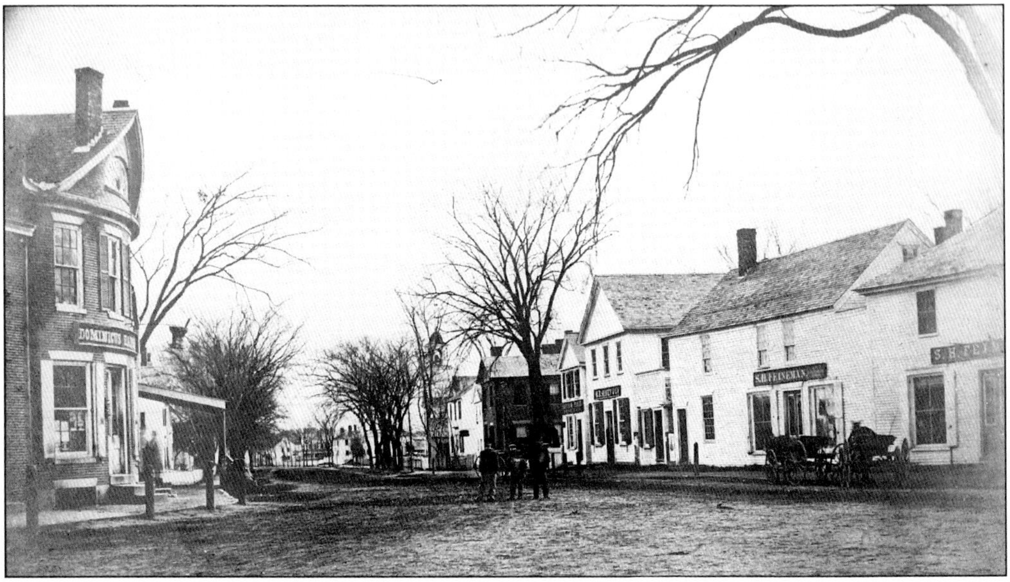

MAIN STREET PRIOR TO 1868. The three white buildings on the right were moved to Charles Street in 1868 to make room for the McDuffee Block. One of the houses still stands on the corner of Charles Street and the Portland Street Extension.

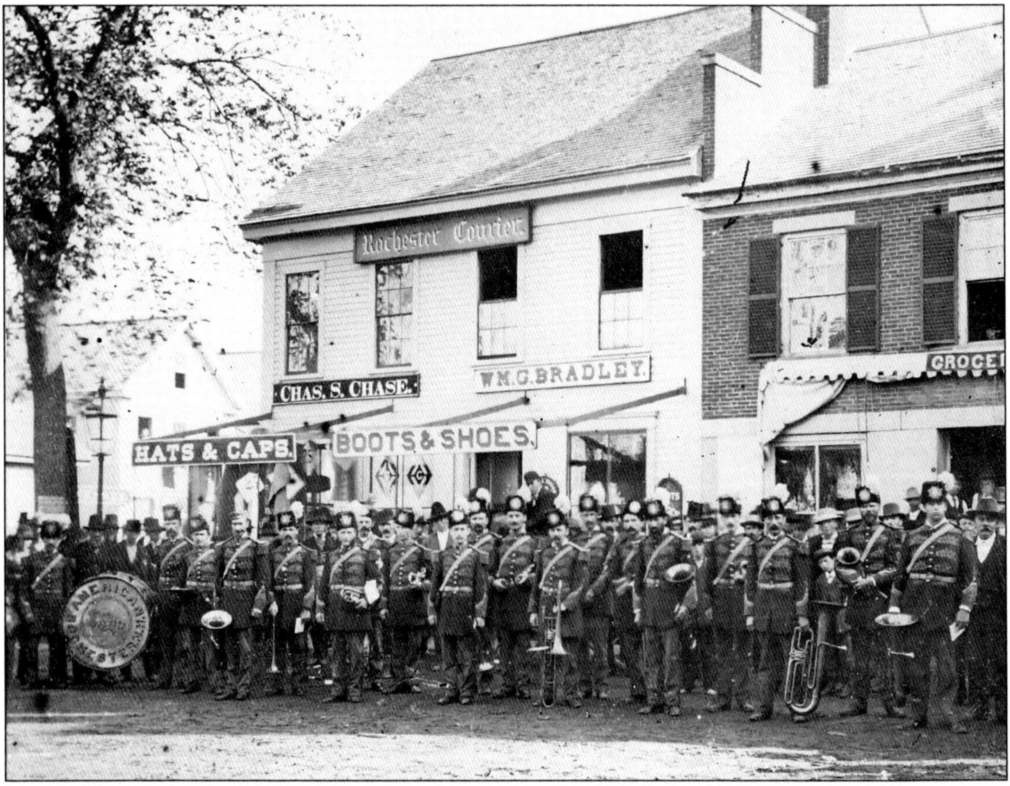

THE AMERICAN BAND. Formed in 1871, this popular band played at many events including concerts, parades, the Rochester Fair, club and business openings, and the dedication of monuments and parks. They were often called upon to perform in neighboring towns.

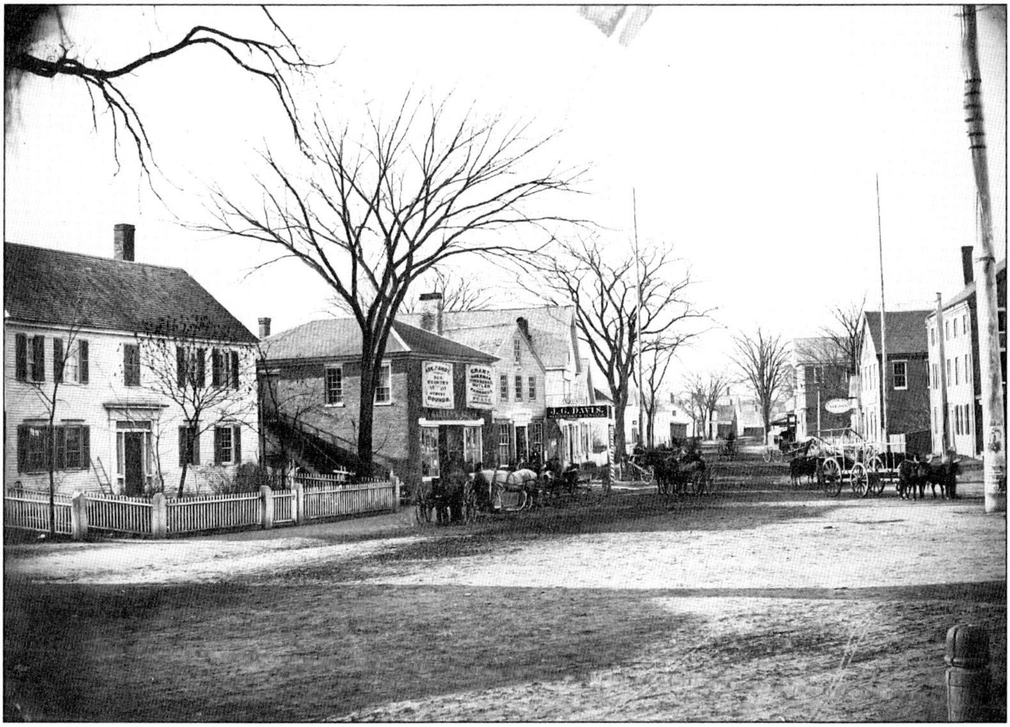

MARKET STREET LOOKING NORTH. The Charles Chase building is on the left. The political poster on the first liberty pole reads, "Abe & Andy—Our Country to its Utmost Bounds." The poster on the second pole reads, "Grant, Sherman, Sheridan, Butler & Farragut. Union-Peace."

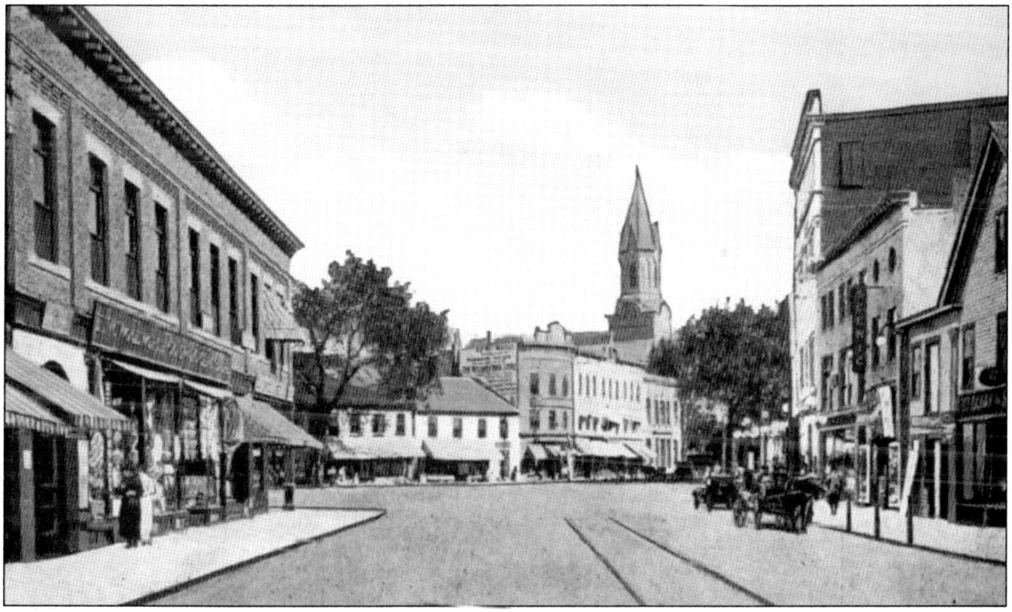

NORTH MAIN STREET LOOKING SOUTH. Woolworths moved into the Dodge Block in 1912 and the Scenic Theatre was built by Louis McDuffee the same year. Henry Berry and Edwin Shorey opened a hardware store at this location in 1898.

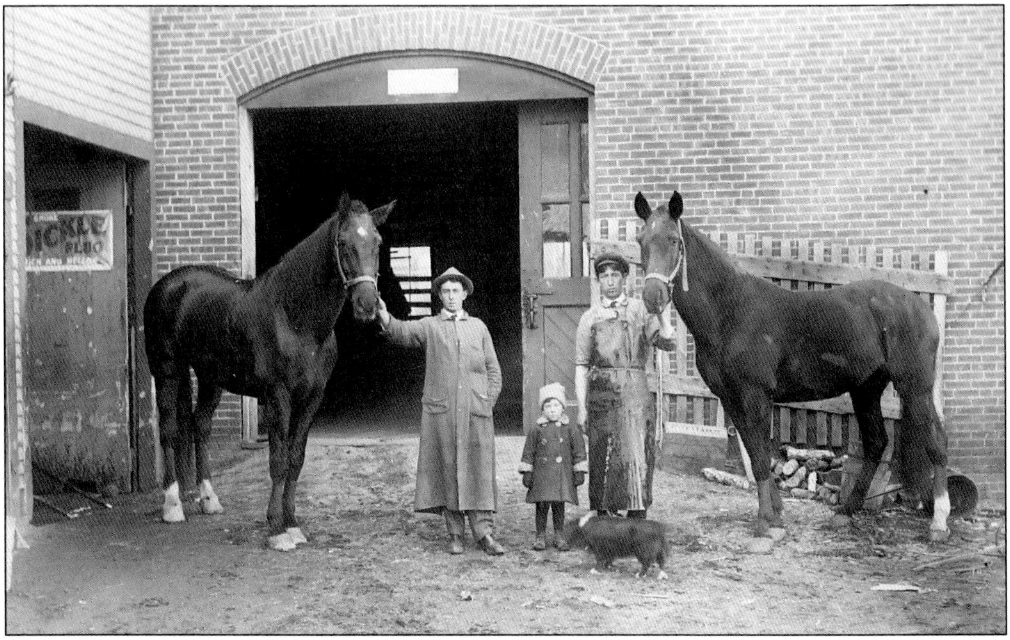

WRISLEY STABLES. The brick stable next to the Wrisley Hotel was owned by Charles and Homer Lowe when this photograph was taken in 1910. Homer Lowe, Robert Lowe, and Bob Meiser are pictured. Today, this is the museum of the Rochester Historical Society.

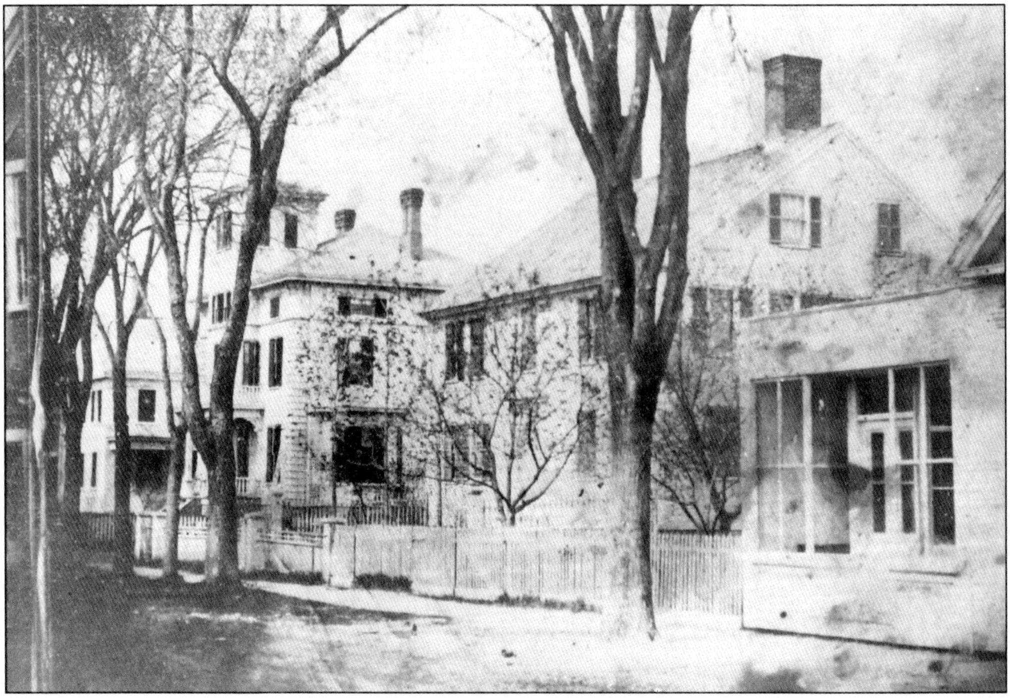

LOOKING UP WAKEFIELD STREET. From the left are the homes of Louis McDuffee (former mayor of Rochester), Dr. James Farrington, and Dominicus Hanson. These buildings have been replaced by the Farmington National Bank, Grange Mutual Insurance, and the Realty Building.

Two

Railroads

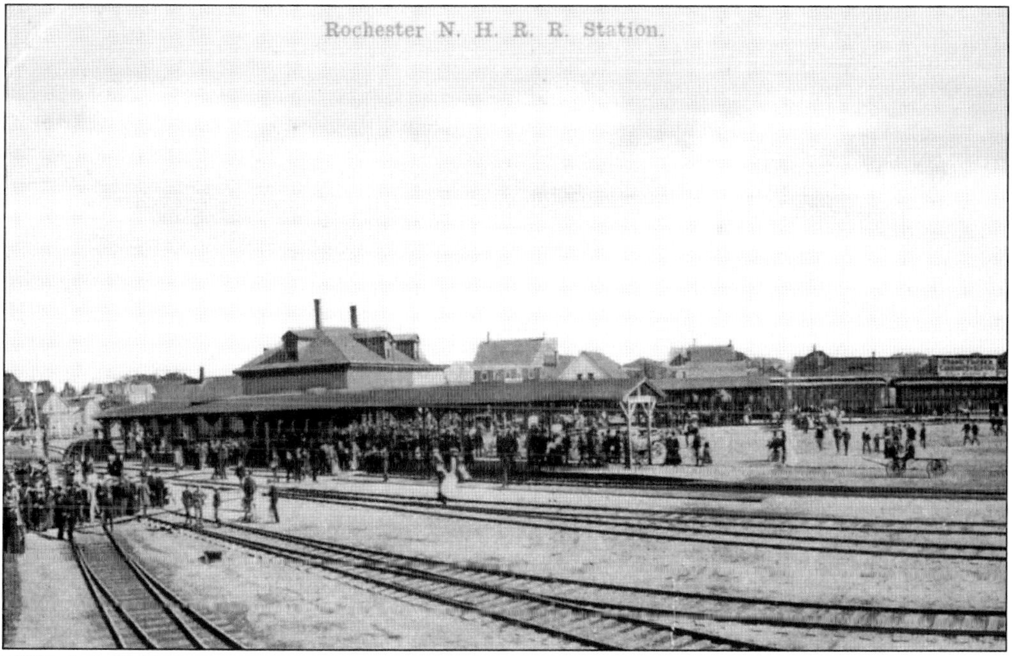

THE ROCHESTER RAILROAD STATION. The arrival of the railroad in Rochester on March 6, 1849, marked the beginning of the rapid growth of the town. Union Station, built in 1885, was later renamed the Boston & Maine Station.

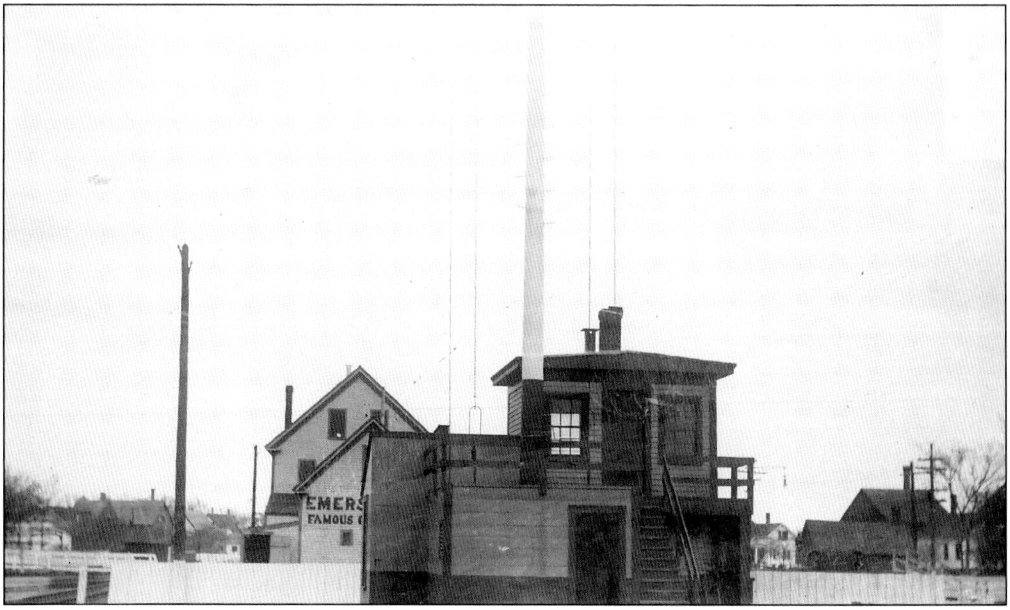

THE RAILROAD SIGNAL TOWER. The signal tower stood just above the depot. Colored balls raised or lowered informed engineers whether to proceed or stop.

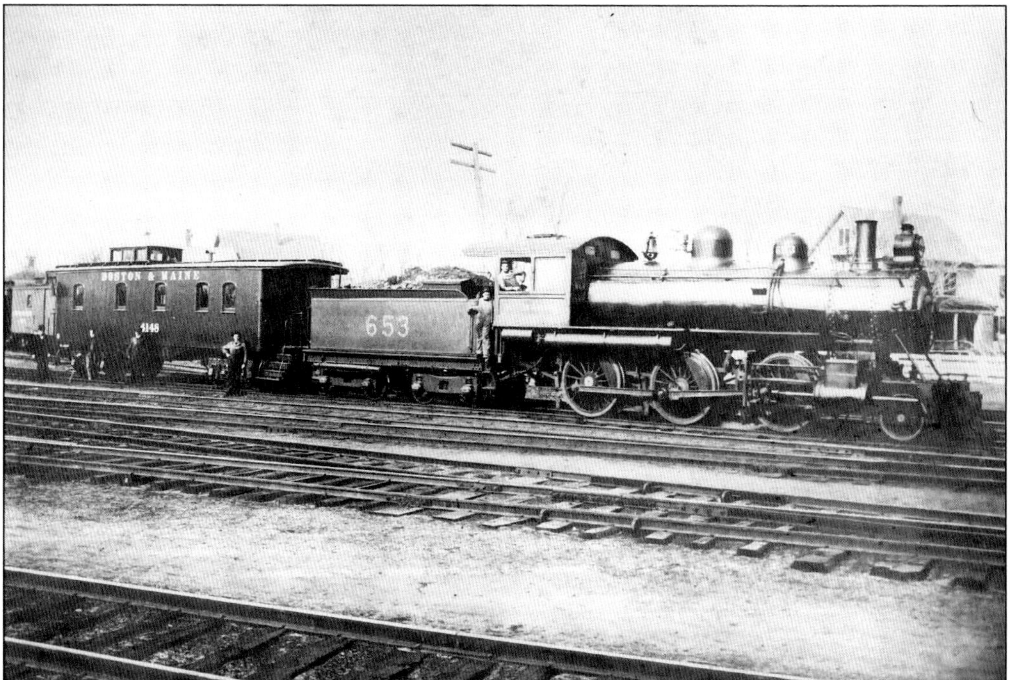

STEAM ENGINE 653. Coal-fueled steam engines pulled trains through Rochester and were joined by diesel engines in the 1930s. After World War II, traffic gradually declined and the tracks were eventually removed.

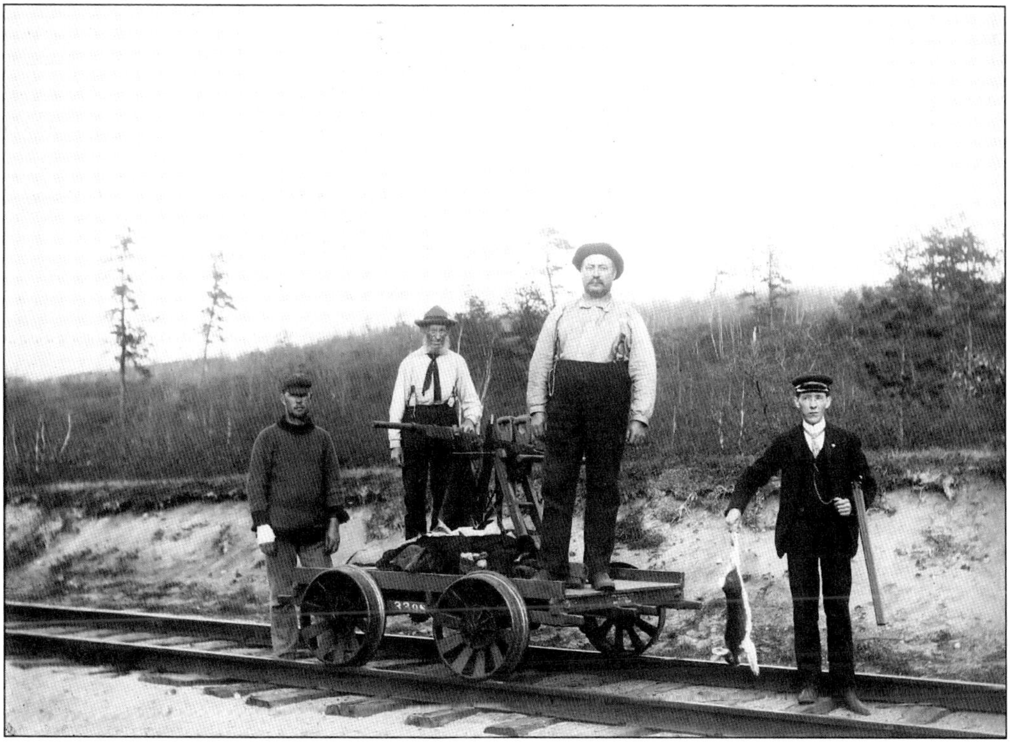

A TRACK REPAIR CREW. The section hands working on the railroad were constantly engaged in keeping the railroad tracks in condition. They were transported to work sites on hand cars like this one. One of these workers seems to have done some hunting.

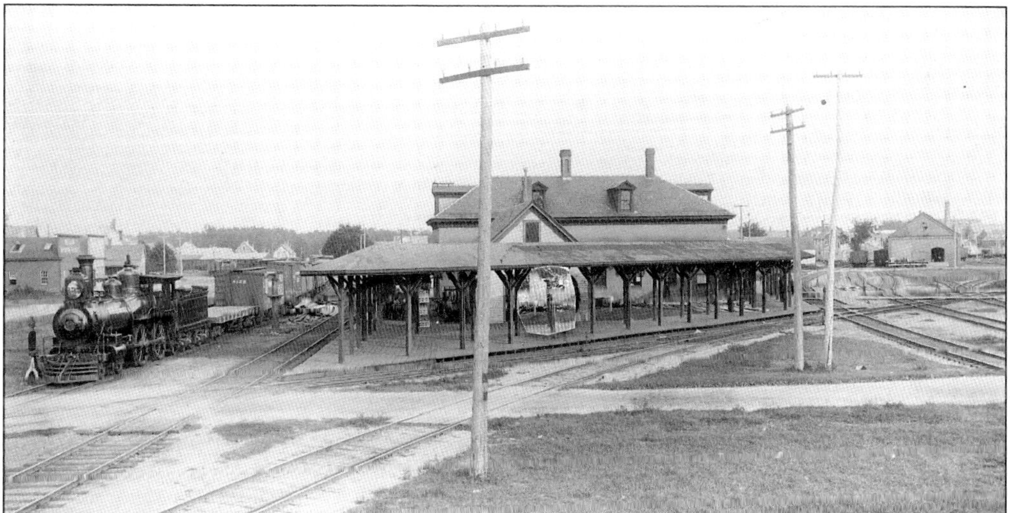

A FREIGHT TRAIN ARRIVING AT UNION STATION. By 1900 Rochester was a major rail center and the junction of four railroads. About fifty passenger and freight trains arrived and departed daily, including eleven passenger trains to Boston every day.

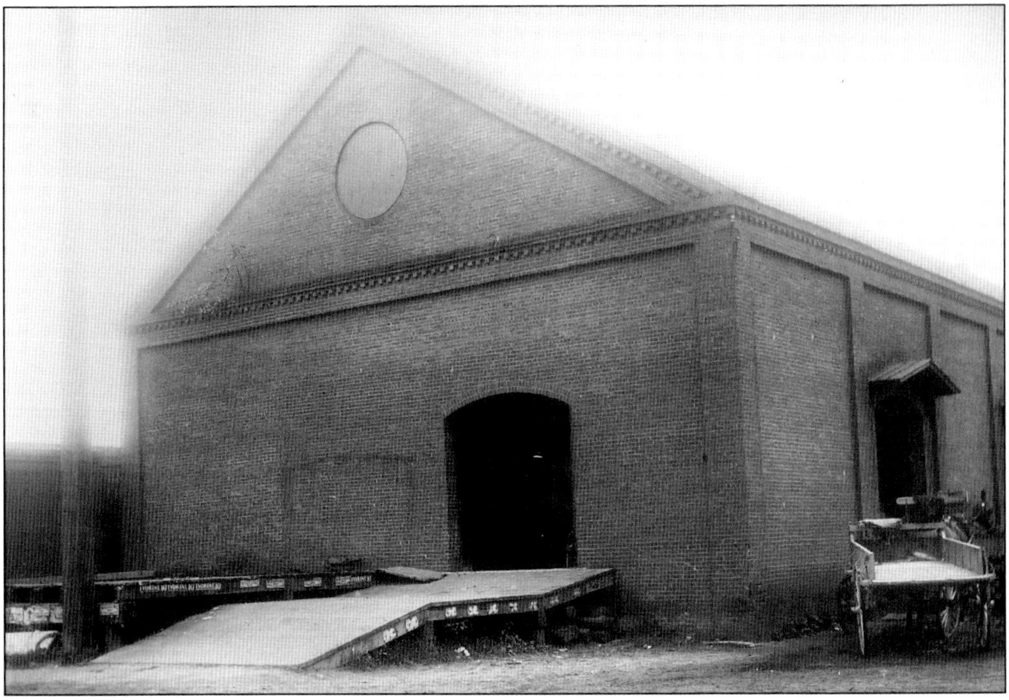

THE BOSTON & MAINE FREIGHT HOUSE. This freight house on Portland Street was closed on October 24, 1975, and is now the Knights of Columbus Hall.

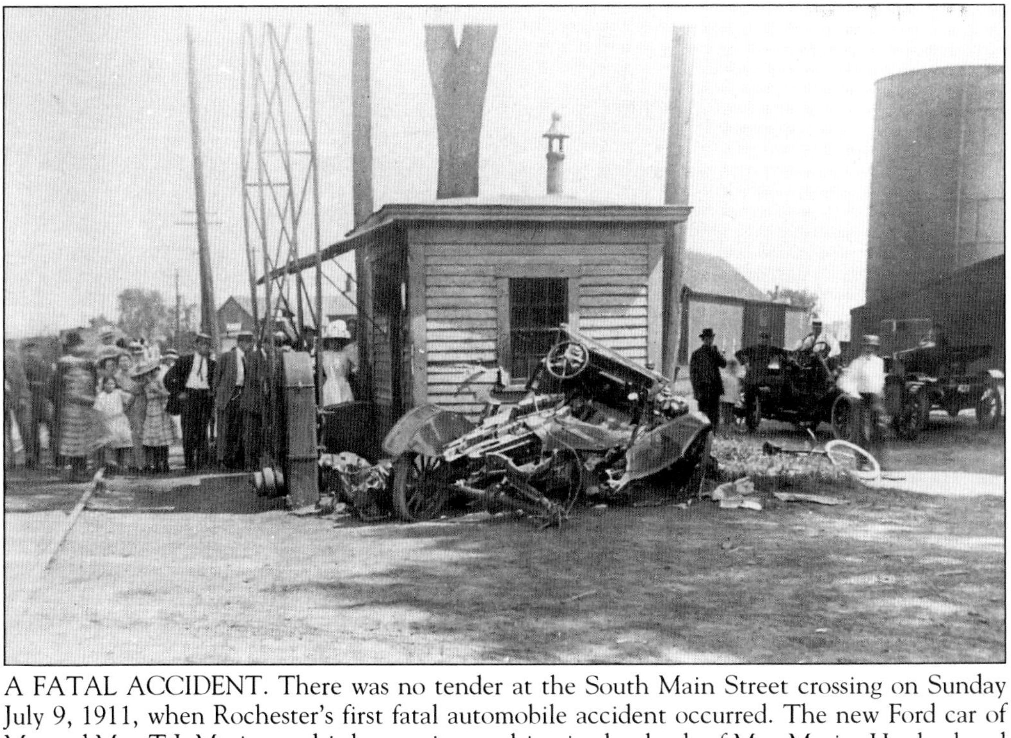

A FATAL ACCIDENT. There was no tender at the South Main Street crossing on Sunday July 9, 1911, when Rochester's first fatal automobile accident occurred. The new Ford car of Mr. and Mrs. T.J. Morin was hit by a train, resulting in the death of Mrs. Morin. Her husband was seriously injured but he survived.

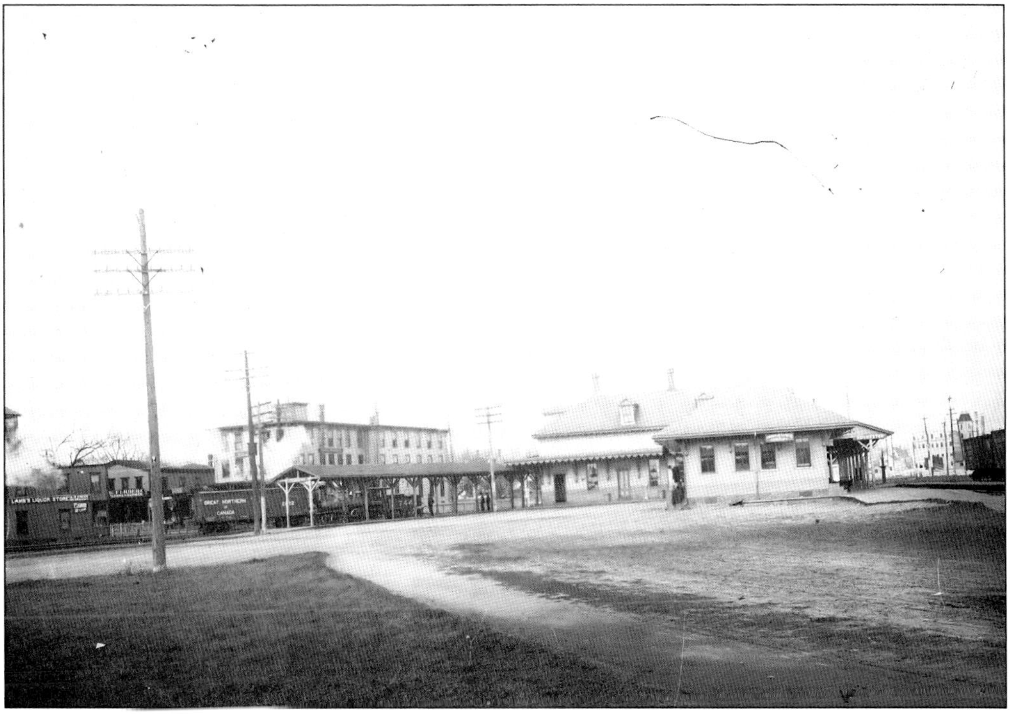

THE PASSENGER STATION. Once a major rail center, this property was sold by the Boston & Maine Railroad in December 1959 to All State Realty of Boston. The buildings were razed and in January 1962 Jerry's Supermarket opened on the site.

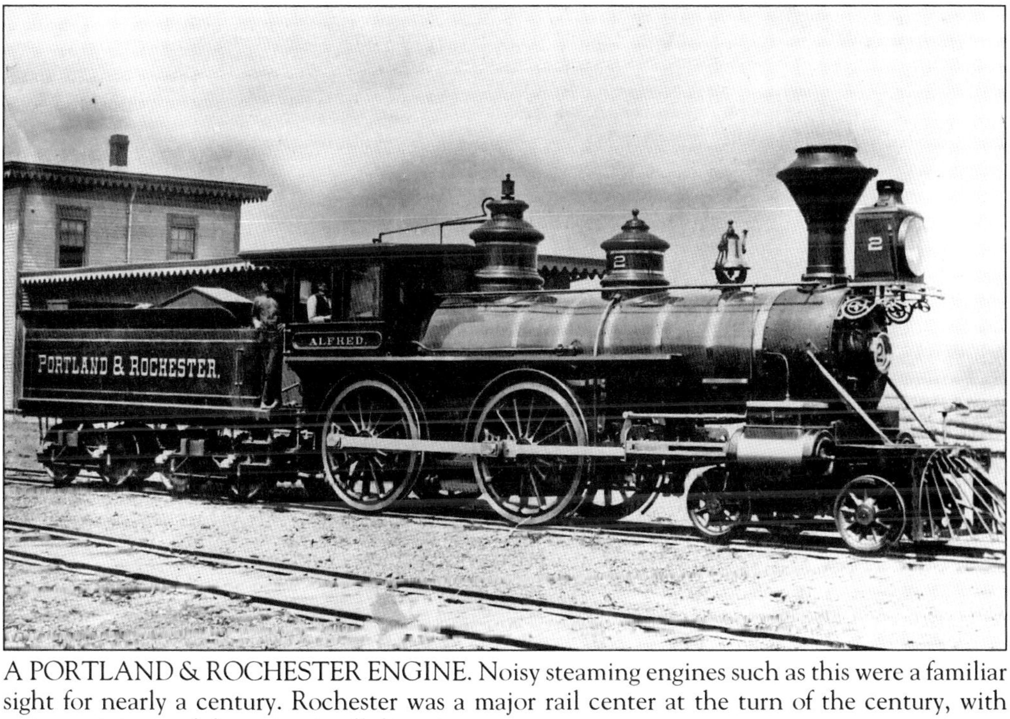

A PORTLAND & ROCHESTER ENGINE. Noisy steaming engines such as this were a familiar sight for nearly a century. Rochester was a major rail center at the turn of the century, with trains arriving and departing in all directions.

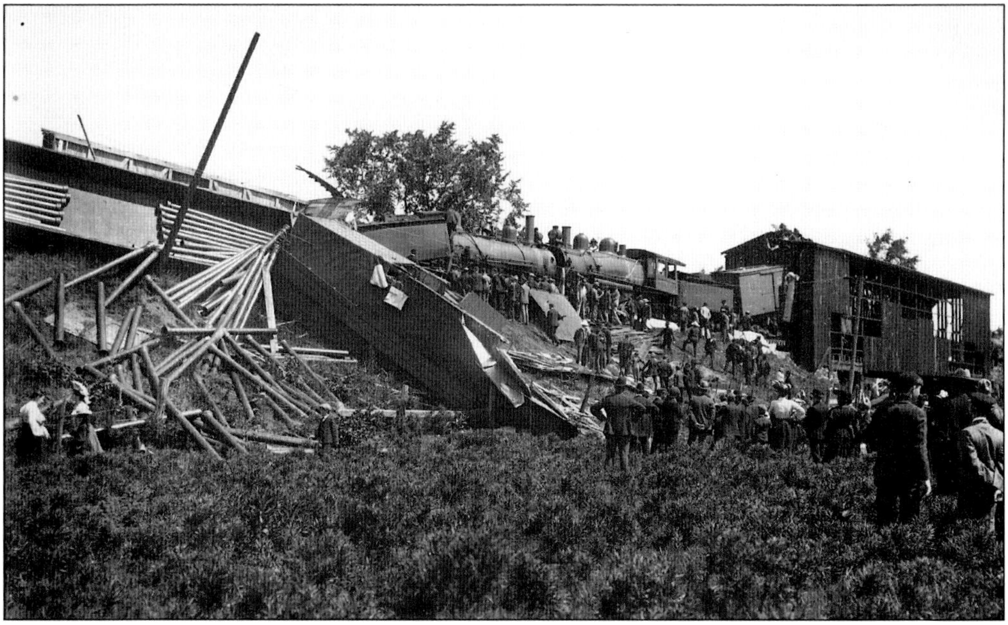

A TRAIN WRECK IN GONIC. Shortly after 4 am on Sunday, July 3, 1904, two freight trains collided head-on at the bridge behind the old gas house on Gonic Road. Neither engine left the track and no one was injured, even though a number of cars were hurled down an embankment.

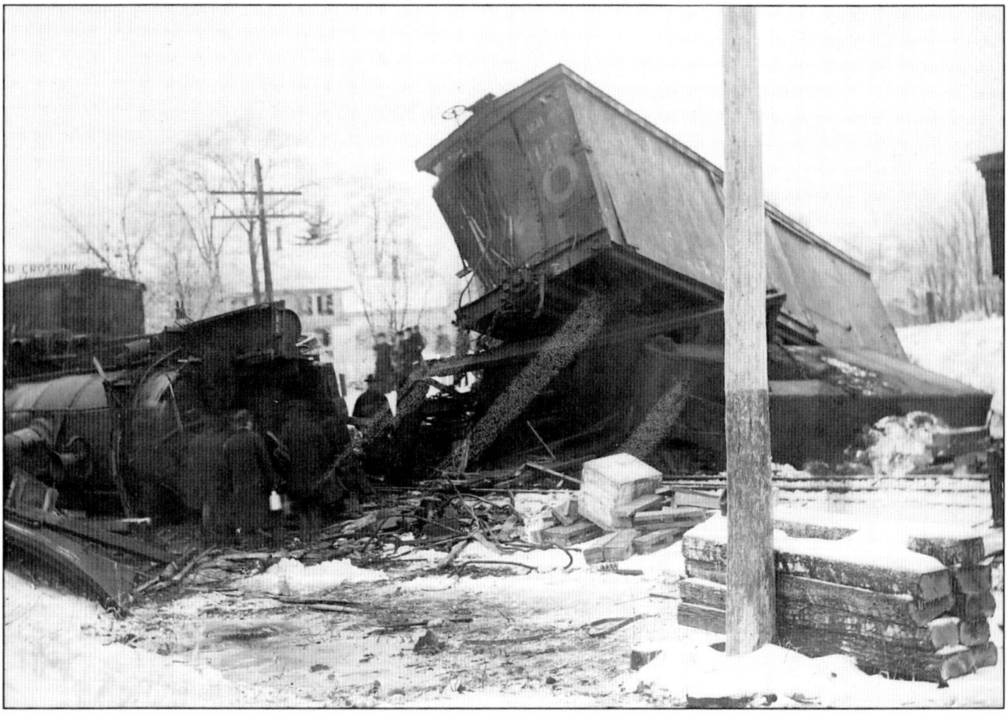

A TRAIN WRECK IN EAST ROCHESTER. A freight train derailed on December 14, 1906, at the Autumn Street crossing in East Rochester. An engineer and the fireman from Nashua were killed.

Three

Public Buildings

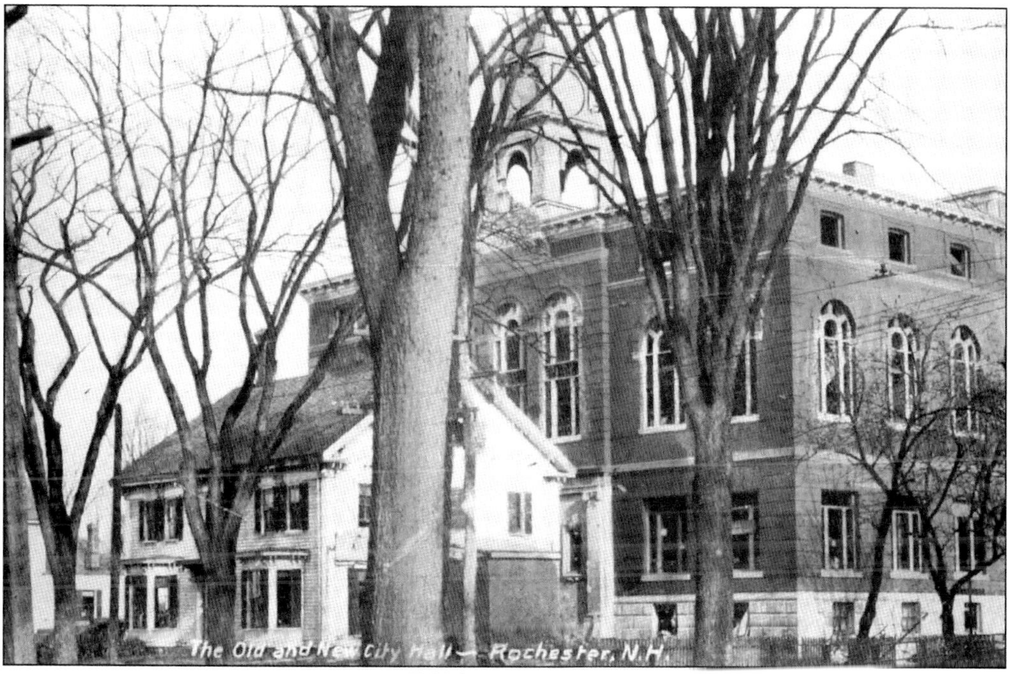

CITY HALL AND THE MCDUFFEE HOUSE. The City of Rochester purchased the John McDuffee estate on Wakefield Street in August of 1896. The deed stipulated that no city hall could be built on the lot for at least ten years. In the interim, the old McDuffee house was used for city business.

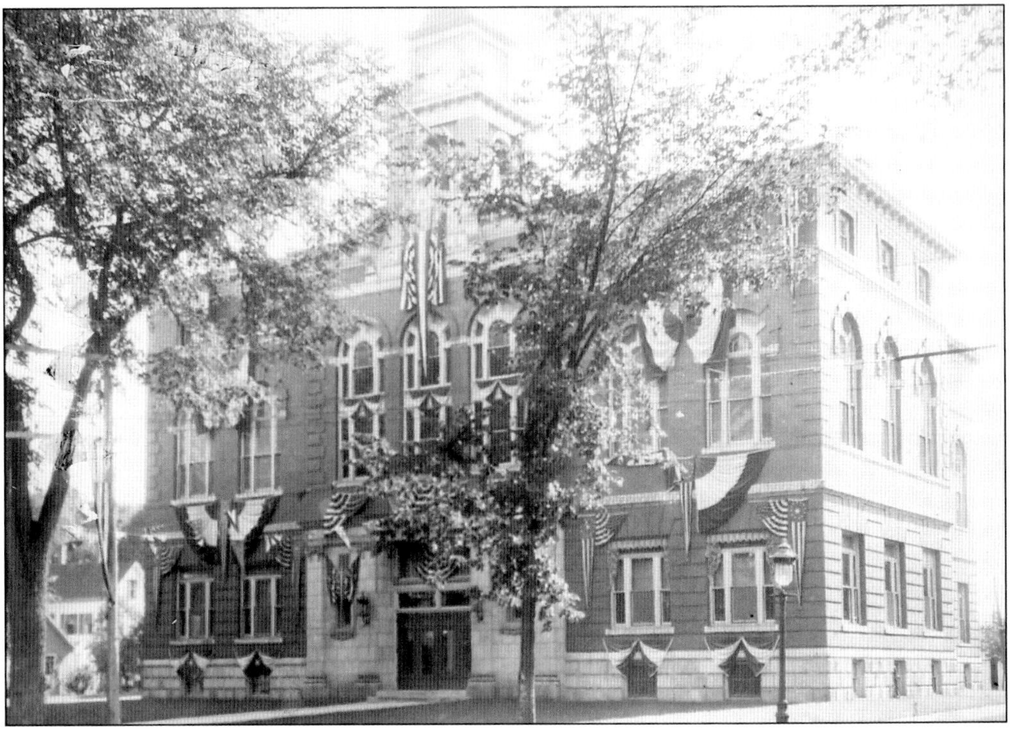

CITY HALL COMPLETED. After the Municipal Building was completed in May of 1908, the old house was sold to Jedediah Morrill and moved to 113–115 Portland Street where it was converted into a two-tenement building.

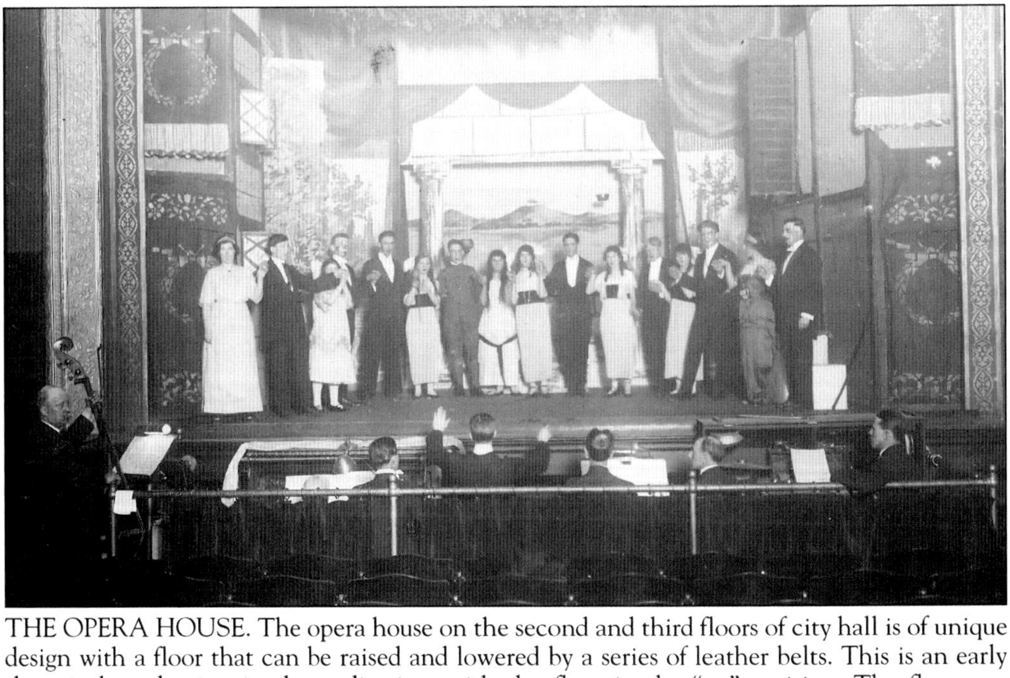

THE OPERA HOUSE. The opera house on the second and third floors of city hall is of unique design with a floor that can be raised and lowered by a series of leather belts. This is an early theatrical production in the auditorium with the floor in the "up" position. The floor was lowered for events such as dances and basketball games.

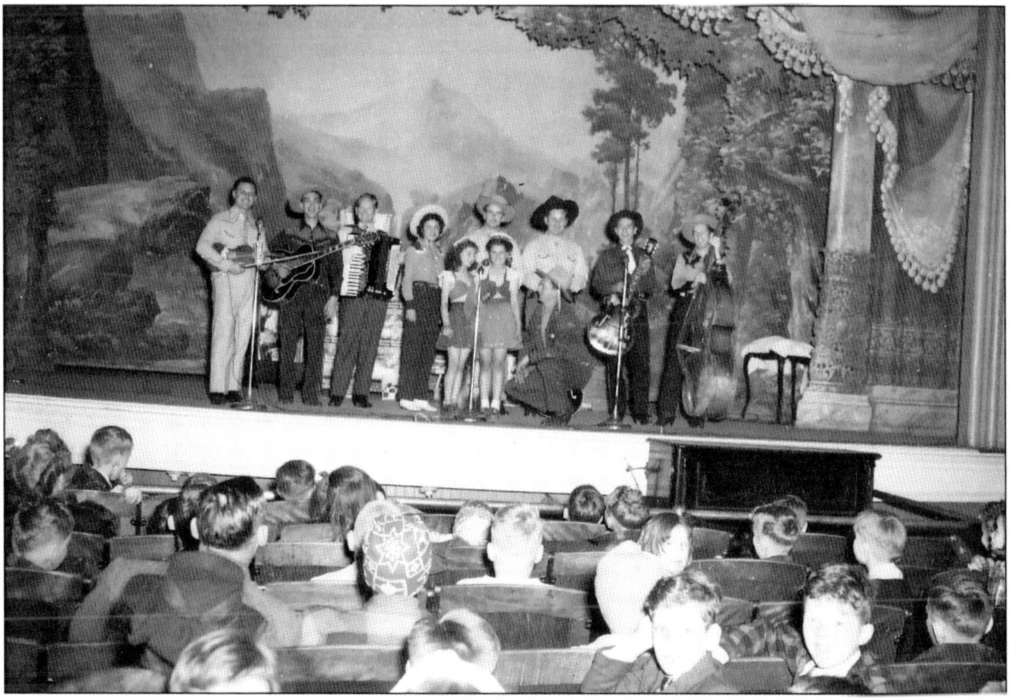

THE BUD BAILEY SHOW, MARCH 14, 1942. Western shows were well-attended in the early 1940s. Adults as well as children gathered in the opera house auditorium on Saturday afternoons.

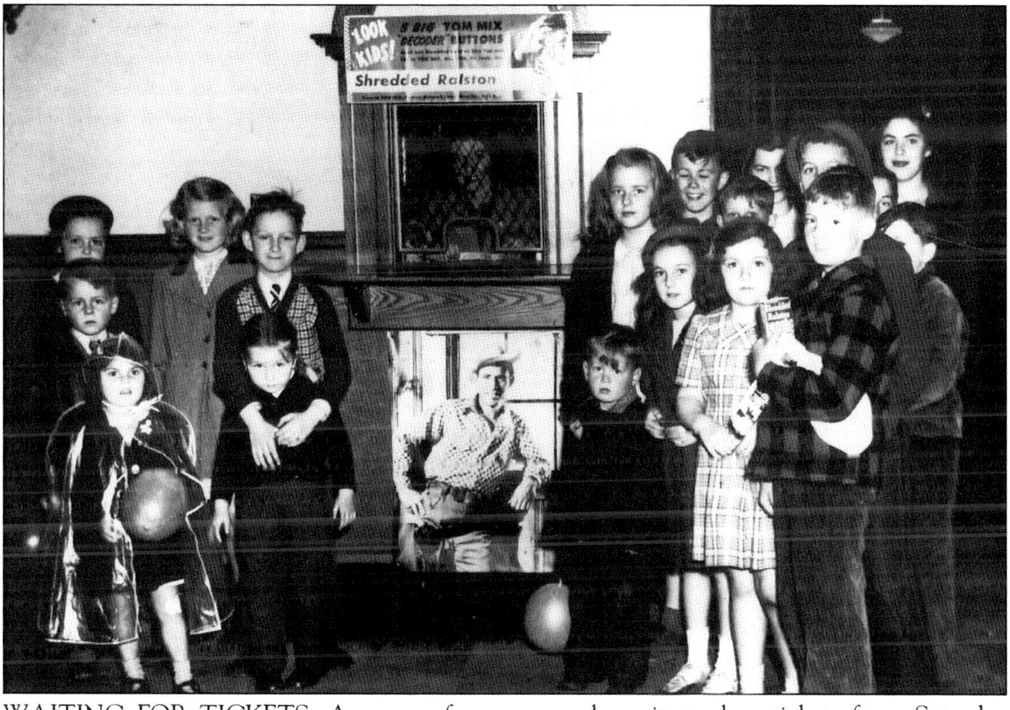

WAITING FOR TICKETS. A group of young people waits to buy tickets for a Saturday afternoon show in 1943.

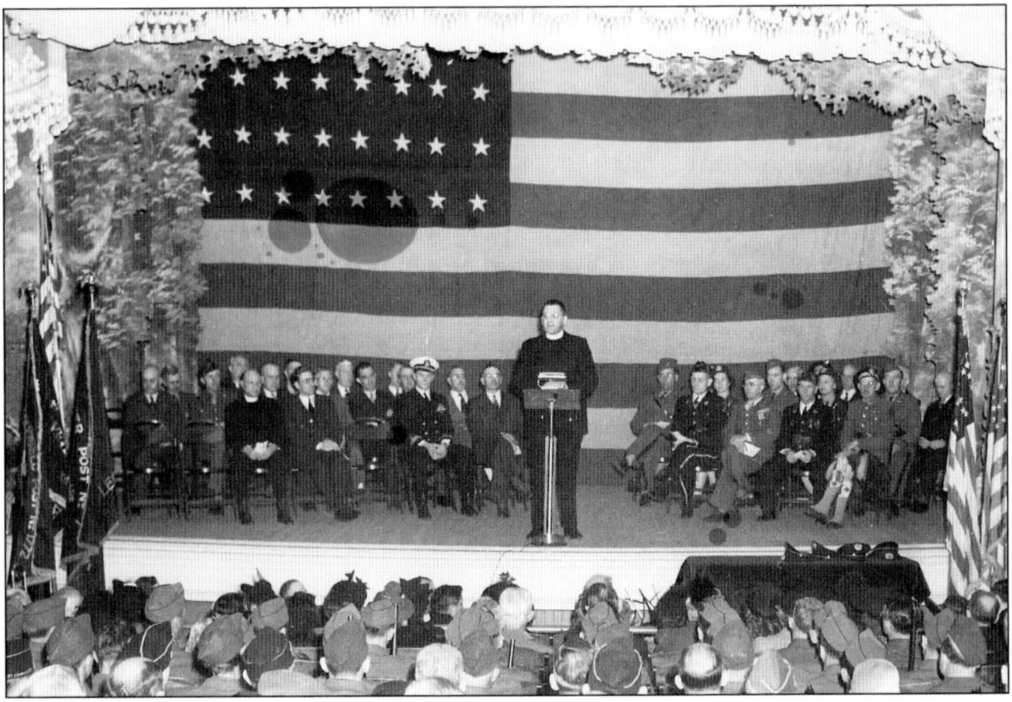

THE HONOR ROLL CEREMONY IN THE OPERA HOUSE. Mayor Walter Wood, the city council, and guests listen to an address by Reverend Charles Trudel of the Holy Rosary church on October 24, 1943.

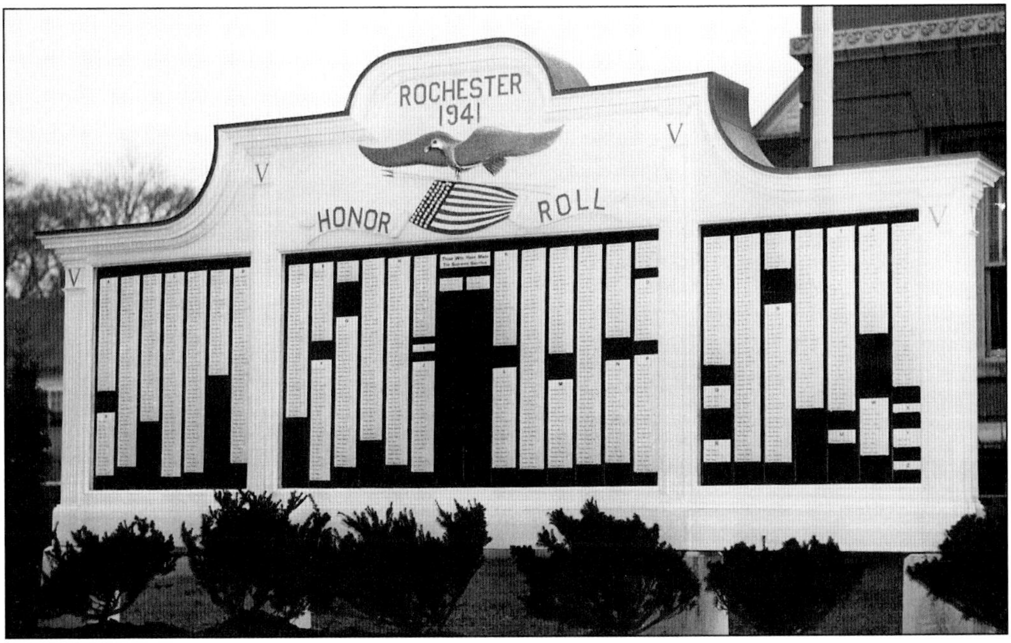

THE HONOR ROLL. On June 1, 1943, Mayor Wood and the Rochester City Council resolved that an Honor Roll monument be built for those who entered the service in World War II. George Potvin, Maurice Jones, and Wesley Lyons were the appointed committee and the monument was constructed by George Blake, Alfred Ouellette, and Adelard Ouellette.

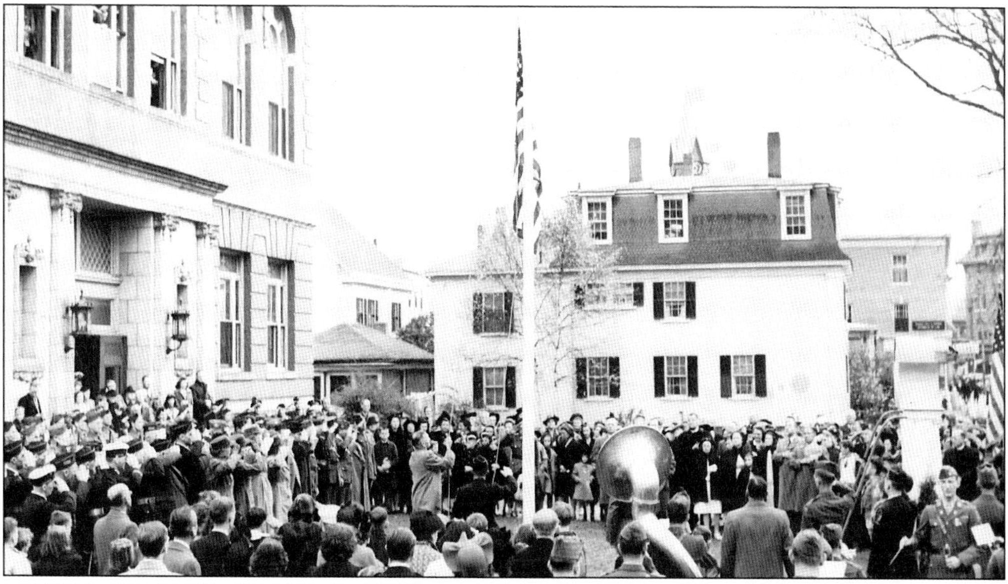

MAYOR WALTER WOOD RAISES THE FLAG. At the conclusion of the ceremonies inside the opera house, the group, consisting of public officials, veterans groups, service men and women on leave, the Rochester City Band, the Spaulding High School Band, and others, gathered on the lawn of city hall for the unveiling of the Honor Roll monument.

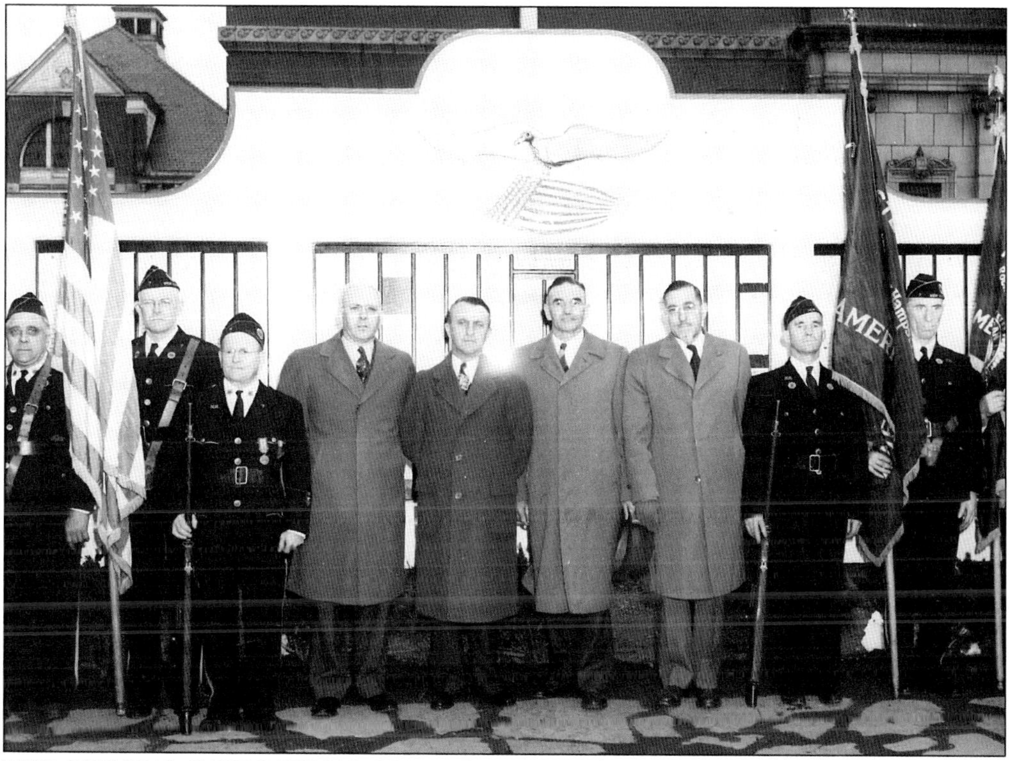

THE OFFICIAL DEDICATION COMPLETE. Posing before the Honor Roll are the mayor, committee, and honor guard. We have identified Phil Hubbard, Aldo Garland, Albert Foster, George Potvin, Maurice Jones, Mayor Wood, and Wesley Lyons.

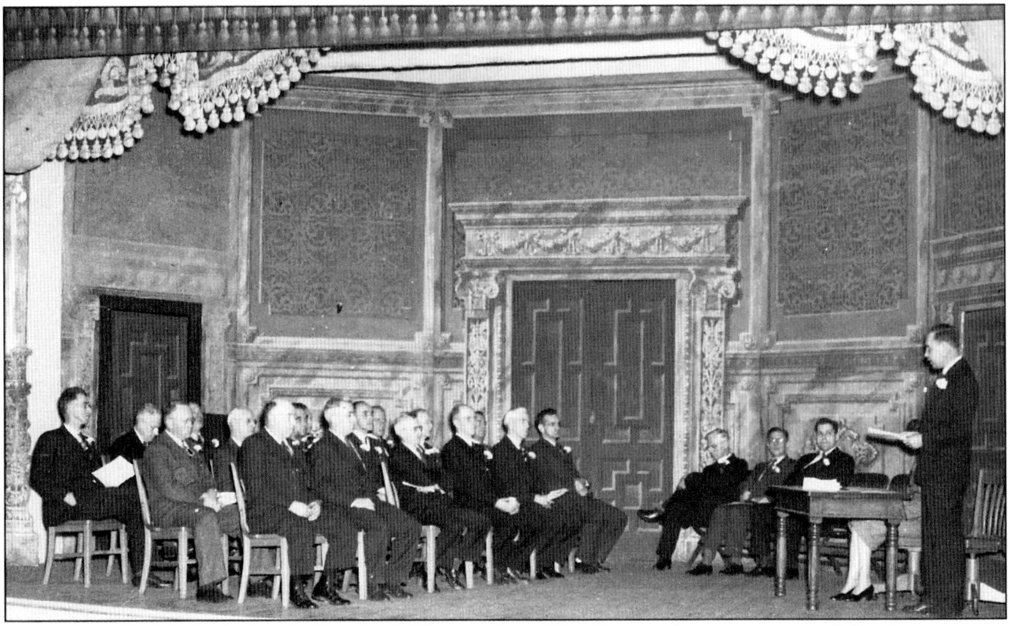

INAUGURAL IN OPERA HOUSE. The stage of the opera house was used for many civic events, including the inauguration of Mayor Thomas Burbank on January 7, 1948.

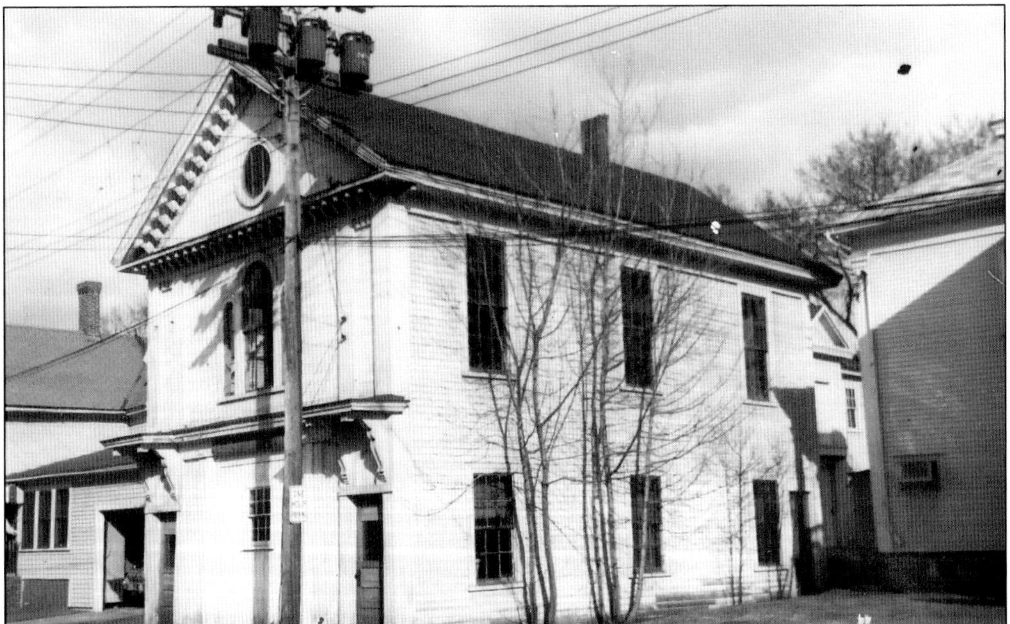

TORRENT FIRE HOUSE #2. The town hall was built in 1851 on the corner of South Main and Wentworth Streets. The firehouse on Wentworth Street was added a few years later. The Rochester Fire Department stopped using this building in 1926 and it became a Ward 6 voting place. Since 1969, Dr. David Dreyer has had his office located here.

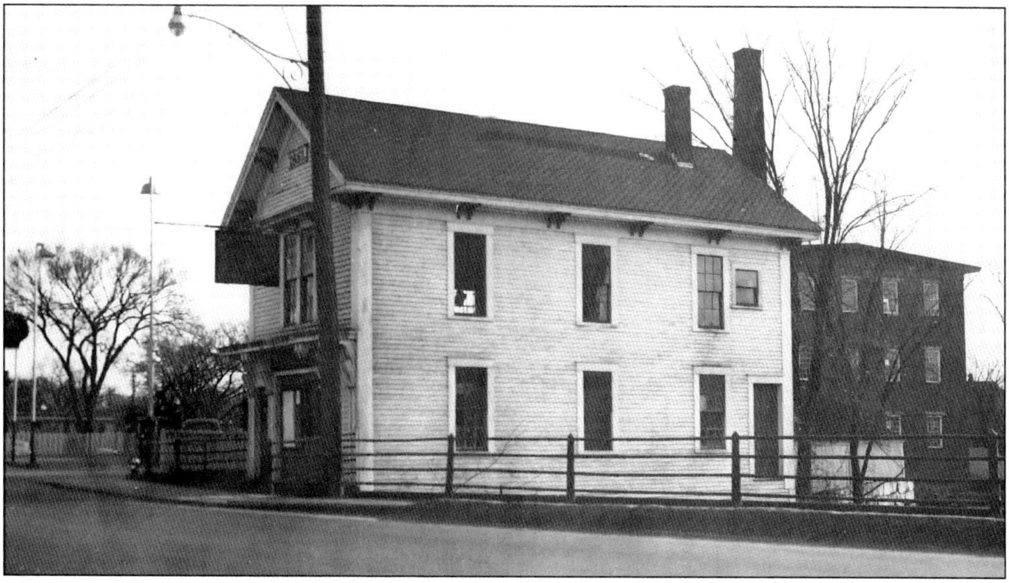

THE COCHECO FIREHOUSE. The building located beside the bridge on North Main Street was not used as a firehouse after 1926 and became a Ward 4 polling place. It was later purchased by Jerry Stuart, who set it up as a workshop in Farmington beside his house at 7 Garfield Street.

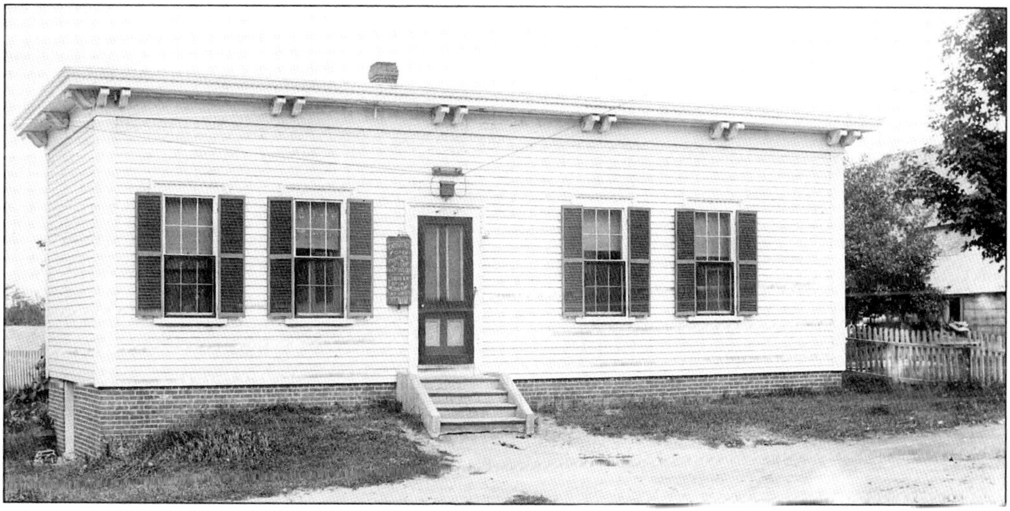

THE EAST ROCHESTER LIBRARY. The counting room of the Cocheco Manufacturing Company, built in 1868, was no longer needed after a new office was built. In the summer of 1888 the company had the old building moved to Main Street (opposite the Glendon House) and made into a reading room and library.

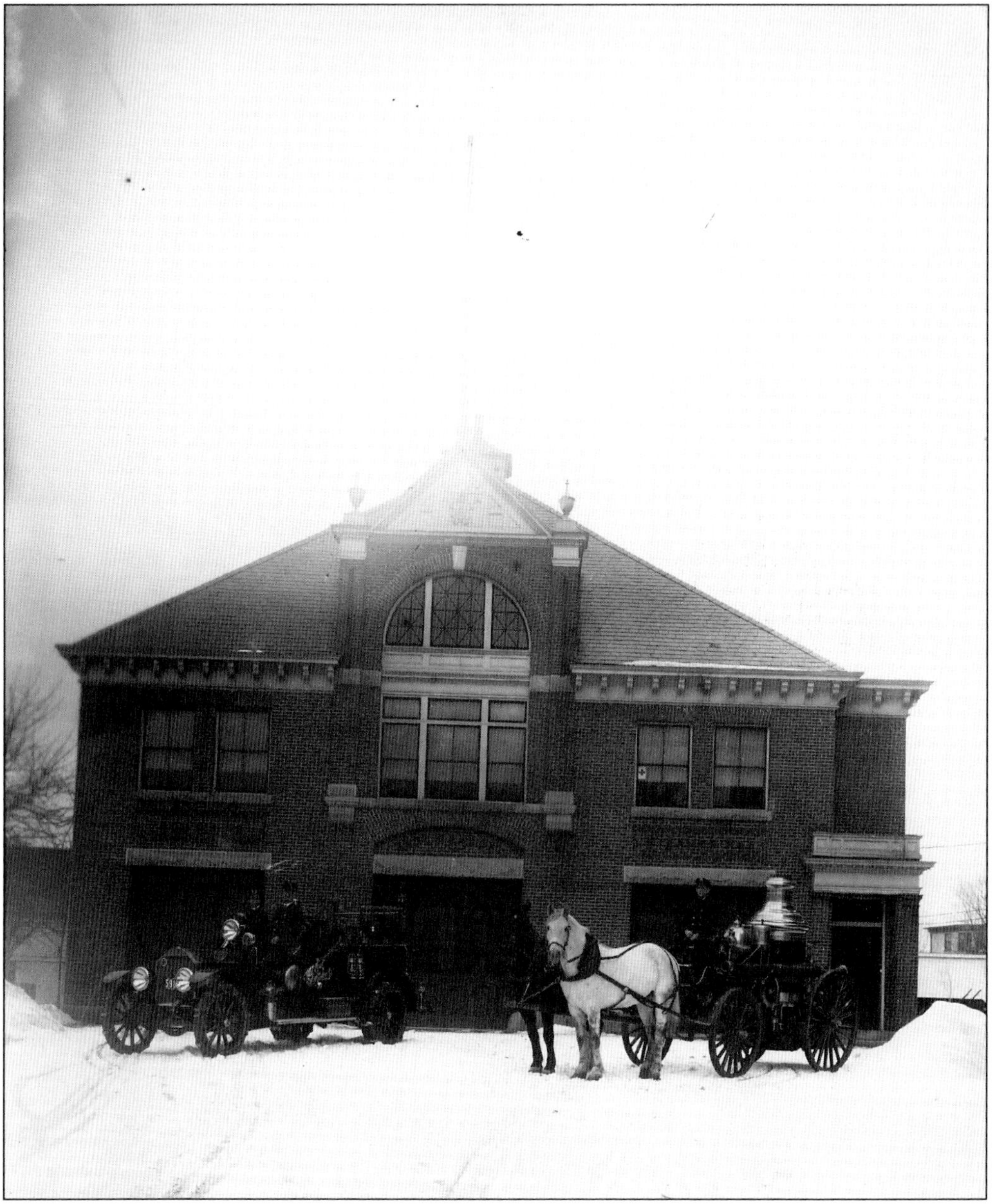

THE CENTRAL FIRE STATION. This building on Wakefield Street was completed in 1905 on the city lot prior to the construction of city hall. The first motor truck was purchased in 1916.

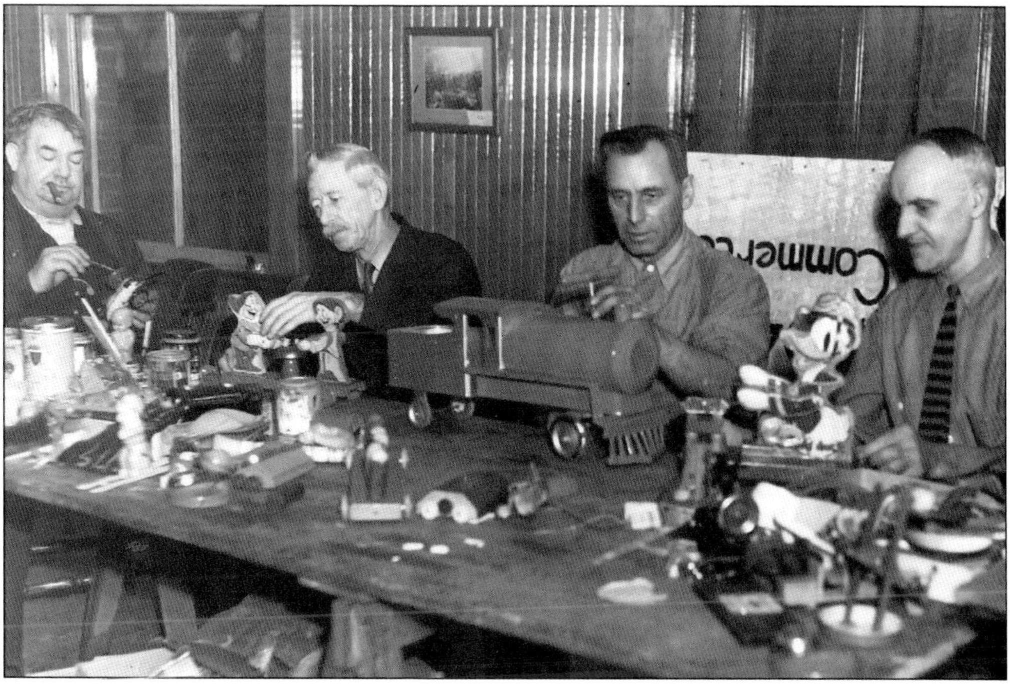

SANTA'S HELPERS. Samuel Locke, F.S. Emerson, Chester Whitney, and Charles Plumer were among the Rochester firemen repairing toys for Christmas distribution in the 1930s.

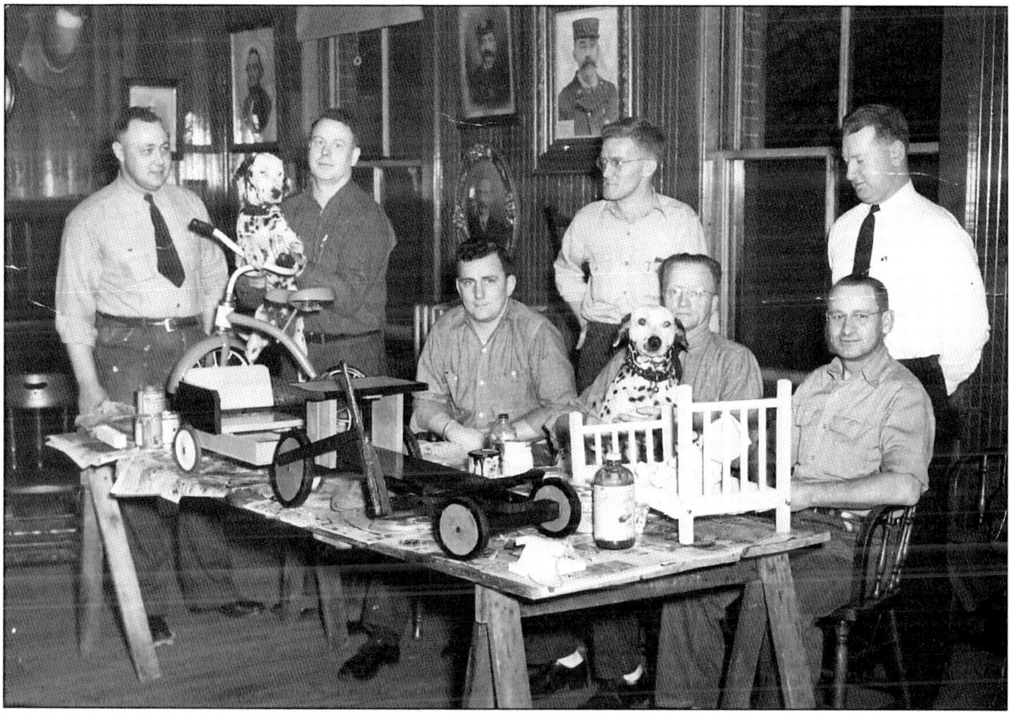

ROCHESTER FIREMEN FIX TOYS. Firemen Fred Cookson, Stanley Ellingwood, Bob Gerry, Harry Lemke, Harold Jenness, George Hussey, and Ralph Seavey are shown here repairing toys in the 1940s.

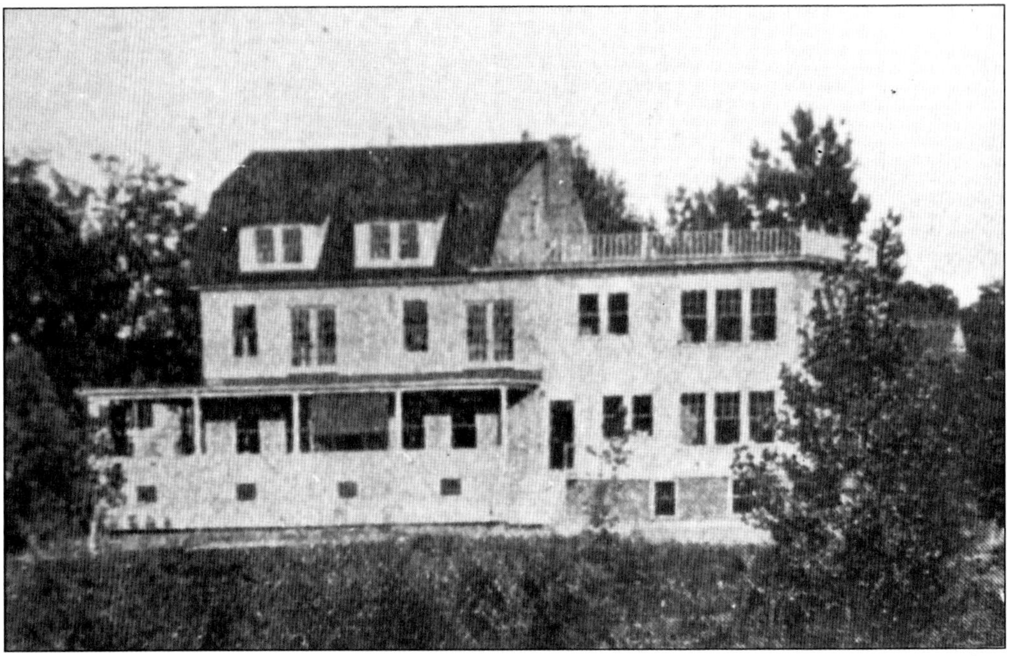

THE ABBOTT HOSPITAL. Dr. Edson Abbott built this twenty-two-room private hospital at 189 South Main Street in 1925. It continued for more than ten years.

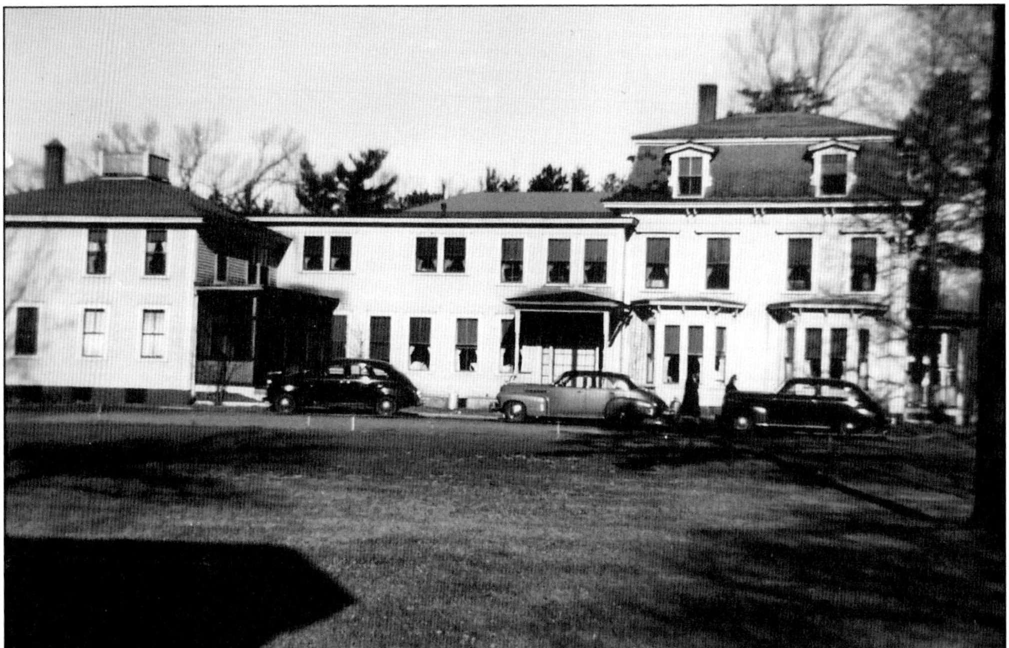

THE ROCHESTER HOSPITAL. The Rochester Hospital, with twenty-four beds, opened in this building on Charles Street on July 26, 1922. In 1926 the trustees accepted a bequest from Jesse Frisbie and changed the name to Frisbie Memorial in honor of his late son, Frank Dunlap Frisbie.

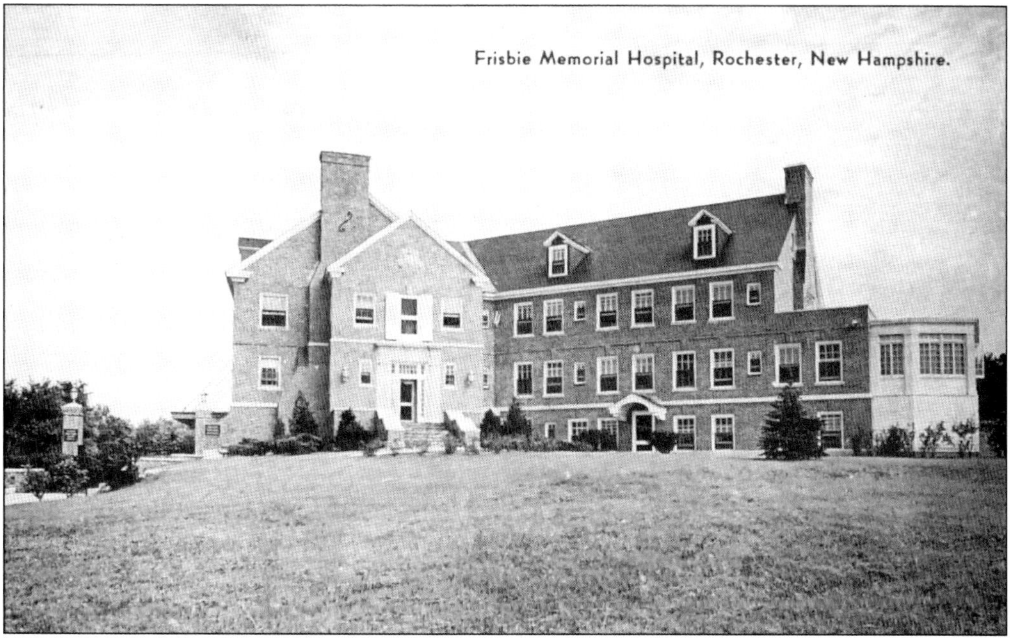

THE NEW FRISBIE HOSPITAL. Patients were transferred in early February 1942 from the old building to this new hospital on Whitehall Road. It was built with a $370,000 gift from the Spaulding families as well as contributions from the public.

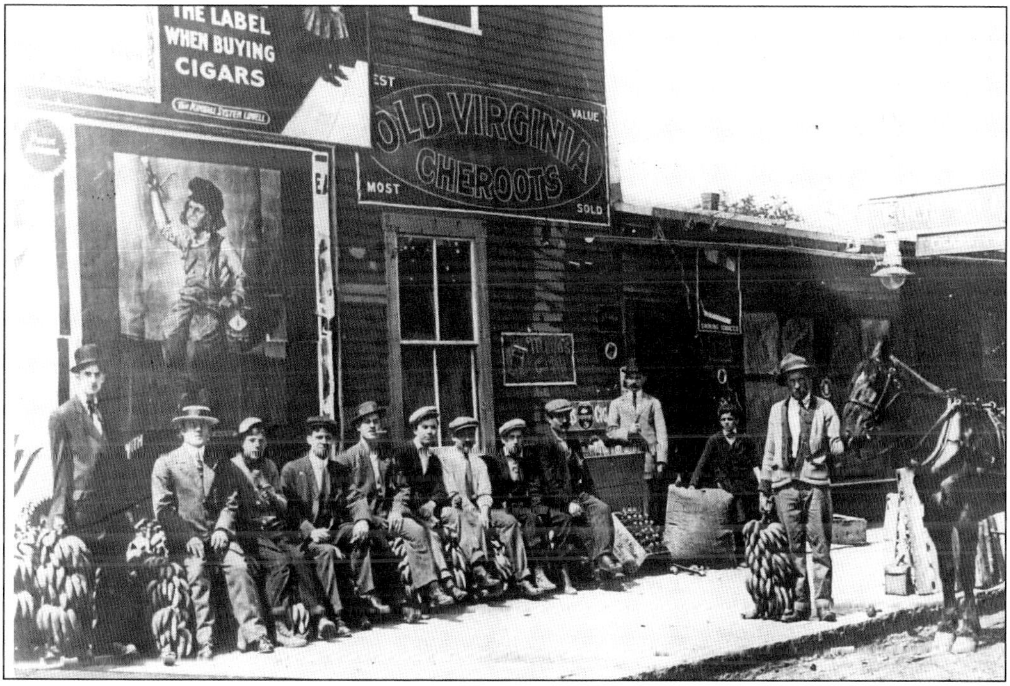

THE POST OFFICE SITE. In 1912 the federal government purchased this land and buildings on the corner of North Main and Bridge Streets for the sum of $15,000. This was to be the site of a new post office. The men seem to be sitting on bananas from the Rochester Fruit Co.

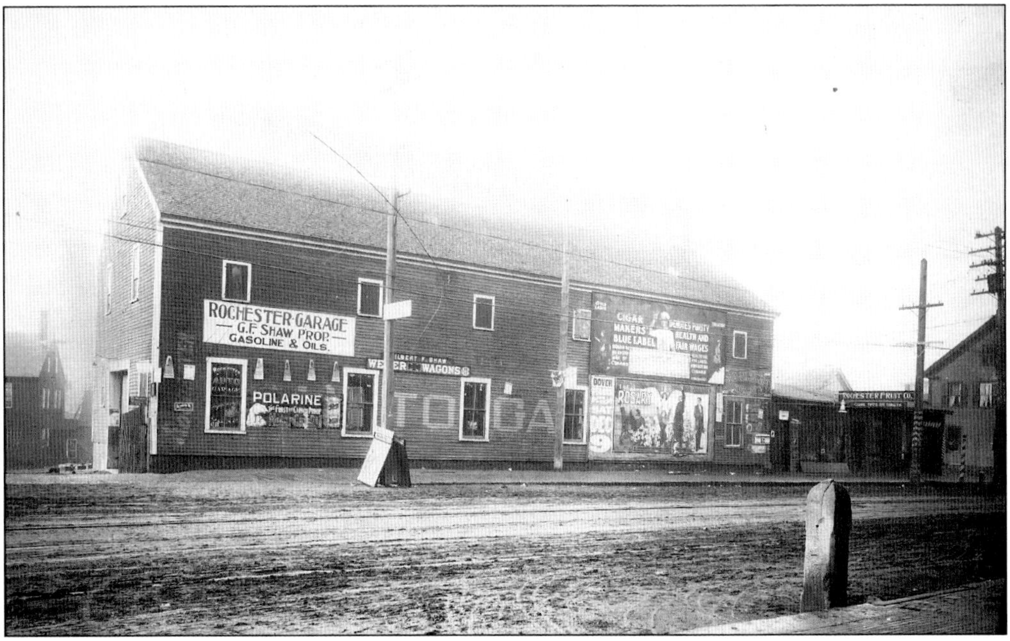

SHAW'S GARAGE. This is a Main Street view of the post-office site. Originally a storage house for the Norway Plains Mill, the large building was occupied by Gilbert F. Shaw, who used the structure to house the first automobile repair garage in the city.

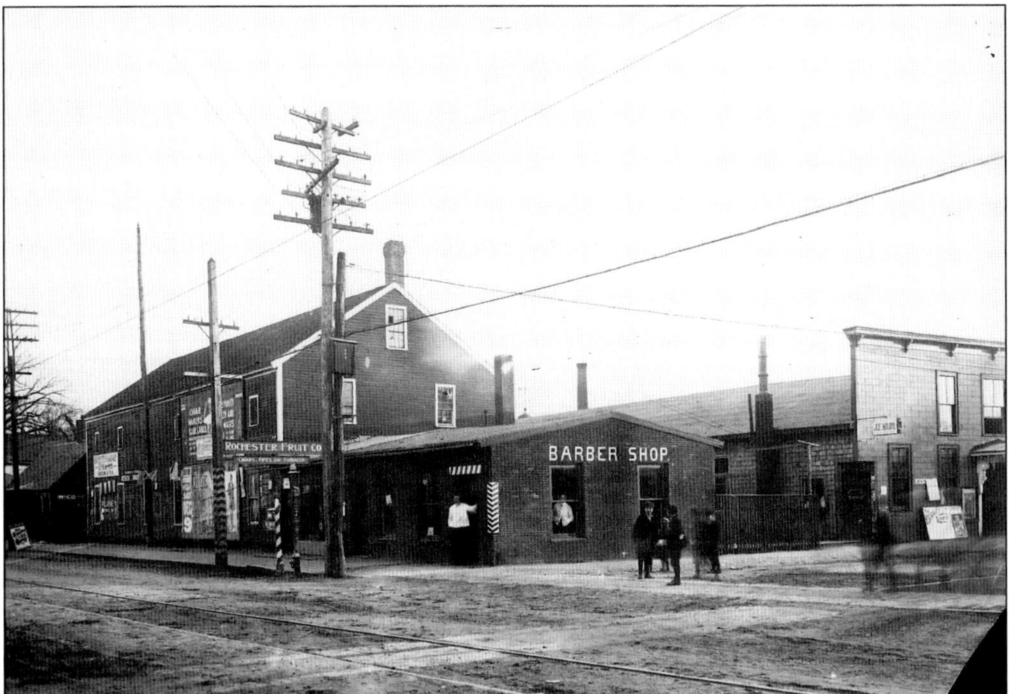

TENANTS TO BE EVICTED. Shaw's Garage, the Rochester Fruit Store, and Maxfield's Barber Shop were on Main Street, and around the corner near the bridge was Lemuel Goodwin's Olympia Theatre. They all had to move to make room for the post office.

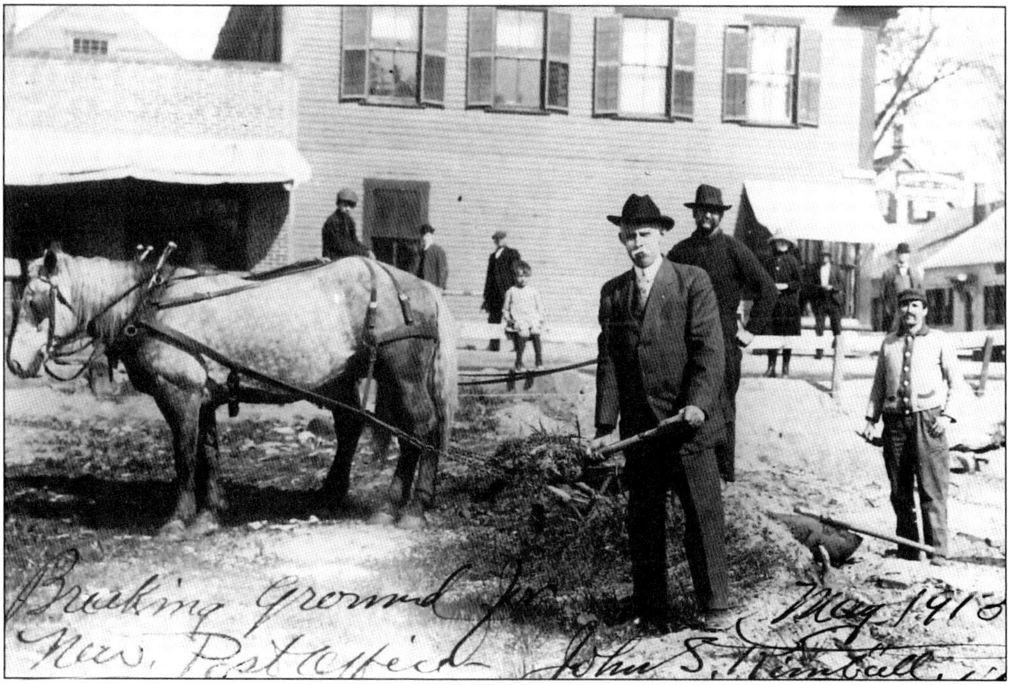

JOHN S. KIMBALL, POSTMASTER. Breaking ground for the post office began in May of 1913. By July the foundation was in place.

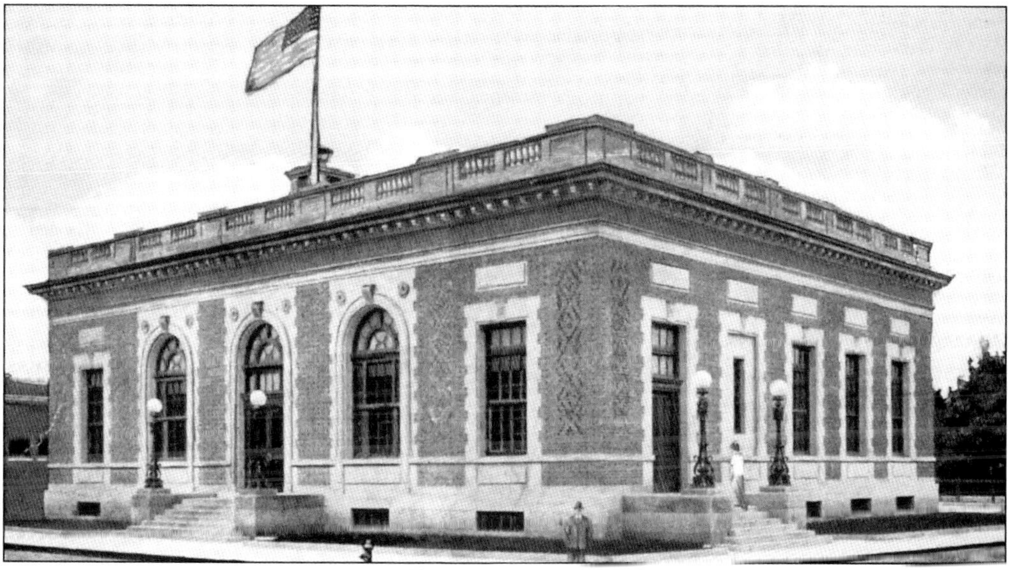

THE POST OFFICE COMPLETED. This new post office opened for business March 15, 1915. It had large revolving doors at both the Main Street and Bridge Street entrances. In the rear was a granite wall with a heavy iron fence and iron hitching rail. This building is now the Rochester District Court at 76 North Main Street.

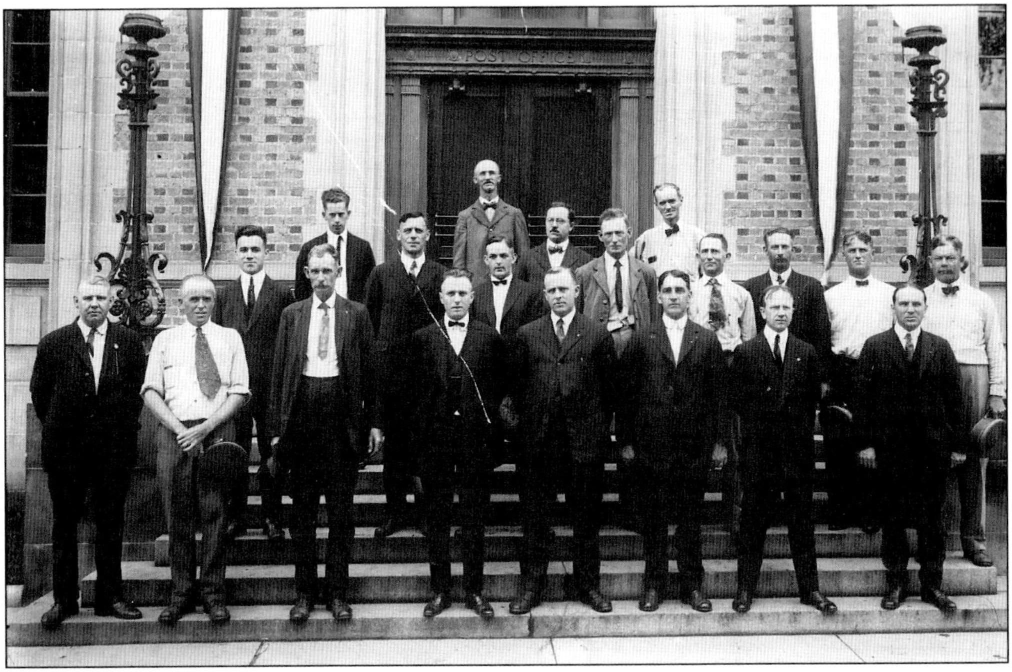

POST OFFICE EMPLOYEES. These post office workers in 1921 include the following, from left to right: (front row) Charles Wood, James Geddes, J. Belmont Allen, Ralph Boyce, Fred Seavy, William Jenness, Albert Nelson, and Robert Blair; (middle row) Will Malone, Robert McClelland, Leon McCombe, Oliver Marble, Henry Grondin, Albert Meader, Dana Meader, and Fred Webber; (back row) Lawrence Goodwin, Clarence Locke, Roland Sanborn, and Ernest Foss.

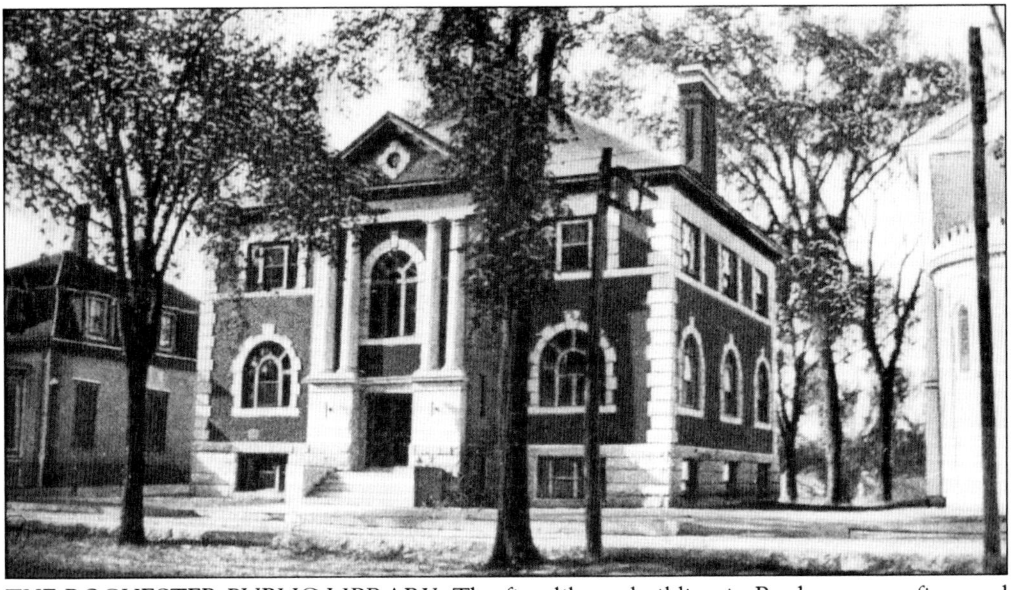

THE ROCHESTER PUBLIC LIBRARY. The first library building in Rochester was financed with a gift of $20,000 from philanthropist Andrew Carnegie. It was built on the lot of the former Main Street School and opened to the public on October 2, 1905. Now, in 1996, the ninety-year-old library has been enlarged and renovated.

Four

Parks and Commons

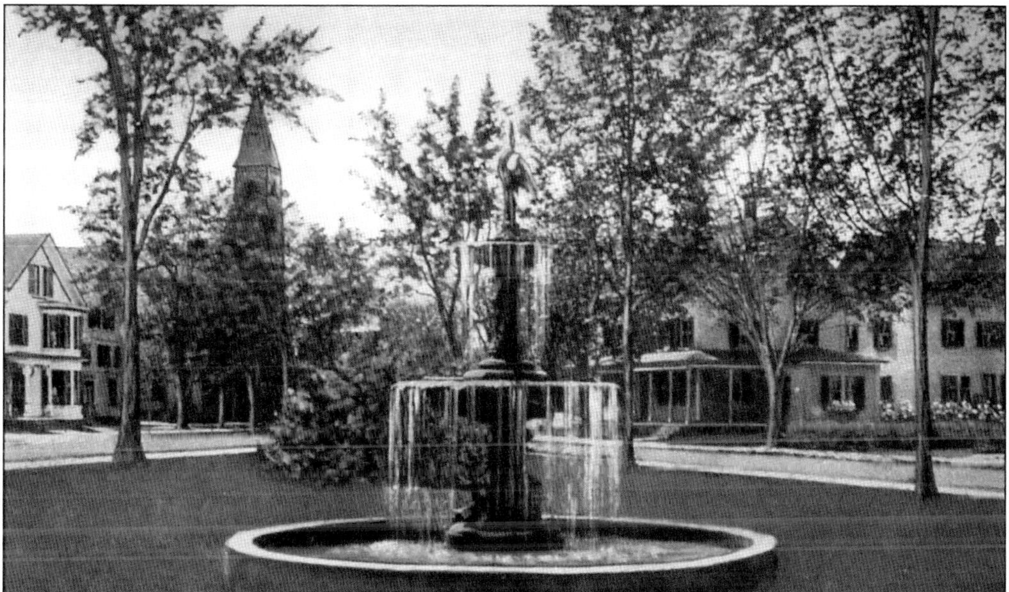

WOODMAN SQUARE. This park on Charles Street was called "Ragweed Park" before 1900. The fountain was installed as part of a beautification project in 1905–10 when the people in the area cleaned and planted the park. The fountain is gone but the base remains, planted with flowers by the Allen School Neighborhood Coalition. This group has brought beauty to Woodman Square once again.

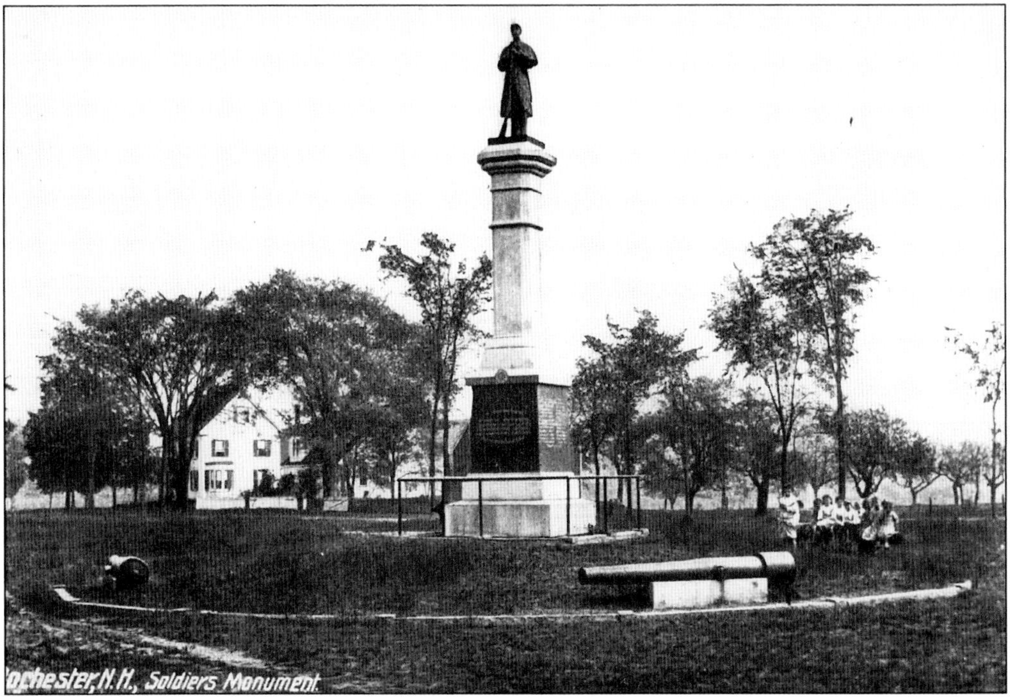

THE CIVIL WAR MONUMENT. This monument to Civil War soldiers, on the Rochester Common, was dedicated twice. The first memorial without the figure of the soldier was dedicated in 1871 but it proved to be unsatisfactory. It was repaired with the soldier added and was rededicated in 1885.

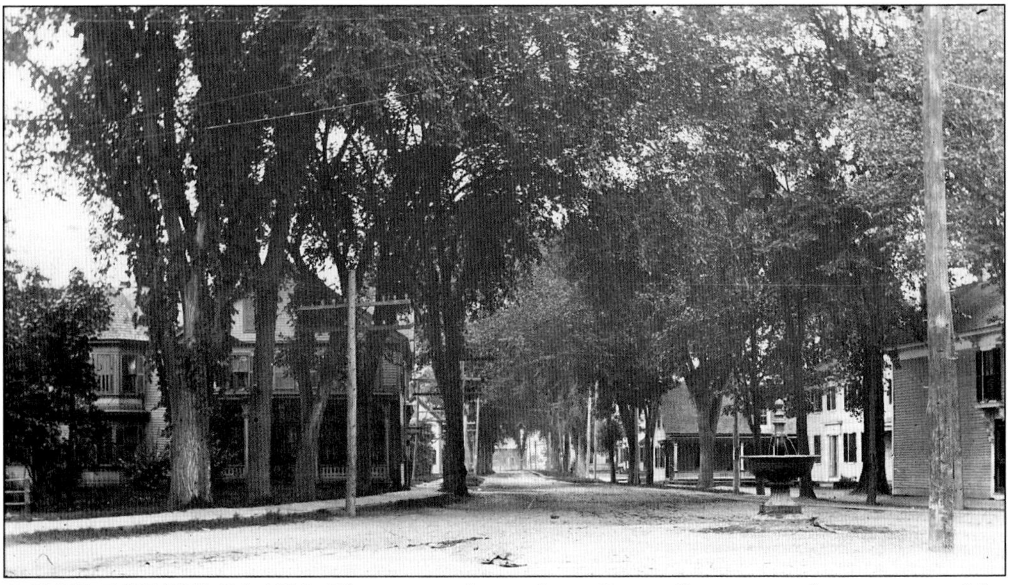

GONIC SQUARE IN 1901. This triangular park in Gonic Square was later improved by the citizens of Gonic with the cooperation of the parks department. In November of 1917 it was officially named in memory of Stephen C. Meader, councilman from Ward 3 from 1896 to 1913.

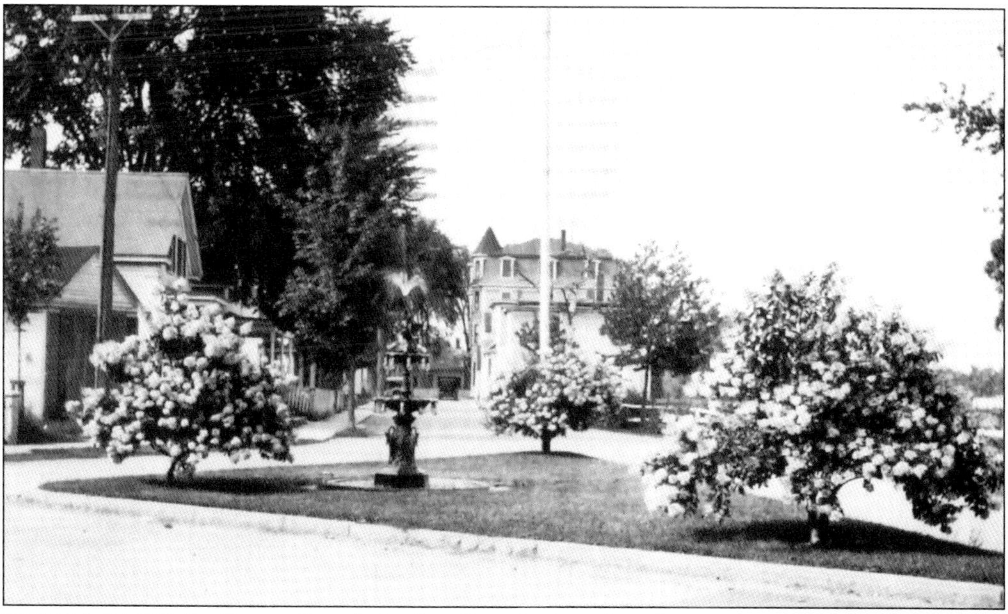

DUVAL PARK. Dr. Ernest Duval, the first French Canadian doctor to come to Rochester, died in 1912 at the age of fifty-two. This park on River Street was built in memory of the beloved doctor. The city donated the land, Mrs. Duval gave the granite curbing, and the people of the neighborhood raised money for the fountain. Duval Park opened in 1914.

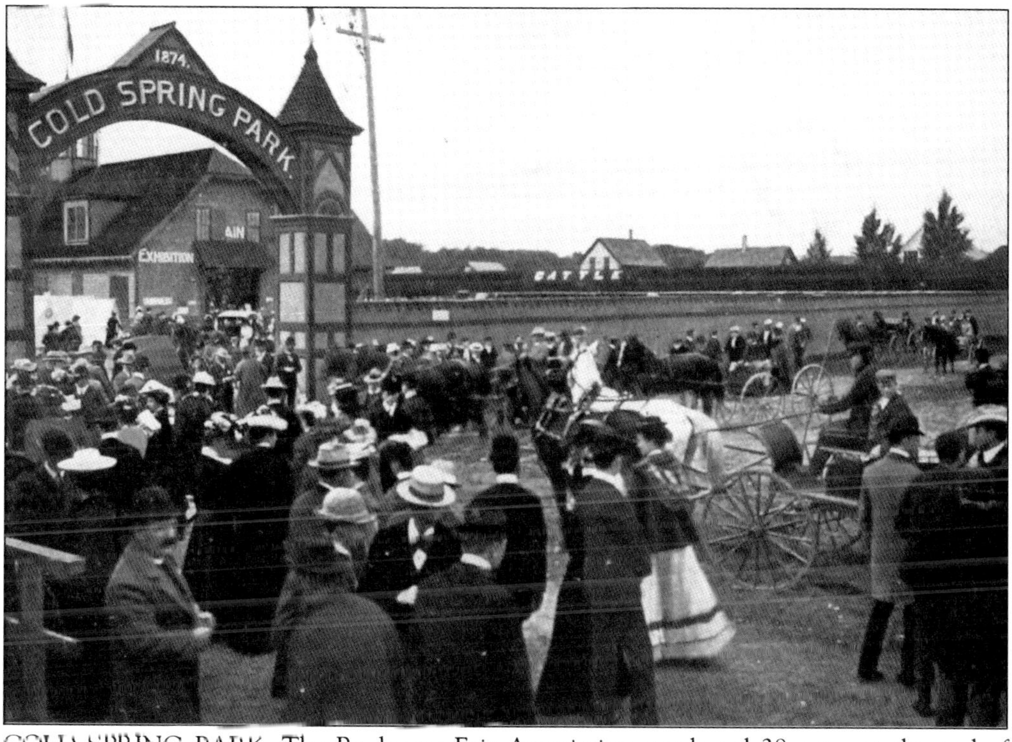

COLD SPRING PARK. The Rochester Fair Association purchased 38 acres at the end of Tebbetts Avenue from multiple owners and, because of the many springs on the land, the area was named Cold Spring Park. Tebbetts Avenue was renamed Lafayette Street in 1898.

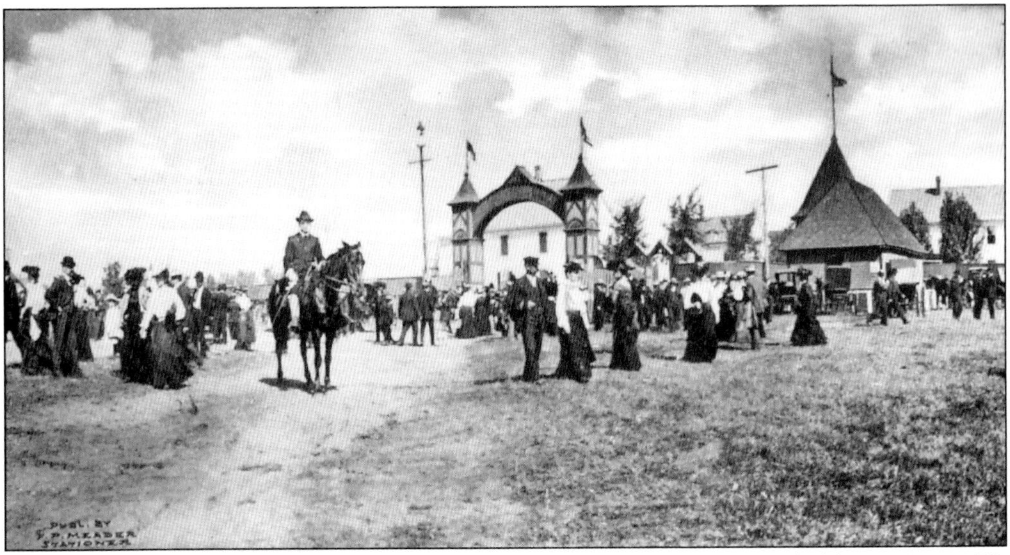

THE COLD SPRING PARK ENTRANCE. Early agricultural fairs were held in 1874, 1877, and 1878 at the Riverside Trotting Park near the river in the Park Street area. The first fair at Cold Spring Park was held in 1879.

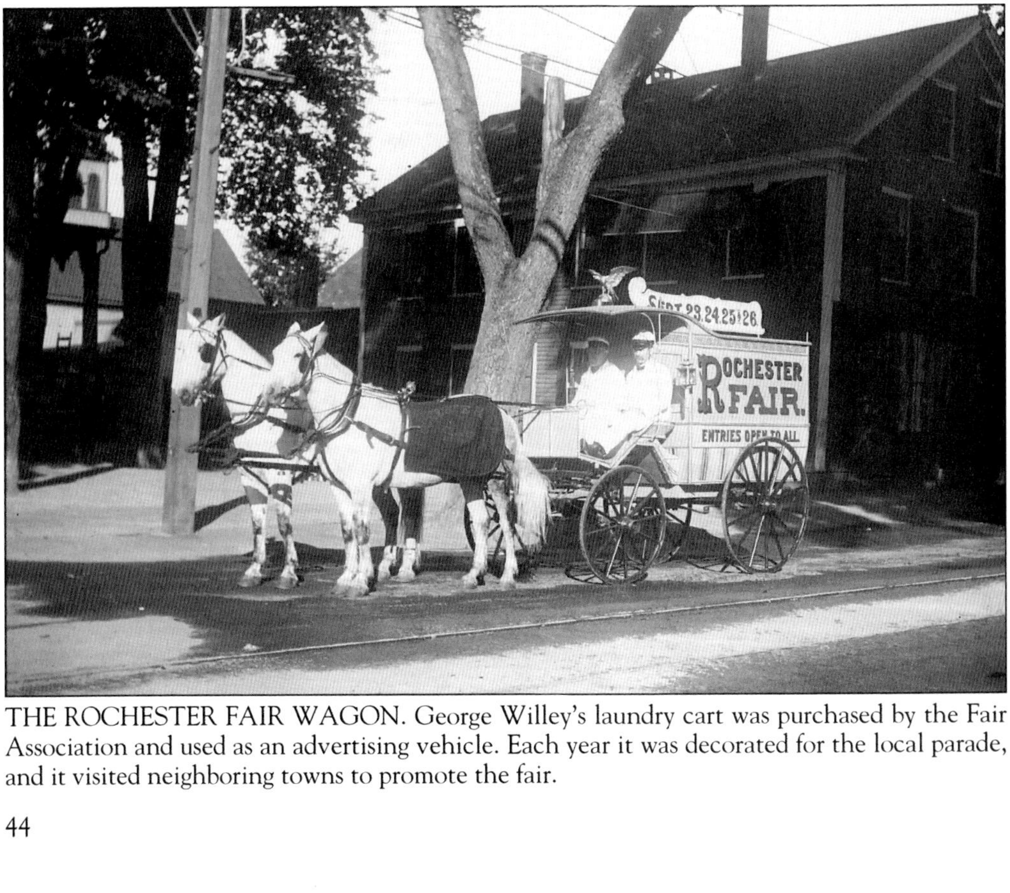

THE ROCHESTER FAIR WAGON. George Willey's laundry cart was purchased by the Fair Association and used as an advertising vehicle. Each year it was decorated for the local parade, and it visited neighboring towns to promote the fair.

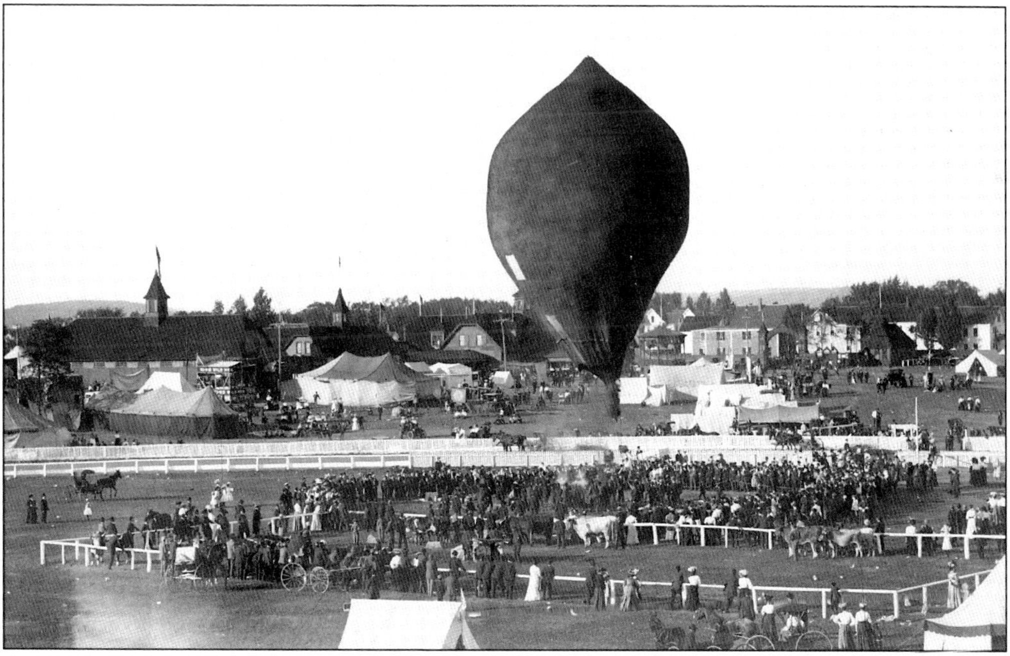

A FAIR BALLOON. The hot-air balloon was an awaited attraction during fair week. A parachutist jumped from the balloon each afternoon and landed somewhere in the city. Charles Dame, a local teenager, made his first jump in 1927. This was the beginning of a love for parachuting that brought him recognition throughout the country.

A FAIR SCENE, c. 1910. The Rochester Fair attracted thousands of people from the city and surrounding areas. From a small agricultural show in a tent it grew to an annual event that was anticipated and enjoyed by the large crowds that attended each year. Notice the Ferris wheel.

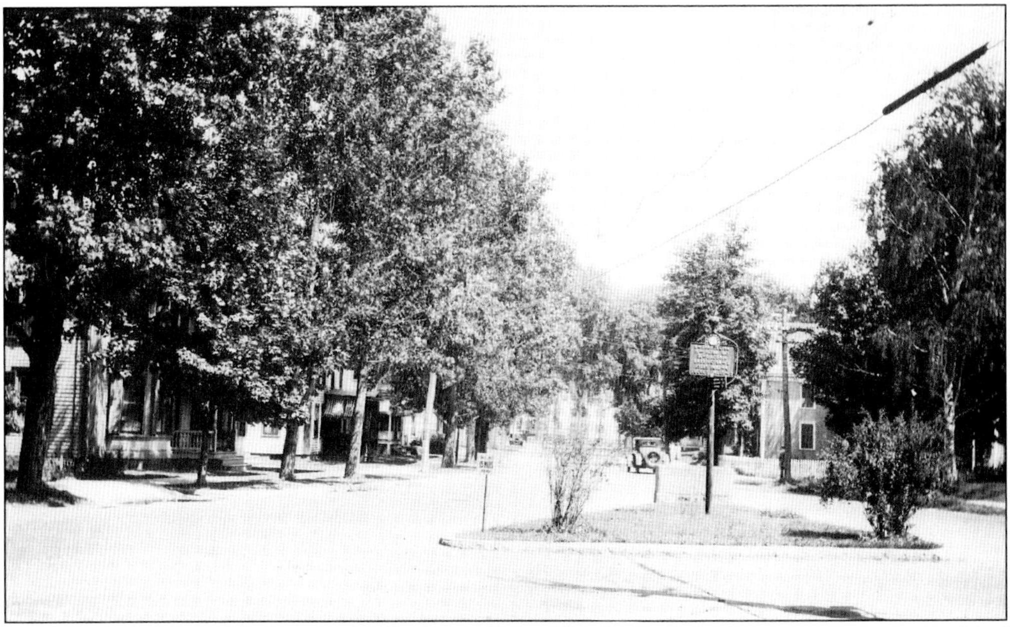

STRAFFORD SQUARE PARK. In 1913 a plot of land was set apart for a park at Strafford Square. A watering trough cut from a single piece of granite was set in place and connected to city water. Horse-drawn wagons that passed by each day often stopped so the horses could drink. The trough is now at the Rochester Historical Society on Hanson Street.

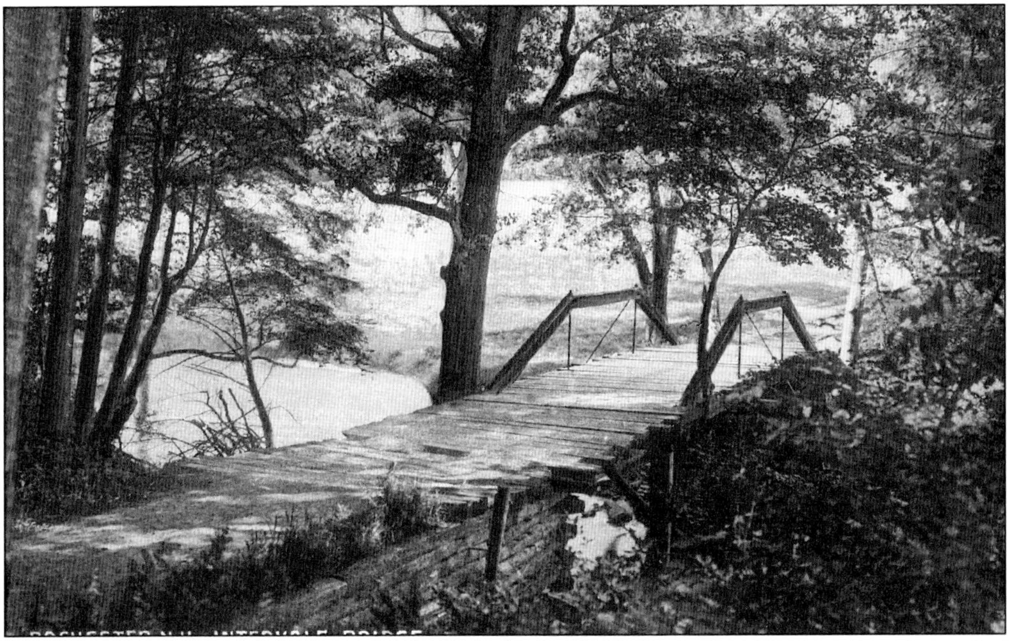

THE INTERVALE BRIDGE. This bridge over the Cocheco River in the intervale at the end of Granite Street was used by pedestrians to walk to and from Cold Spring Park.

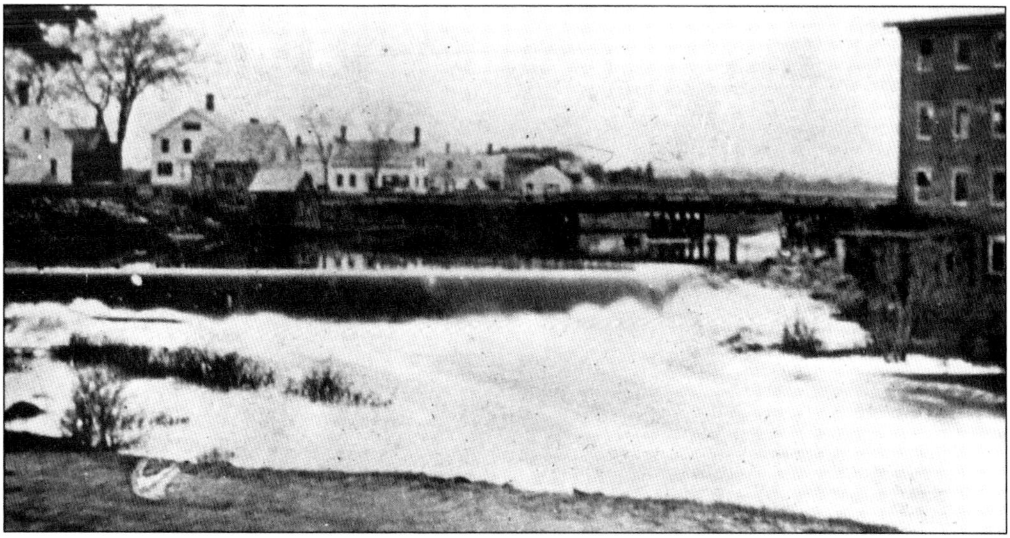

THE OLD WOODEN BRIDGE OVER THE COCHECO. This old bridge over the Cocheco River on Market Street was built in 1754. By the time this photograph was taken the wooden bridge had been in poor condition for some time and was beyond repair.

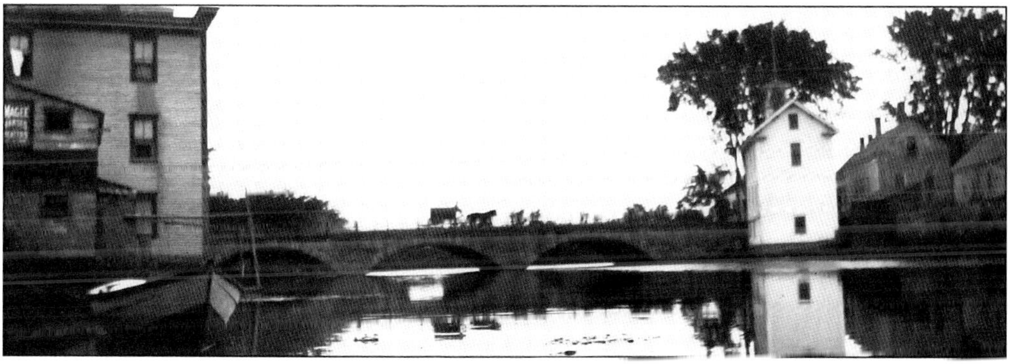

THE STONE ARCH BRIDGE. A new stone arch bridge replaced the old wooden bridge in 1883. Silas Hussey, a local stonecutter, completed this bridge in twenty-seven months at a cost of $14,014.59. During the construction the road was fenced off and traffic was rerouted over Bridge and River Streets.

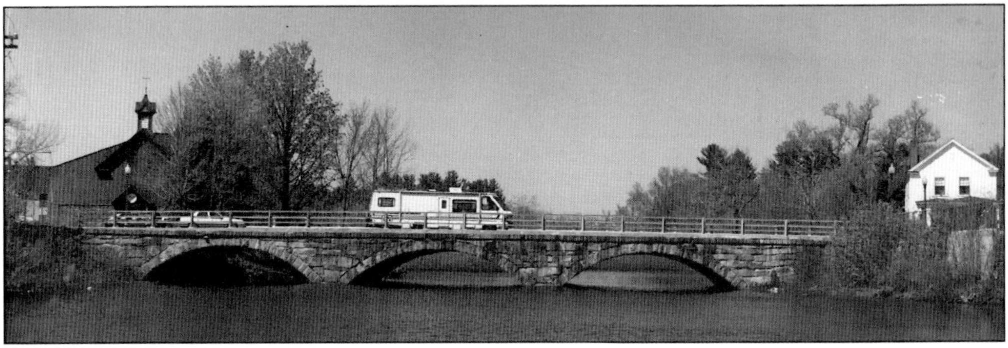

THE BRIDGE TODAY. For over a century this bridge has served the city well and is a excellent monument to the fine craftsmanship of its builder, Silas Hussey.

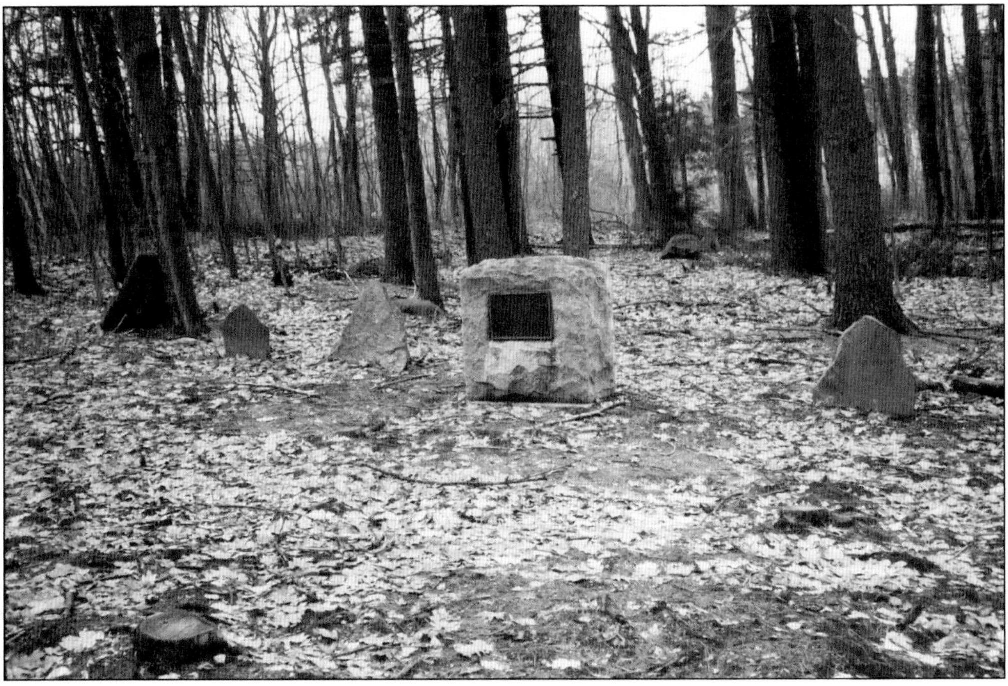

HODGDON PARK. This park honors Mrs. Jonathan Hodgdon, who died on May 1, 1748, the last resident of Rochester to be killed by Indians. The monument was moved to a wooded location near the Anchorage Motel and dedicated on December 10, 1994.

Five

Blocks and Clubs

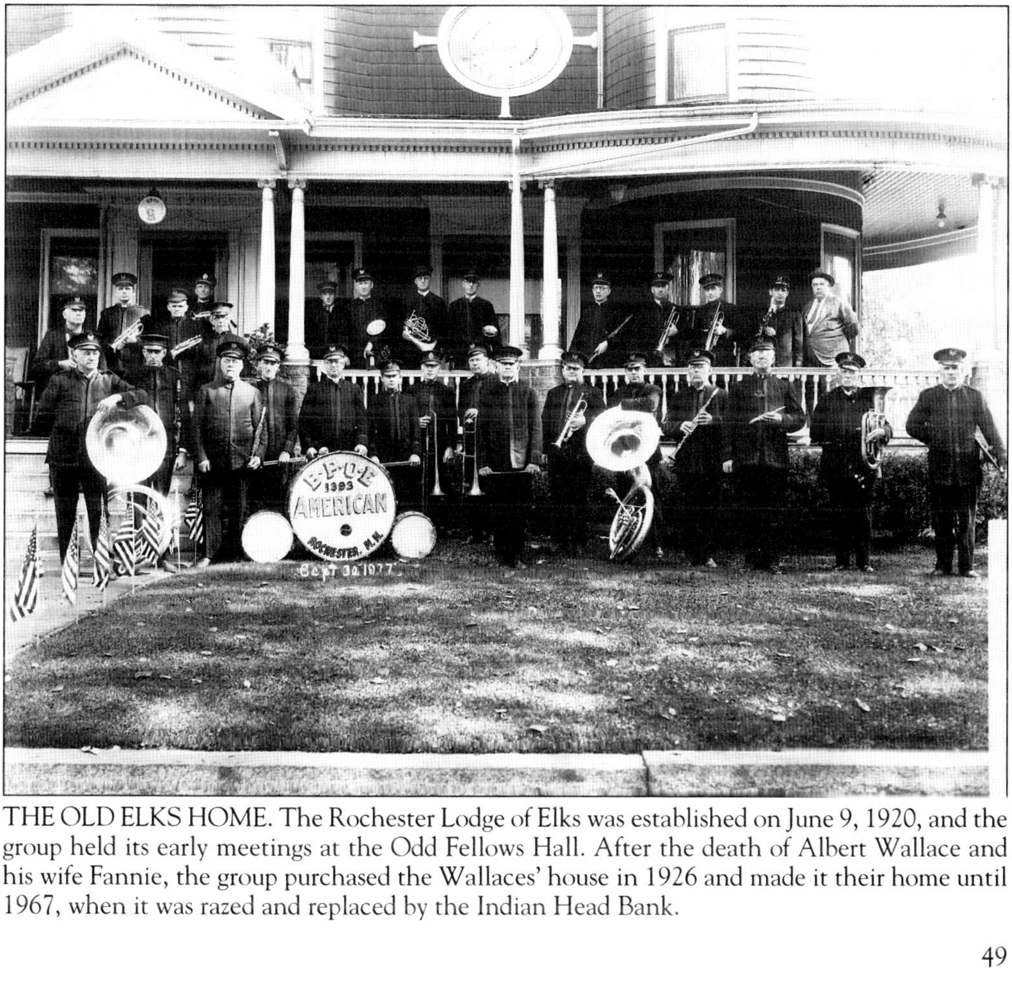

THE OLD ELKS HOME. The Rochester Lodge of Elks was established on June 9, 1920, and the group held its early meetings at the Odd Fellows Hall. After the death of Albert Wallace and his wife Fannie, the group purchased the Wallaces' house in 1926 and made it their home until 1967, when it was razed and replaced by the Indian Head Bank.

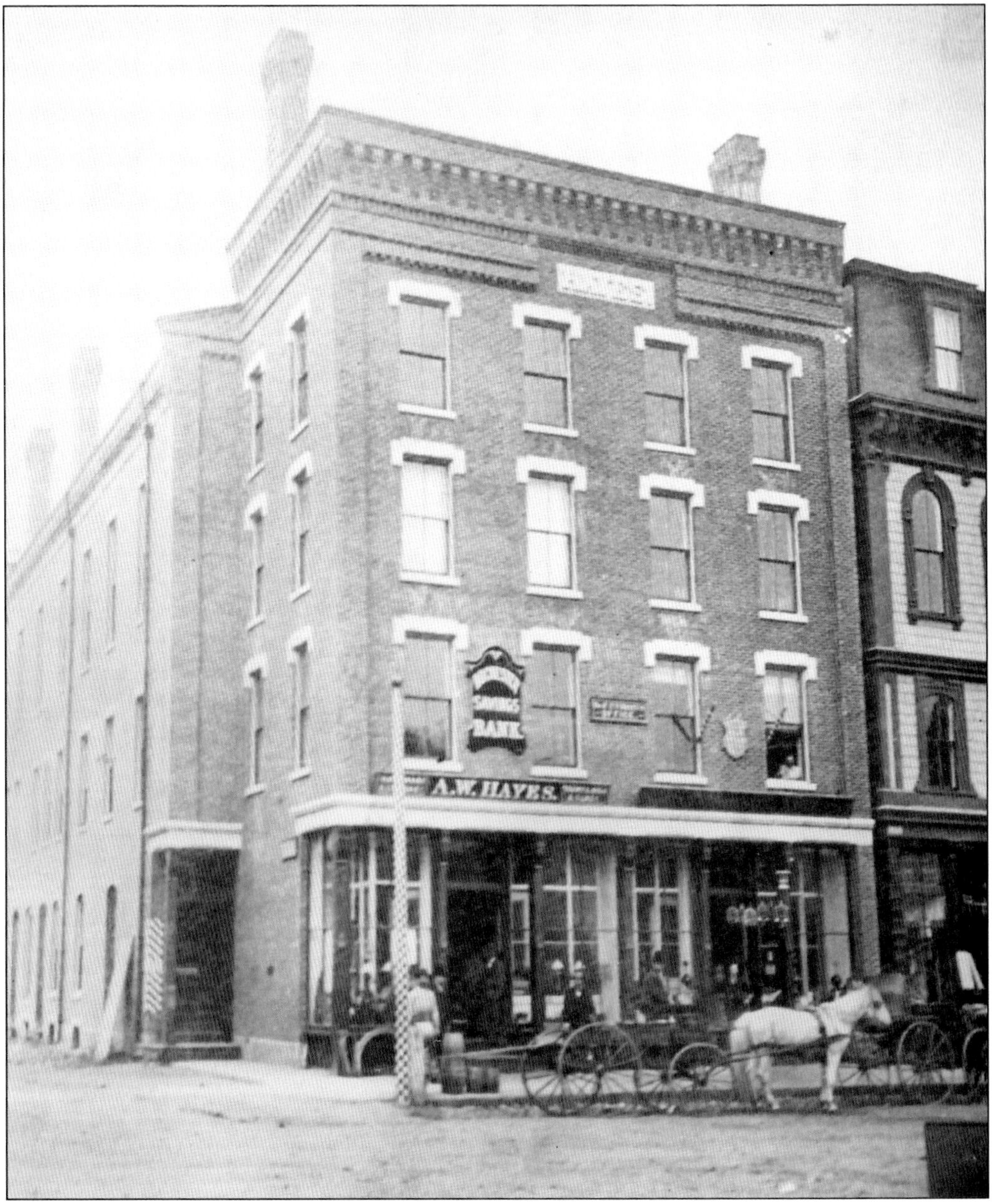

THE HAYES BLOCK. Simon Chase moved his house from Market to Congress Street in 1878. Albert W. Hayes, a prominent businessman, bought the lot and erected a four-story building. The third and fourth floors were occupied by the Hayes Opera House, which was reached by a separate entrance. On at least one occasion, a temporary overhead bridge across Congress Street connected this block with the McDuffee Block for a large party.

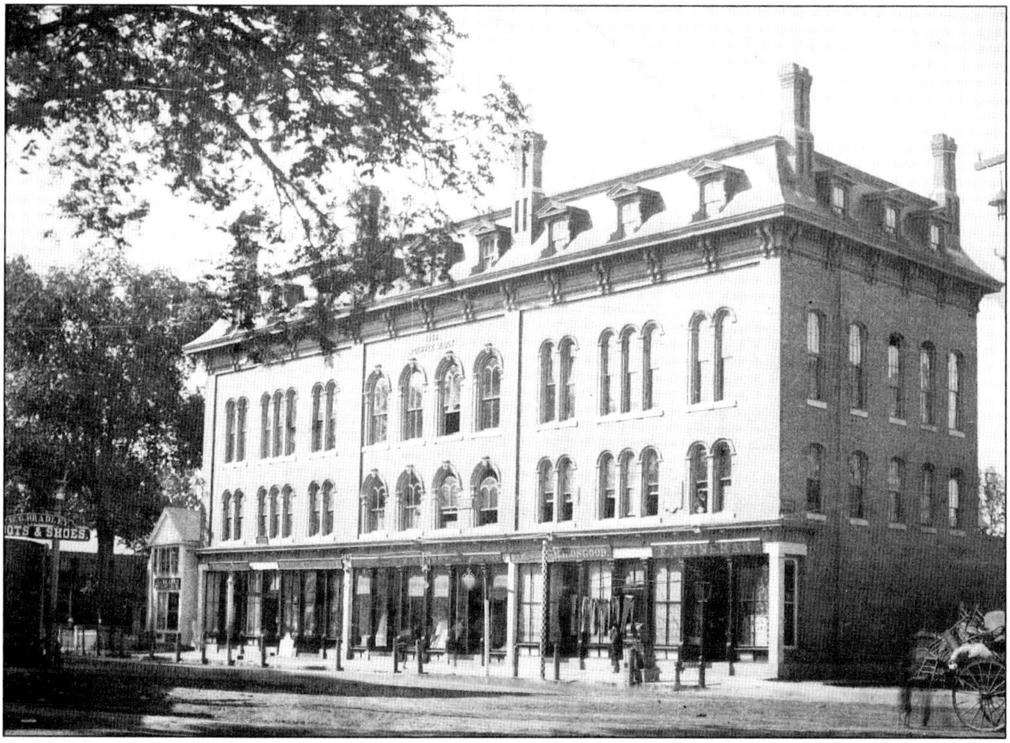

THE MCDUFFEE BLOCK. This 100-foot front, four-story building, built by John McDuffee (left, 1803–1890) in 1868, was the largest block in Rochester. One of the first tenants was the Feineman Brothers company, who purchased the building in 1927. Other longtime tenants were the Lightbody Drug Store and the Fernald Hackett Restaurant. The Armory Roller Skating Rink was on the third floor in 1886. It was opened each Tuesday with dancing following the skating. The Strand Ballroom was there in the 1920s and in the 1940s it was called the Rendezvous. On April 15, 1992, the block was destroyed by arson.

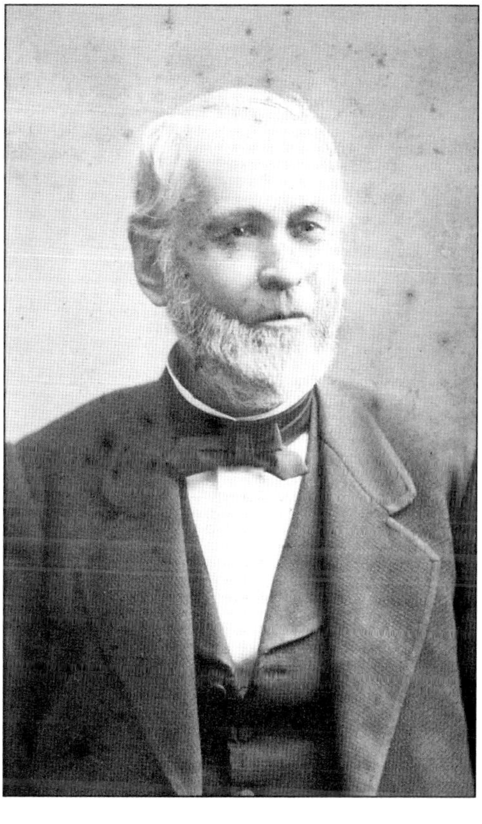

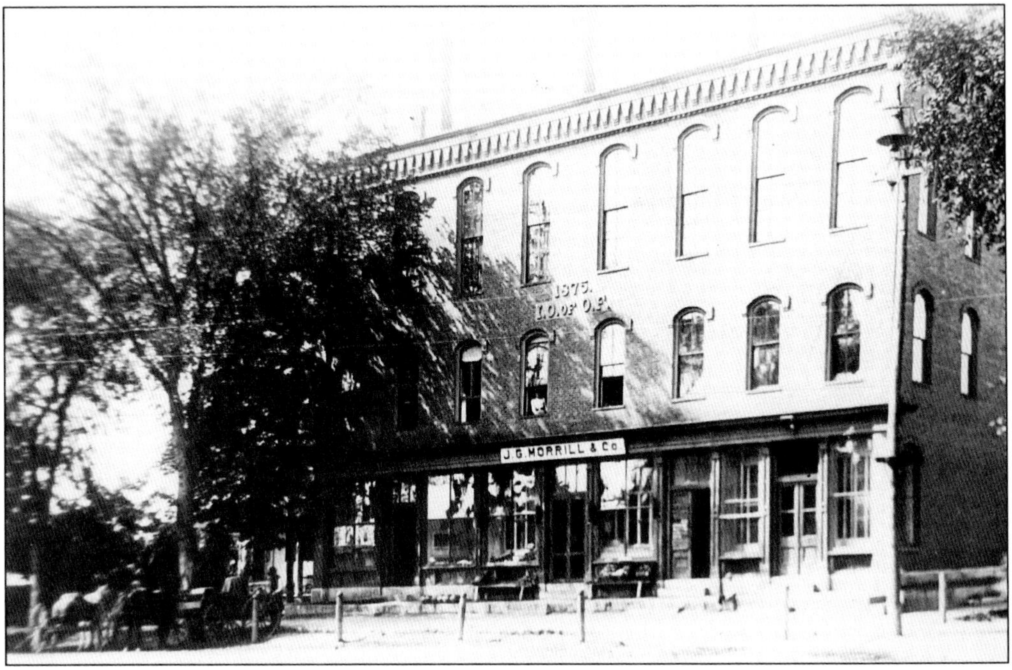

THE INDEPENDENT ORDER OF ODD FELLOWS BLOCK. Motolina Lodge was founded in 1846 and that same year the organization leased the entire second floor of the Rochester Academy. Later when the school closed this block was built on a lot that had been the front yard of the academy in 1874.

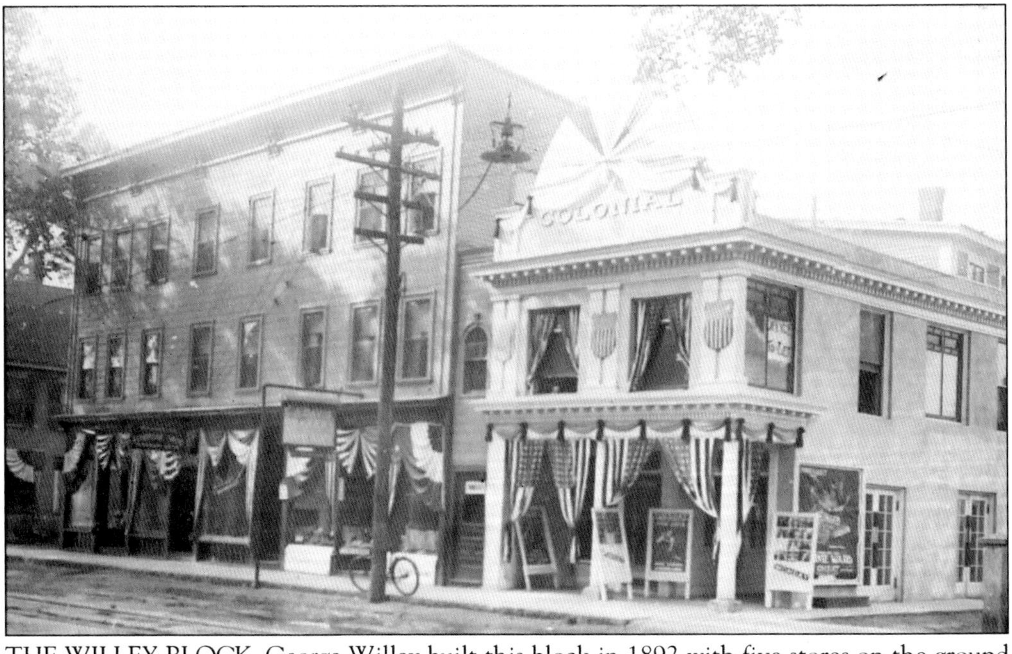

THE WILLEY BLOCK. George Willey built this block in 1892 with five stores on the ground floor and apartments upstairs. George's son Lawrence inherited the property in 1920 and opened a two-story theatre called the Colonial. Later Lawrence leased the theatre to the Interstate Theatre Company who ran the State Theatre that closed in 1948.

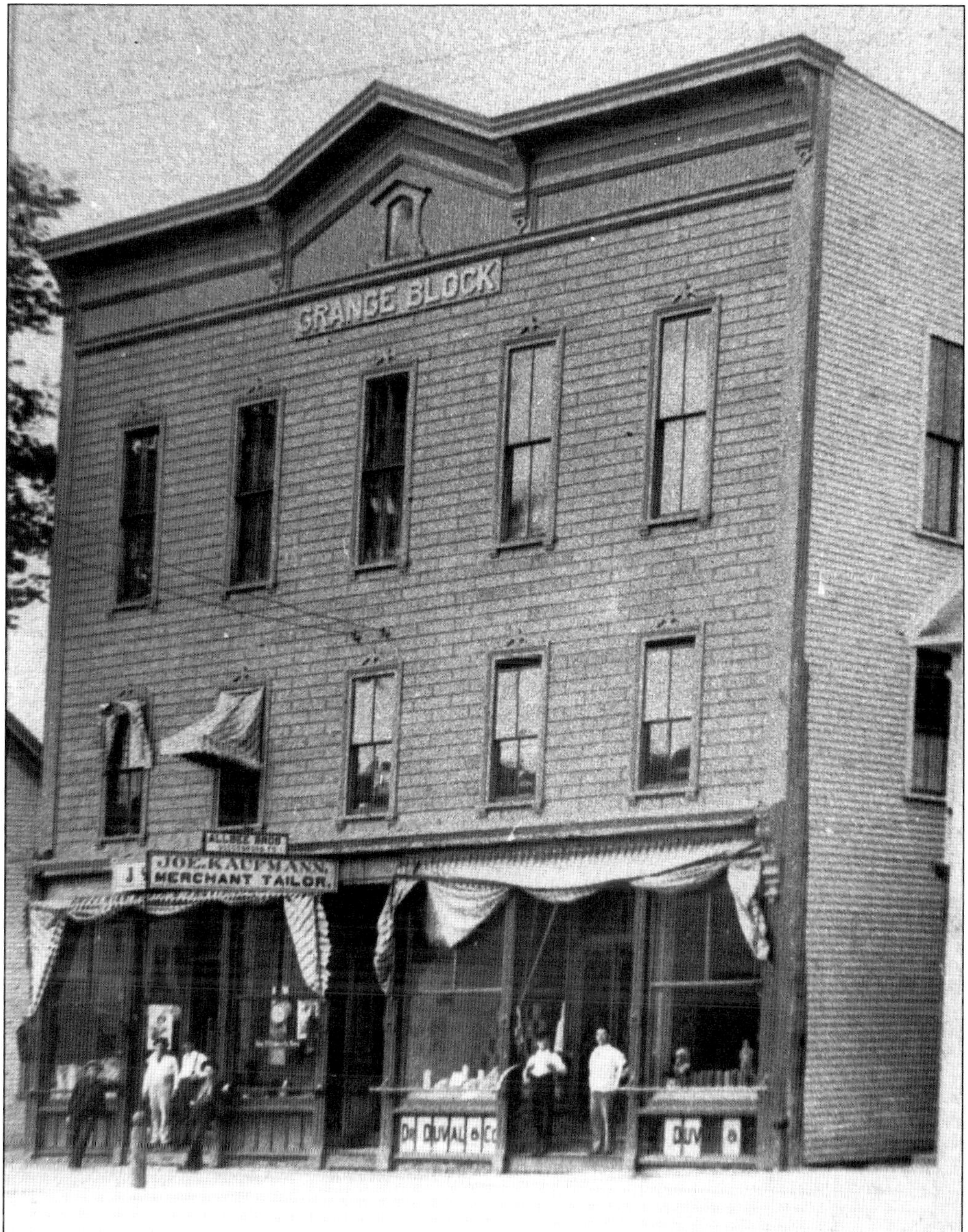

THE GRANGE BLOCK. The owners of this block, all members of the local Grange, provided quarters for the Grange on the third floor when they built it in 1887. Lothrop & Farnums purchased the building at 61 North Main Street in June 1912, when they were evicted from the Dodge Block. The top story was removed in 1967 during renovations for the J.C. Penny Co.

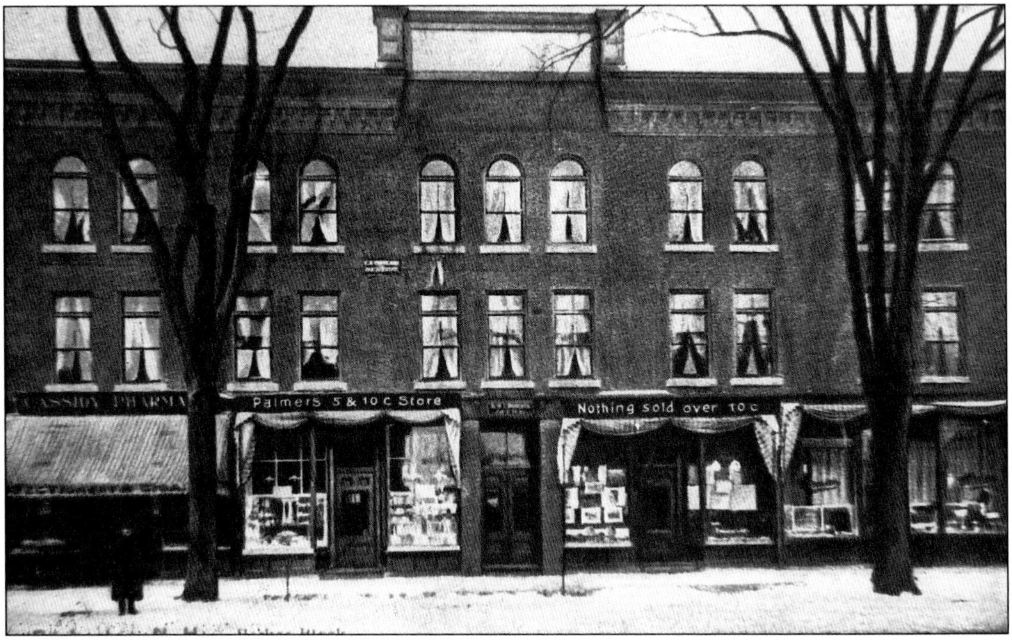

THE BARKER BLOCK. Charles S. Barker purchased the Farrington property on the corner of Portland and Main Streets in 1889 and built this block. His wife Etta, a milliner, opened a shop on the Portland Street corner.

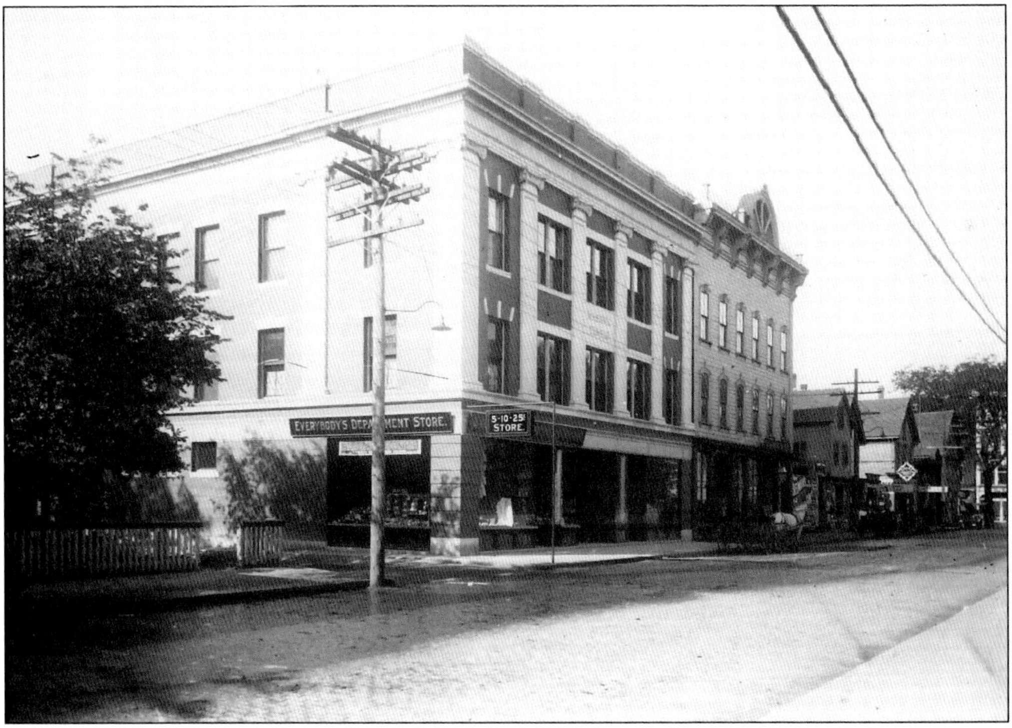

THE MASONIC TEMPLE. Charles A.C. Hanson donated land at the corner of Hanson Street and Central Avenue as a site for a Masonic Temple. The newly completed building was dedicated on July 24, 1911.

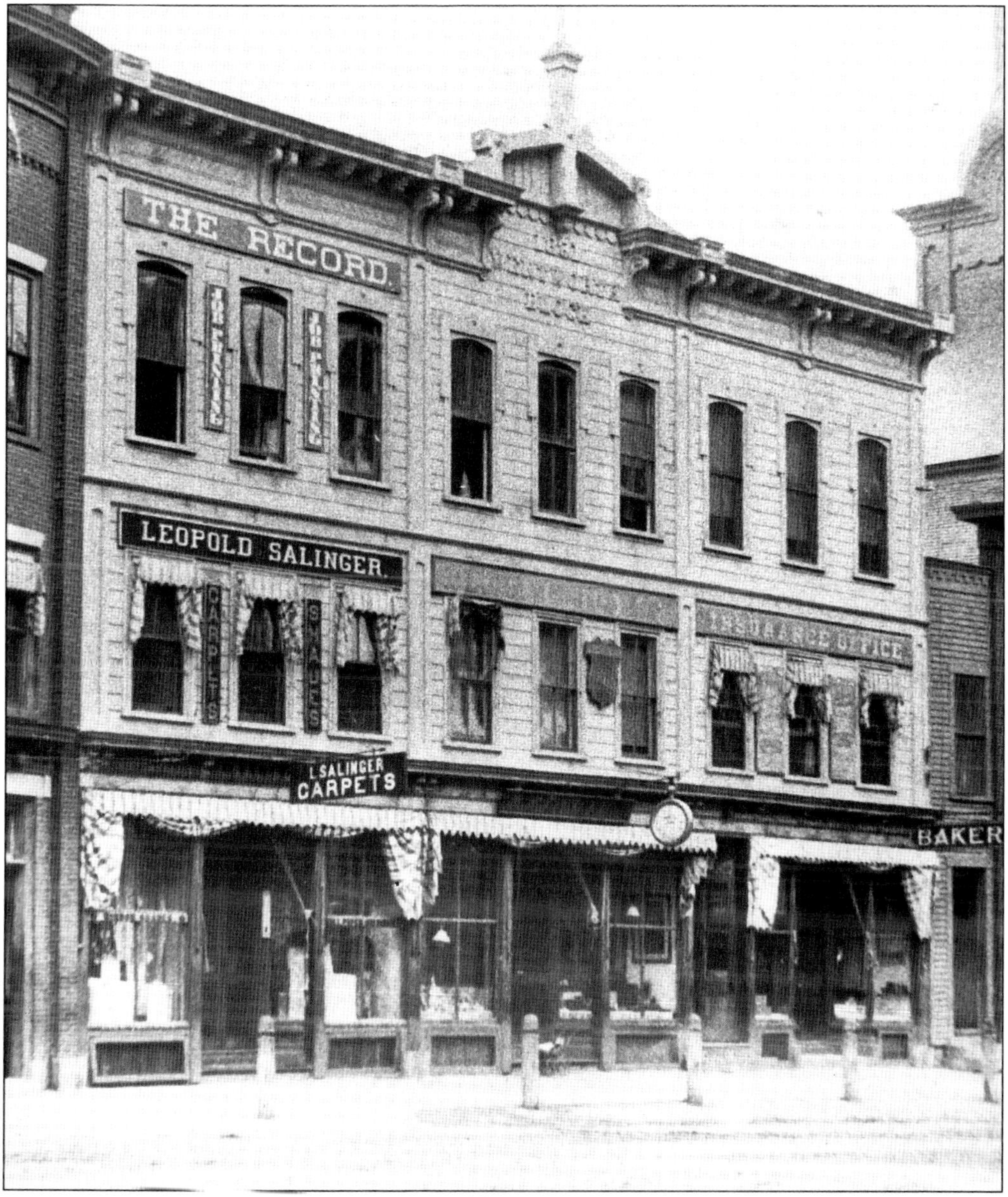

THE WENTWORTH BLOCK. An old building in this location was destroyed in 1880 by the same fire that damaged Hanson's Drug Store next door. Two years later, Ezekiel Wentworth, the owner, had a new brick block built with four large stores on the first floor. Offices occupied the second floor and the third story was the GAR Hall.

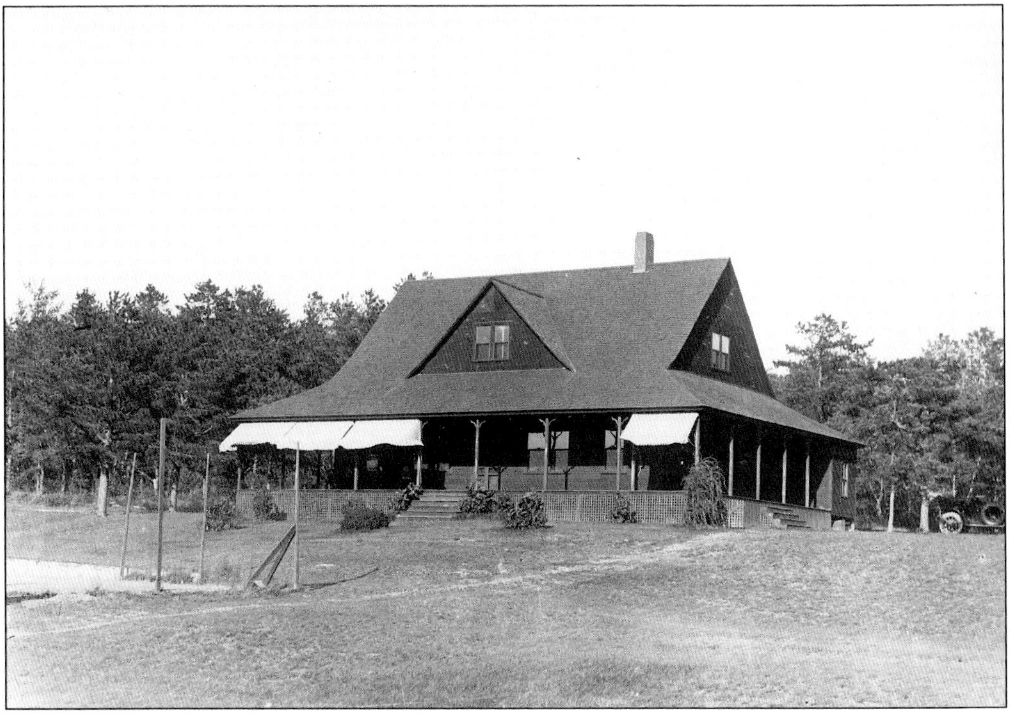

THE FIRST COUNTRY CLUB. This early country club opened in October of 1904 at the end of Snow Street. When the club was closed in 1922, the house was sold to Charles Watson Sr., who used parts of it in his home at 5 Academy Street.

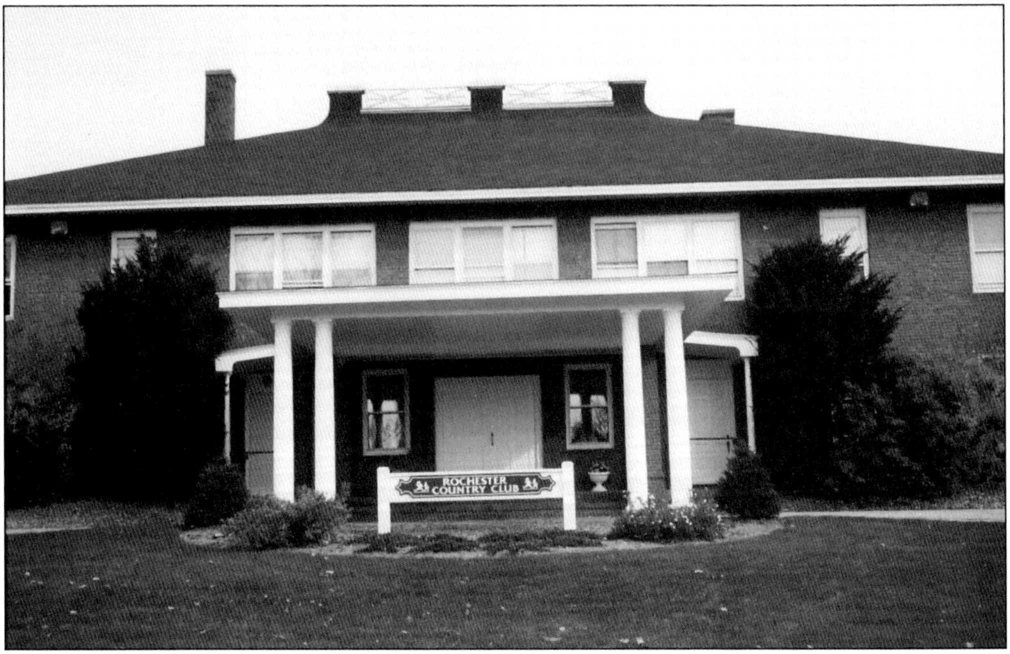

A NEW COUNTRY CLUB. A new country club was opened in Gonic in 1922 on land purchased from Joseph Warren. The club was built with a nine-hole golf course that was later made into an eighteen-hole course.

Six

Merchants

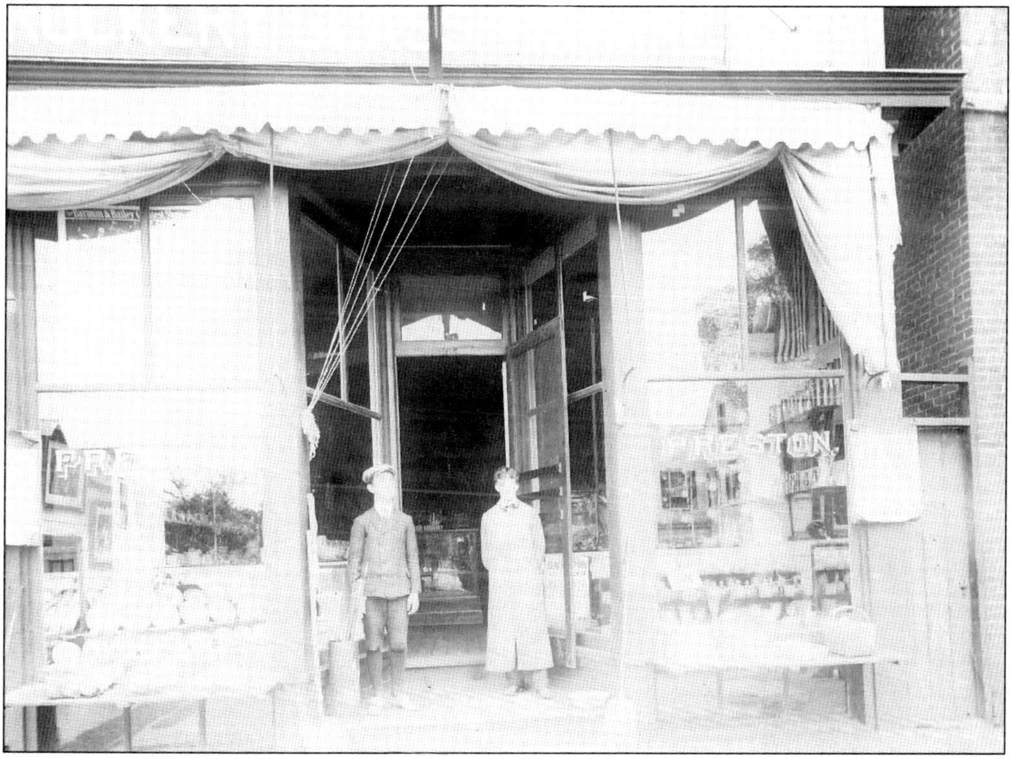

PRESTON'S CROCKERY STORE. Preston's Crockery was located at 45 North Main Street. He sold crockery, glass, china, tinware, lamps, wallpaper, and other household goods. Vinton Preston (right) and Vincent Lamy are pictured here.

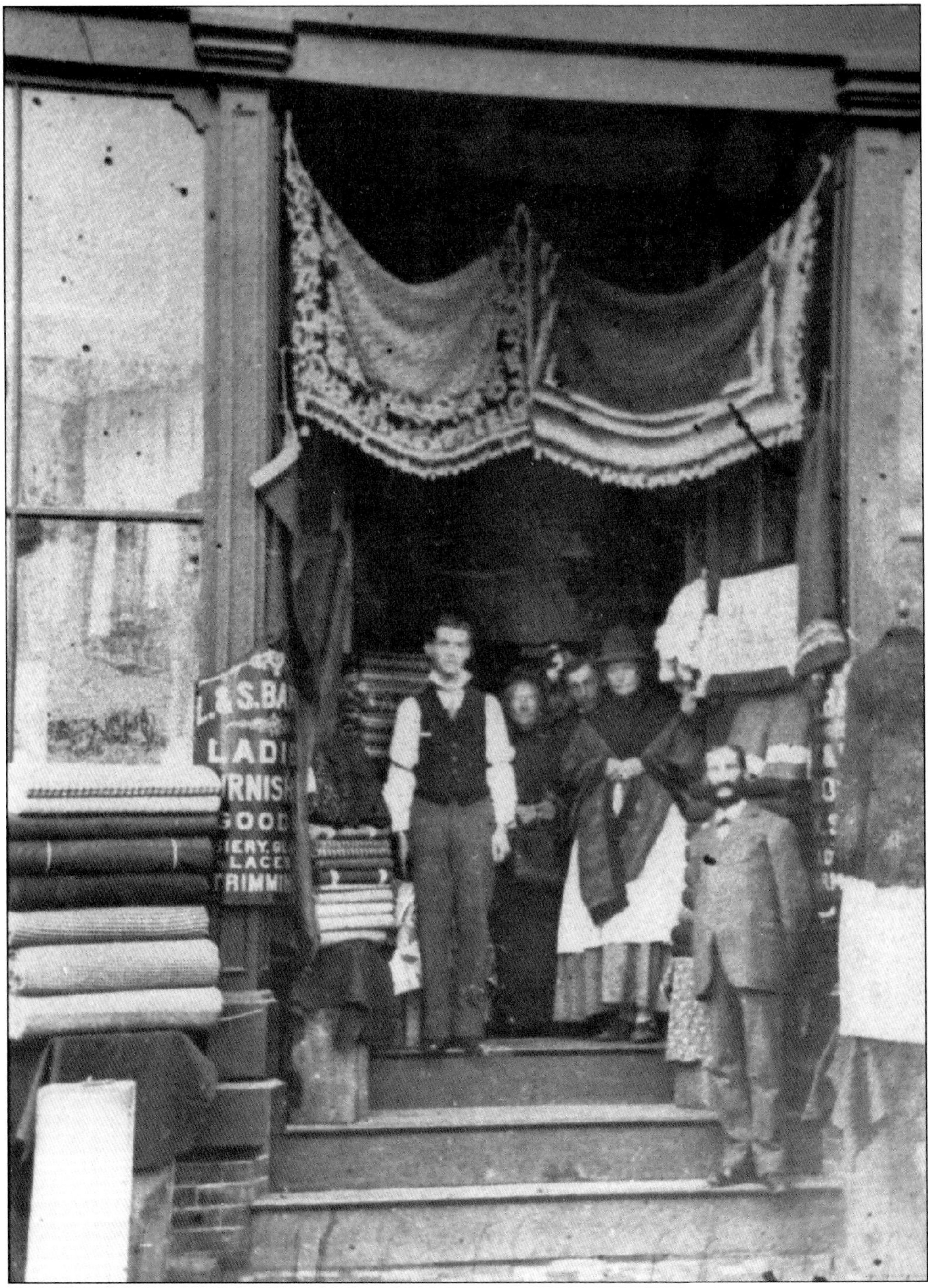

L&S BARUCH'S DRY GOODS STORE. Sophie Baruch came to Rochester from Germany in 1856 to work in the store of her uncle, S.H. Feineman. About ten years later she leased this store in the Chase Block and started her own business. Her brother Lewis arrived in 1873 and joined her in business.

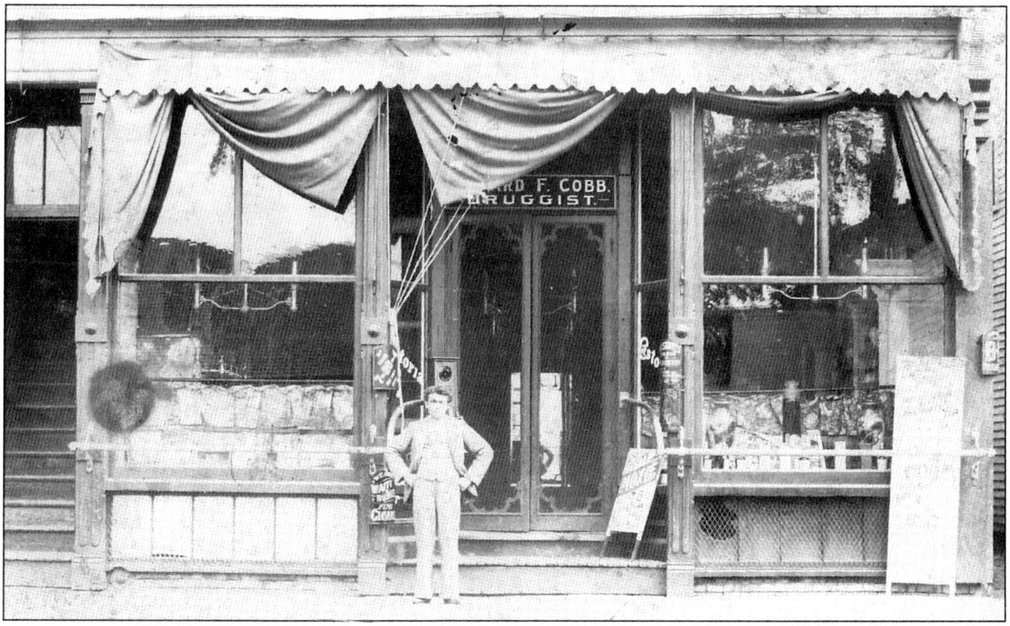

THE COBB DRUG STORE. John Perreault is standing in front of the store of Edward F. Cobb at 6 North Main Street near Union Street. The store, established in 1900, dispensed medicines and sick room supplies.

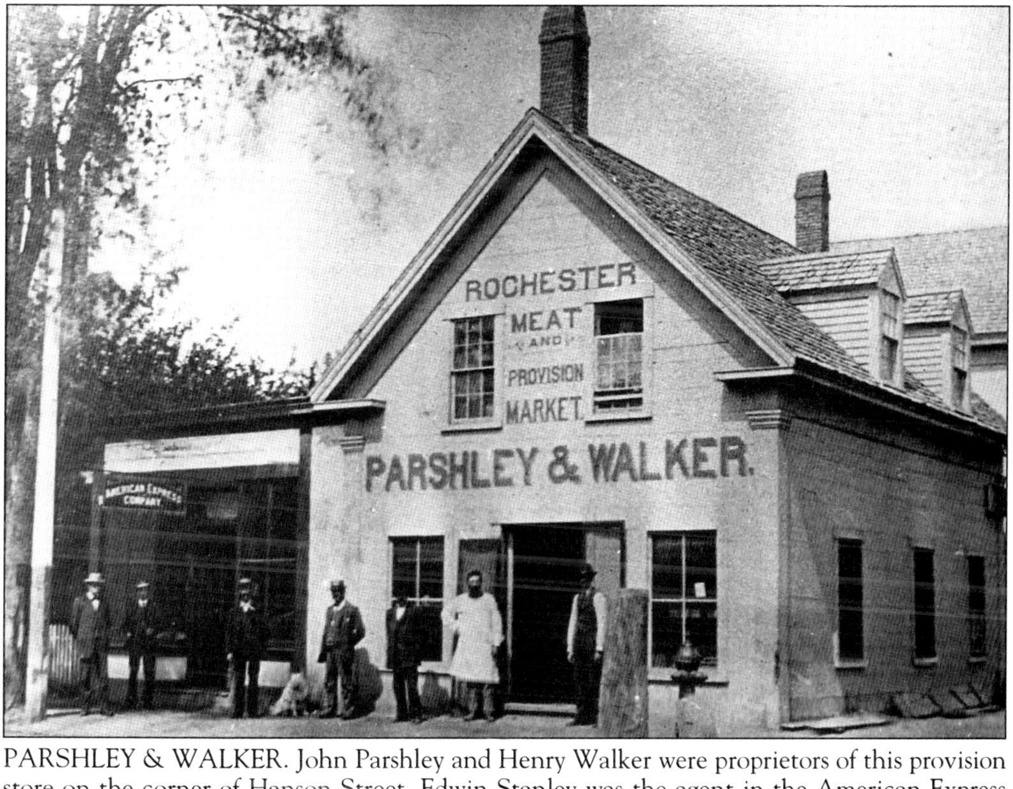

PARSHLEY & WALKER. John Parshley and Henry Walker were proprietors of this provision store on the corner of Hanson Street. Edwin Stanley was the agent in the American Express office on the left.

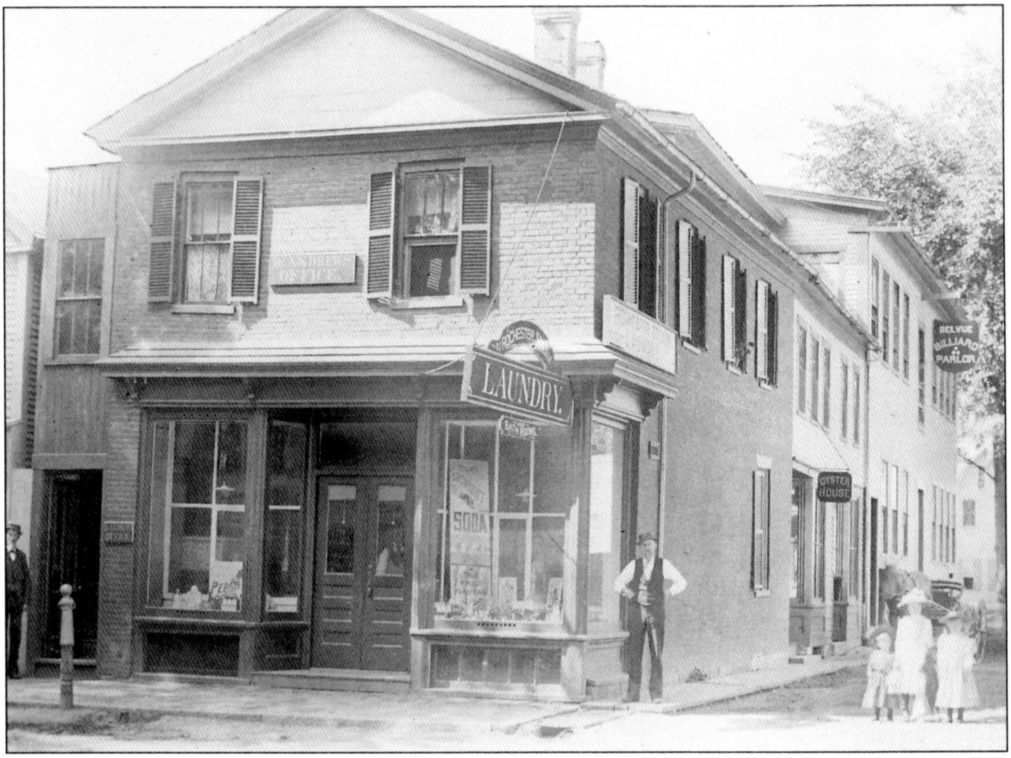

WILLEY'S LAUNDRY. George Willey opened a steam laundry on the square *c.* 1886. After five years he moved the laundry to the old Cole place on Main Street and enlarged the building to include an oyster house and a billiard parlor. Dr. Burt Andrews had an office on the second floor. The children are Lawrence, Mahala, and Gertrude Willey.

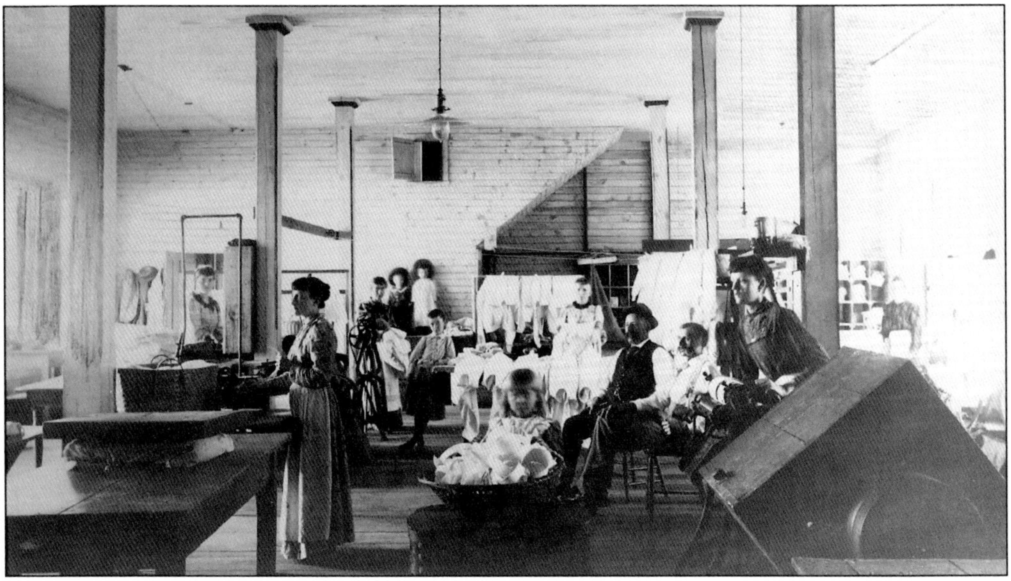

INSIDE WILLEY'S LAUNDRY. George Willey employed fifteen people in his laundry. Customers could order laundry washed and returned wet ready to hang, or have it completely finished. Lace curtains were a specialty.

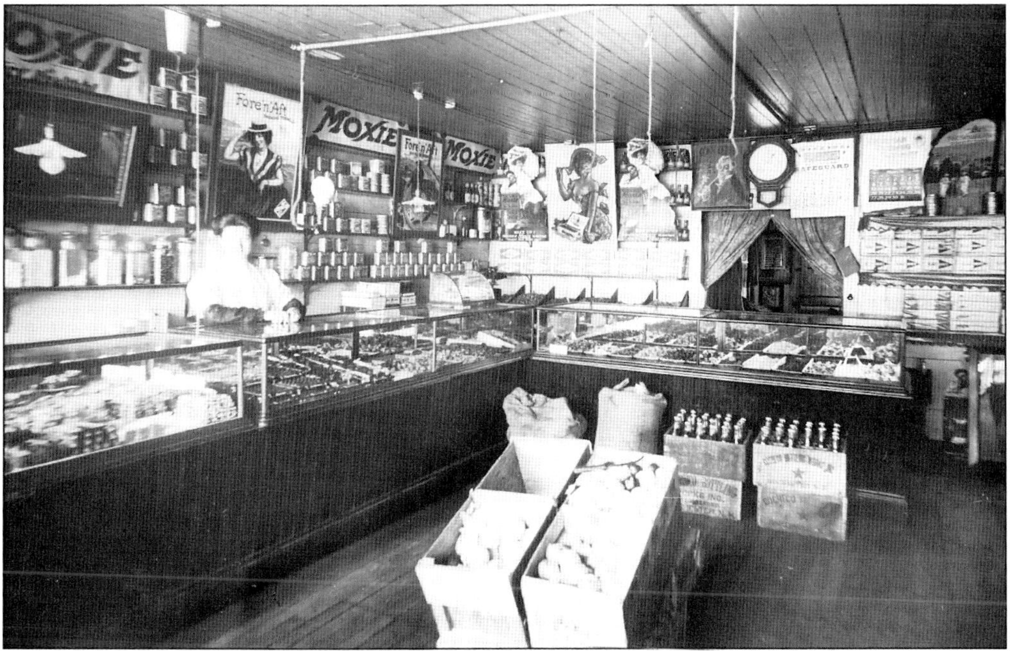

THE ROCHESTER PROVISION & FRUIT COMPANY. Charles Rumazza and his wife Victoria owned this store at 7 Signal Street in the 1920s and 1930s. Josephine Orino, the clerk, was a sister to Mrs. Rumazza.

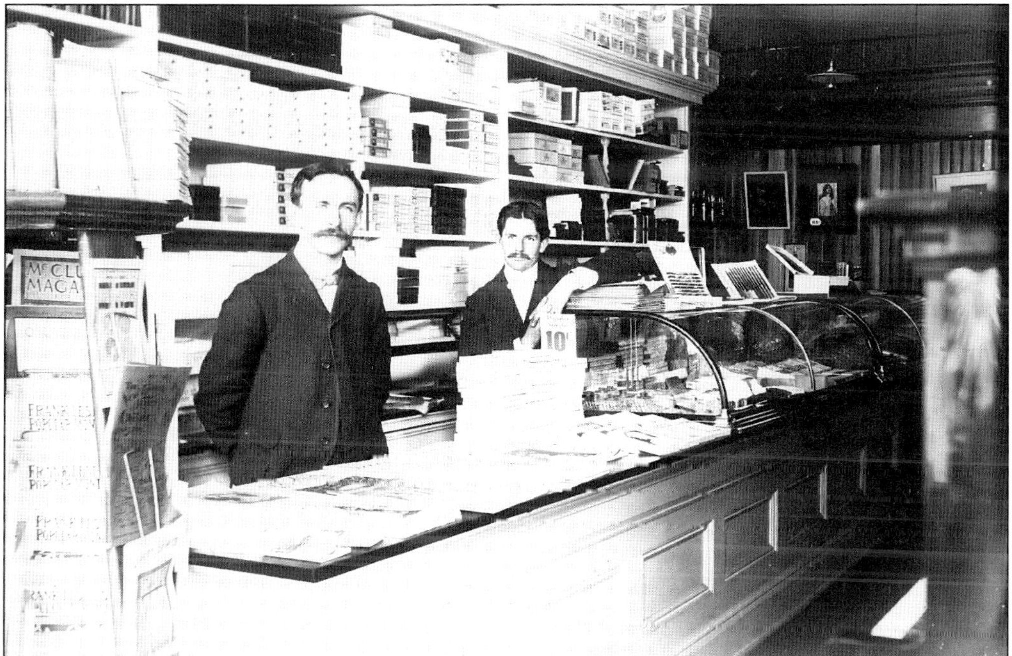

MEADER'S STORE. Constructed in 1873 by Dominicus Hanson especially for a post office, this building was leased to the U.S. government for more than twenty years. Meader's store was located here from 1898 (when Fred Meader moved his music business here) until 1996 (when it closed). Fred Meader (right) and John Horne are pictured.

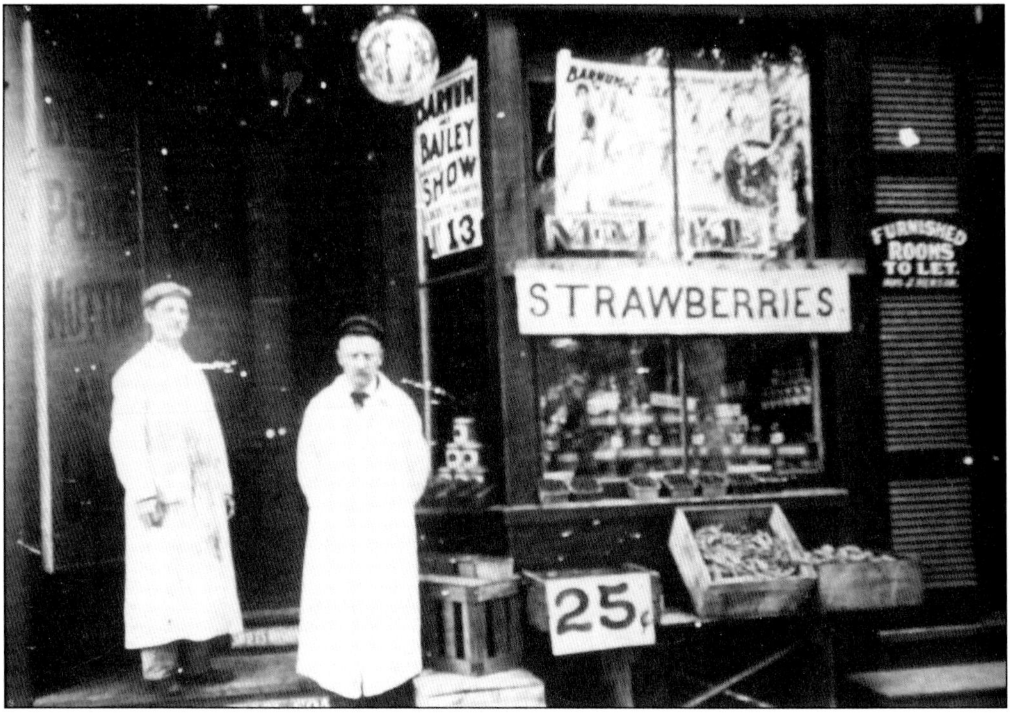

A SOUTH MAIN STREET STORE, *c.* 1900. Clerks John Meserve and John Rickor stand in front of the store located north of the City Hotel. The poster on the left reads, "Barnum and Bailey—the Greatest Show on Earth—A Circus that is a Circus"; the one on the right reads, "Furnished Rooms to Let. Mrs. J. Hersom."

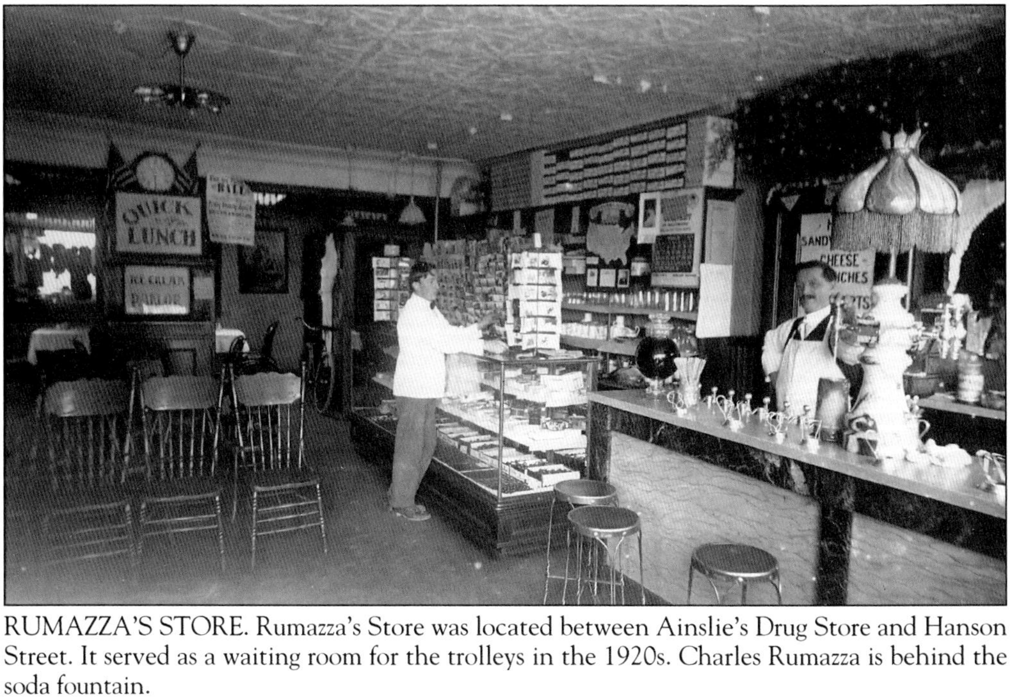

RUMAZZA'S STORE. Rumazza's Store was located between Ainslie's Drug Store and Hanson Street. It served as a waiting room for the trolleys in the 1920s. Charles Rumazza is behind the soda fountain.

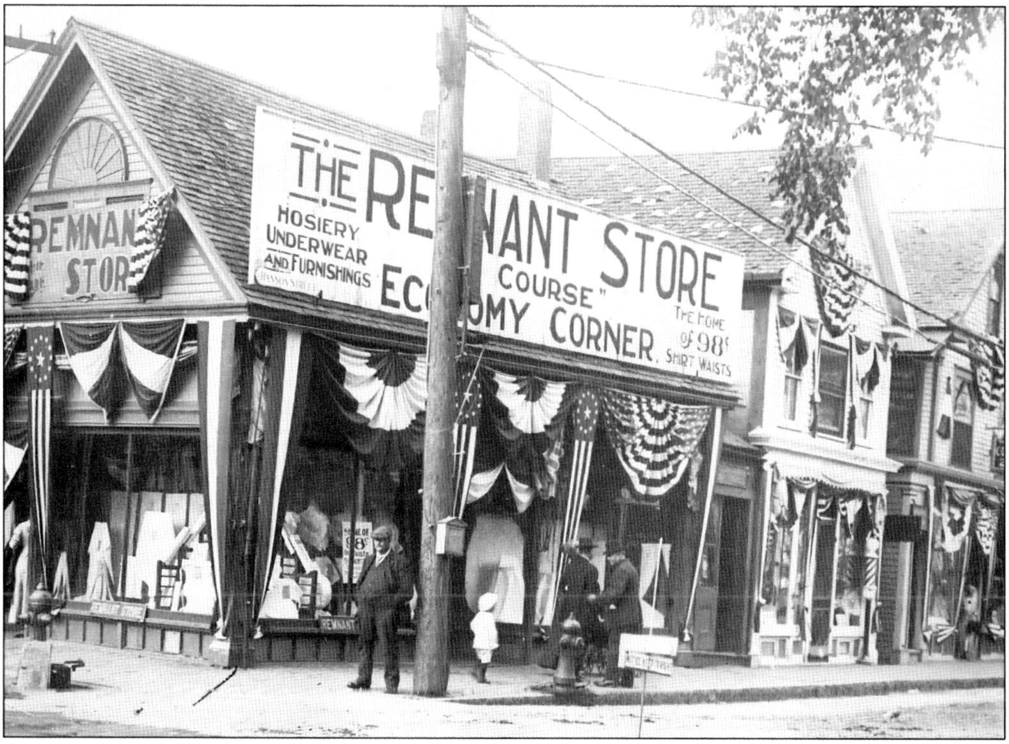

THE REMNANT STORE. The Remnant Store on the corner of Wakefield and Hanson Streets was owned and operated by Charles A.C. Hanson.

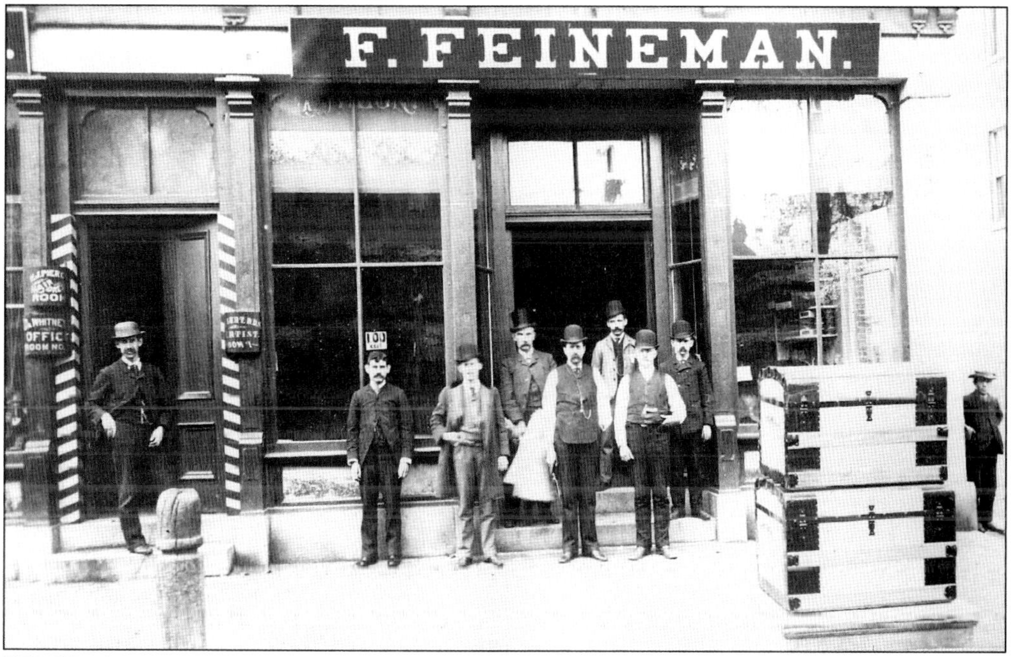

FEINEMAN'S STORE. In 1868 Frederick Feineman moved his business into a store on the Congress Street corner of the new McDuffee Block. Feineman died that same year and his five sons—Herman, Moses, Lewis, Solomon, and Edward—took over management of the store.

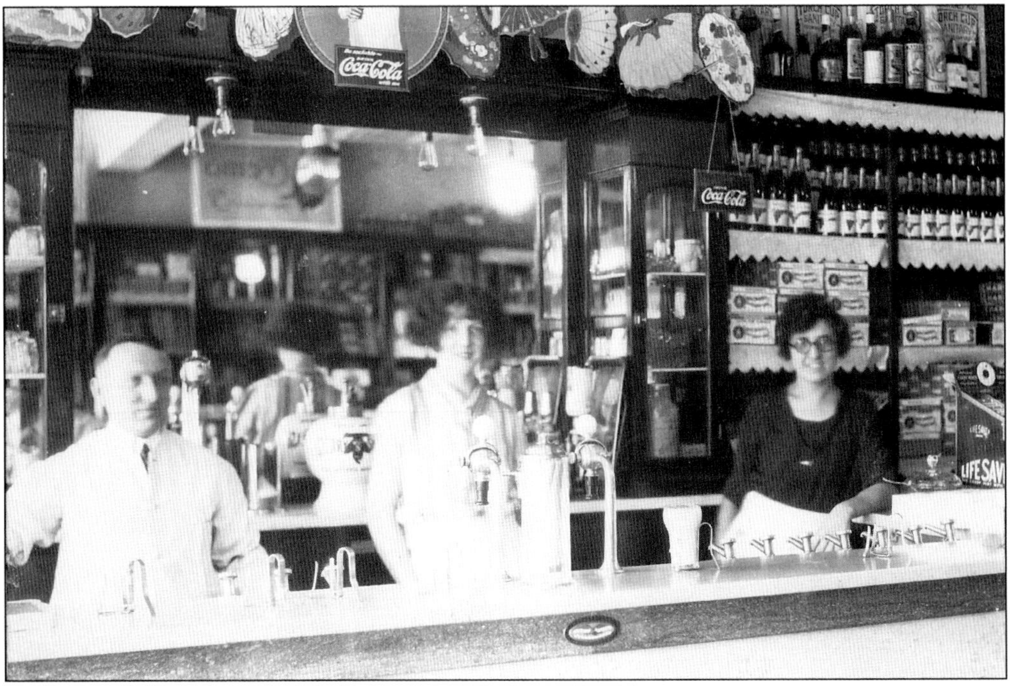

ALIMI'S STORE. This store was located on the corner of South Main and Knight Streets. Pictured c. 1930 are, from left to right, Angelo Alimi (proprietor), Dot Lenfest (clerk), and Mrs. Julia Alimi.

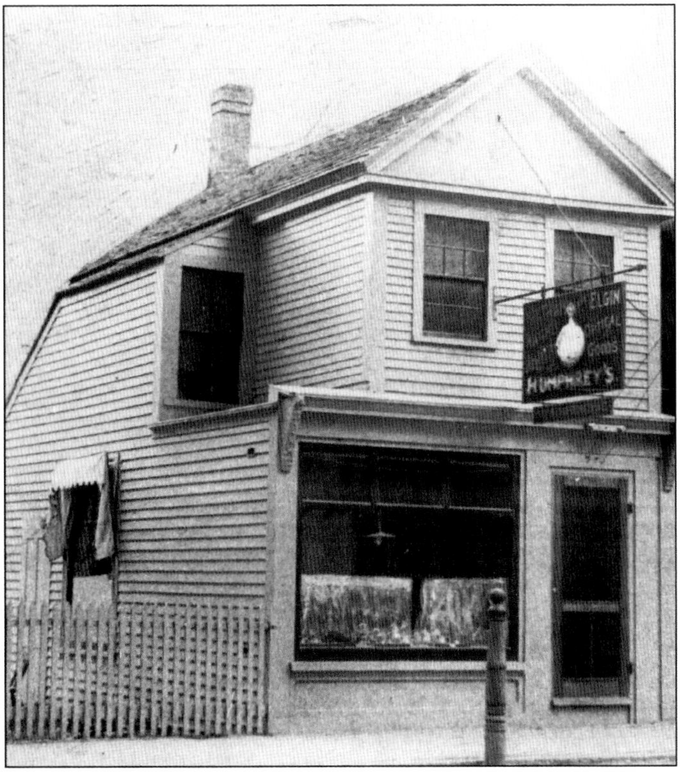

HUMPHREY'S JEWELRY. John M. Humphrey came to Rochester in 1889 and purchased this small store on the corner of Main and Arrow Streets. Mr. Humphrey, an expert on precious stones and a skillful watchmaker, employed two assistants in his successful business. The telephone exchange was in this building in 1890.

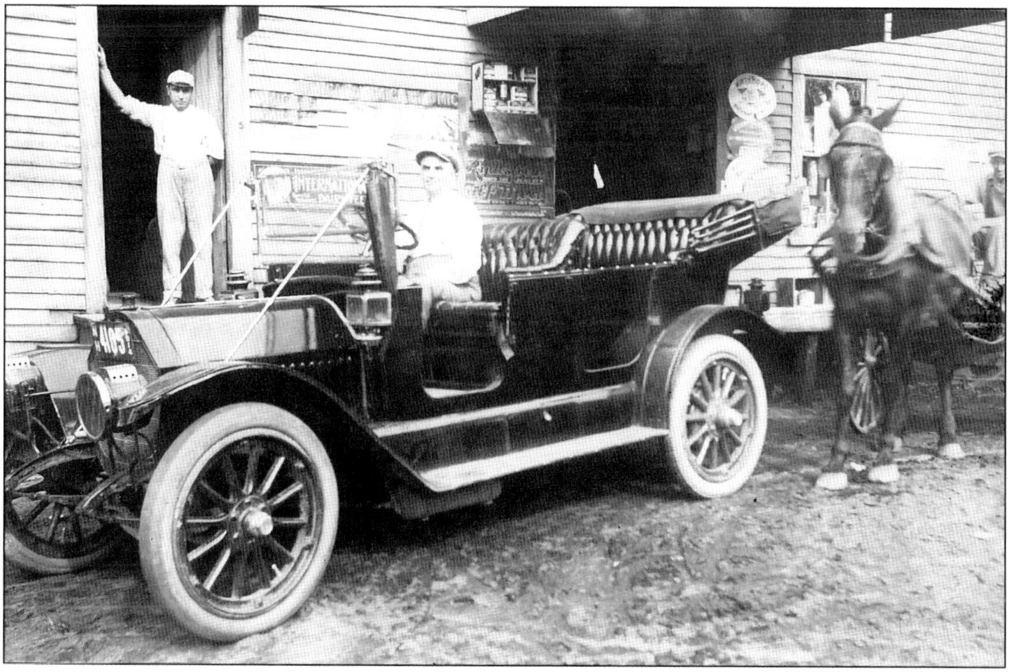

DEAN'S GRAIN STORE. George Dean's grain store was opposite the freight house on Portland Street in 1914. George Dean is in the automobile, Albert Weeks is in the wagon, and Walter King is in the doorway.

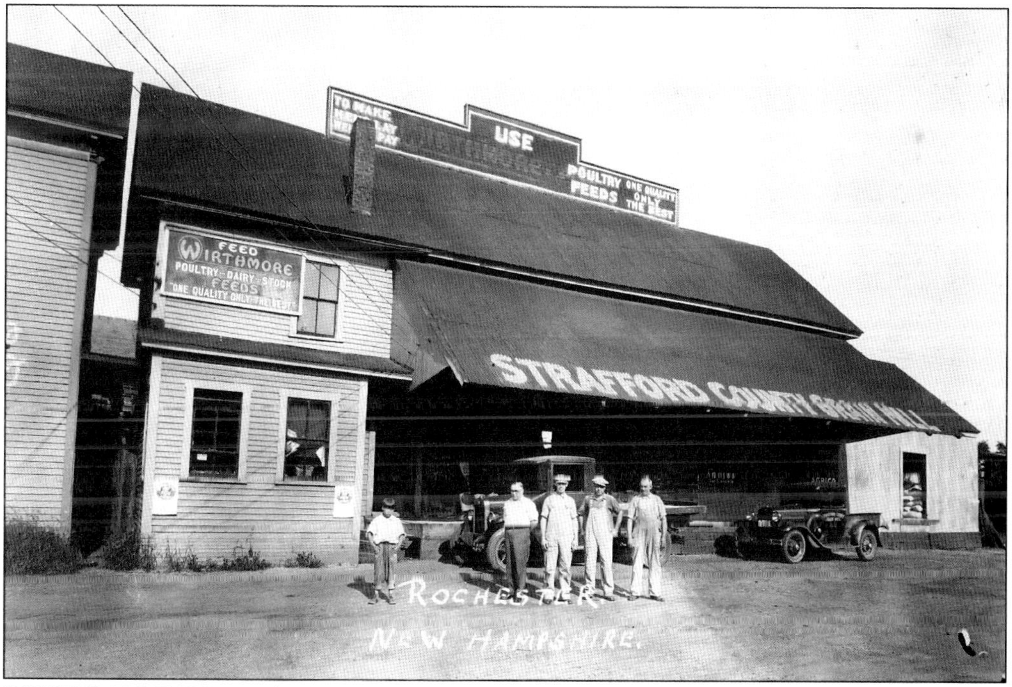

WIRTHMORE FEED. This business was located on Portland Street near the Freight House. The man on the right in front of the truck is Walter King.

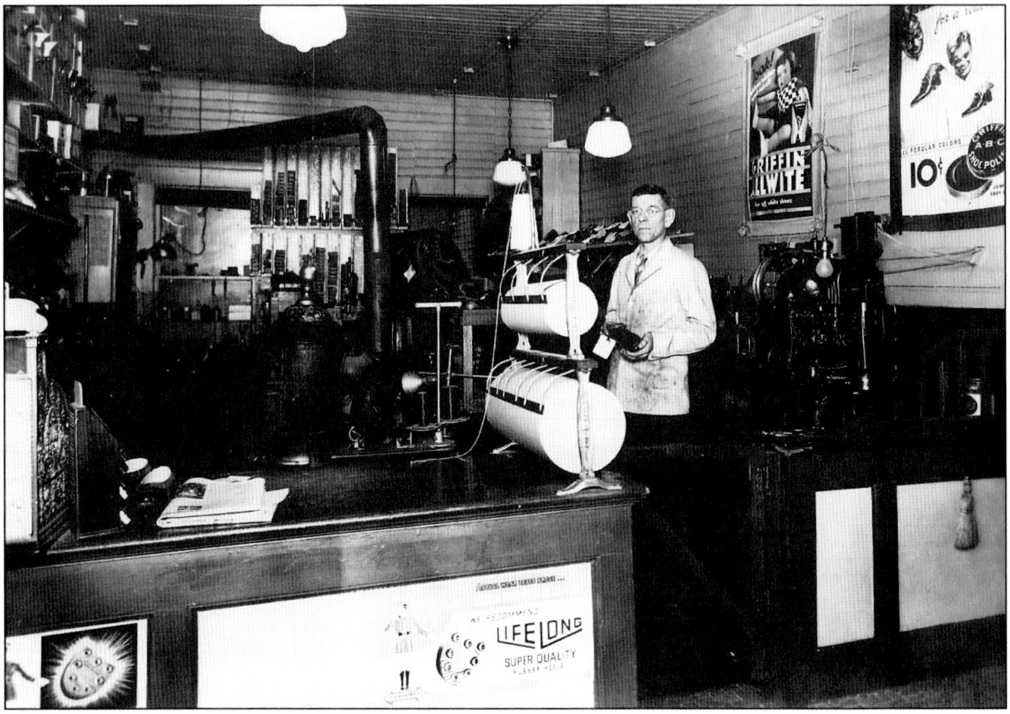

GAGNE'S SHOE REPAIR. Albert Gagne purchased this shop on May 7, 1936, and operated his popular shoe repair business here for more than thirty-five years. Pictured is Albert Gagne, proprietor, in his shop at 1 Bridge Street.

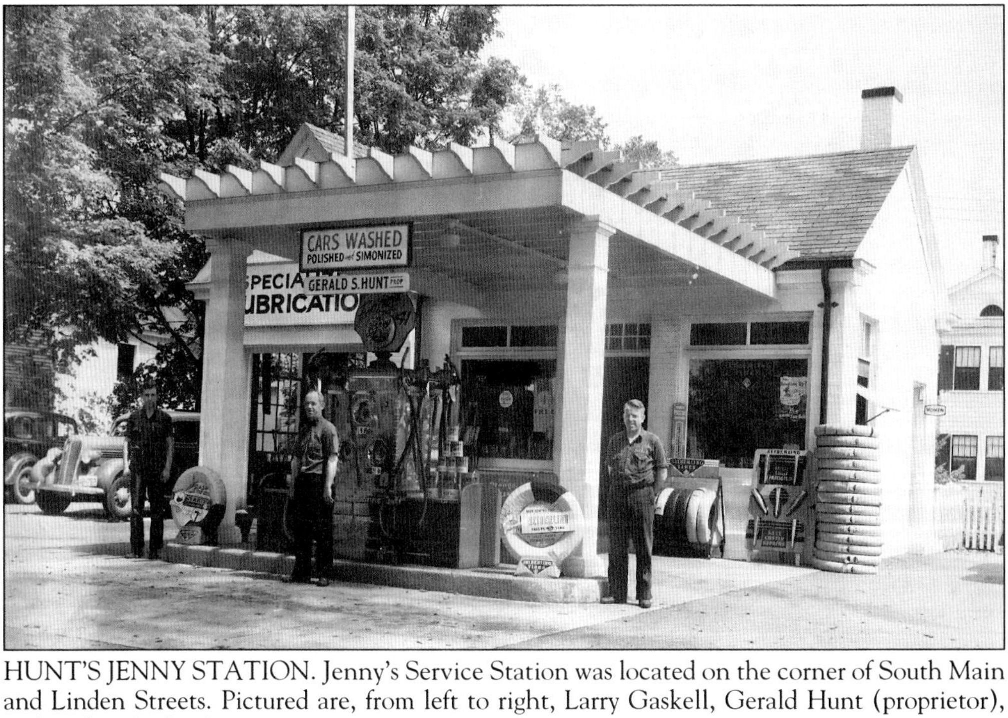

HUNT'S JENNY STATION. Jenny's Service Station was located on the corner of South Main and Linden Streets. Pictured are, from left to right, Larry Gaskell, Gerald Hunt (proprietor), and Luther Garland.

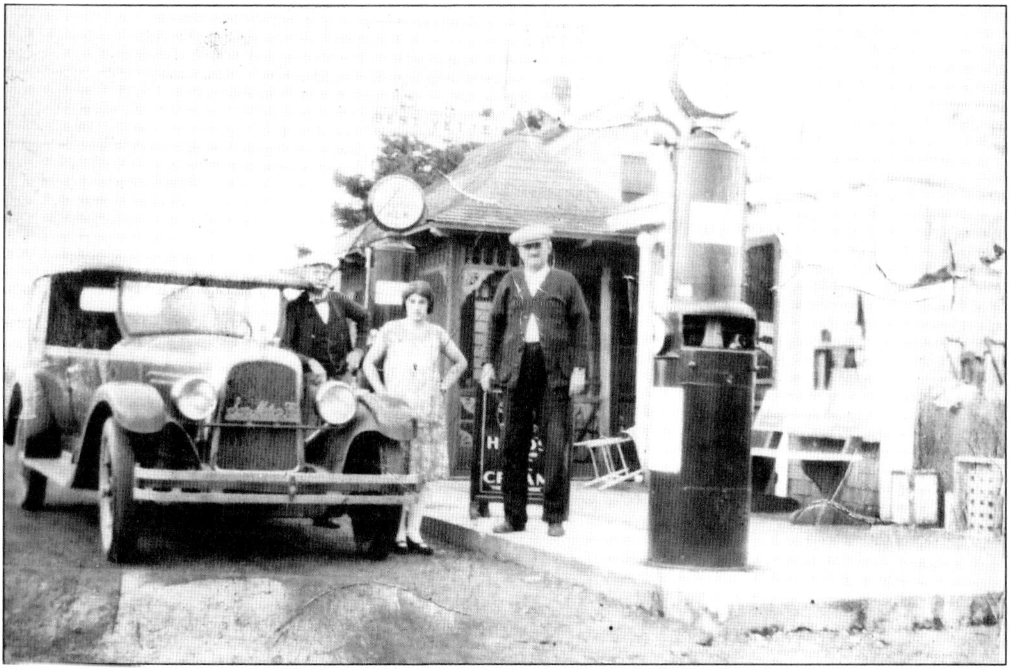

FOSS GARAGE. This image shows Harry Foss at his garage on Wakefield Street. Harry was killed at age fifty-nine in 1929 when he was hit by a train at the Wakefield Street crossing. Pictured are Grampa Foss, Rhona Foss, and Harry Foss.

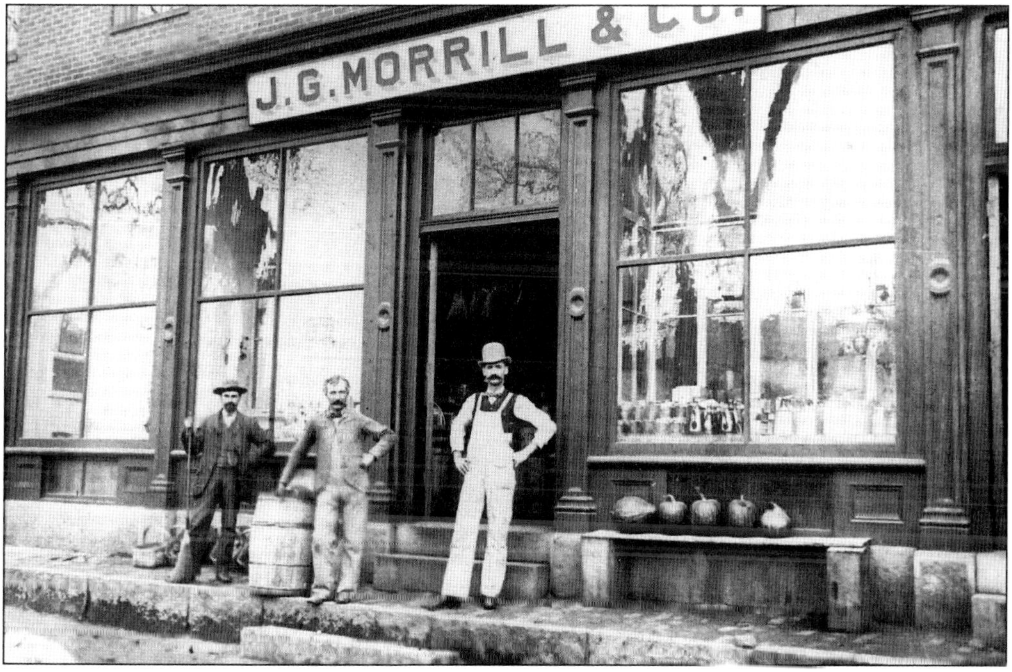

MORRILL'S GROCERY STORE. The J.G. Morrill Grocery Store was in the IOOF Block on South Main Street. He was one of the first tenants when the block was opened in 1874 and his well-stocked store became so popular that by 1901 he occupied three stores—the whole first floor of the block.

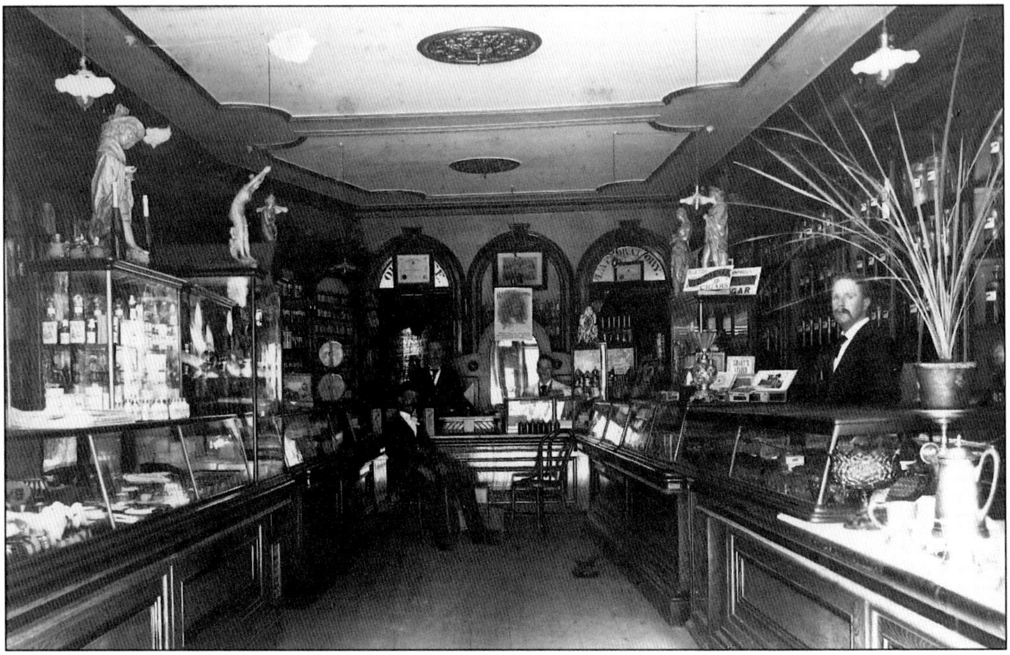

INSIDE BURNHAM'S DRUG STORE. R. Dewitt Burnham leased the old Dominicus Hanson Drug Store in 1882. From the laboratory in the rear right he concocted prescriptions for his many customers. Mr. Burnham is behind the counter on the right.

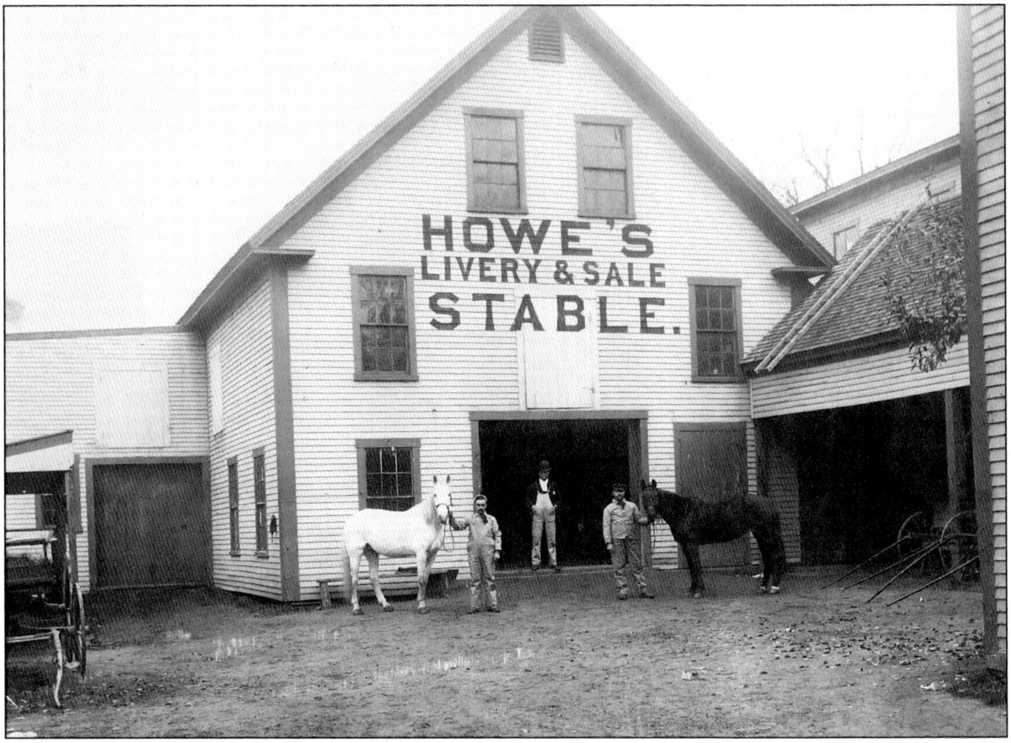

HOWE'S LIVERY. Ithamar S. Howe operated this livery stable behind his house at 90 North Main Street in 1890.

Seven

Industries

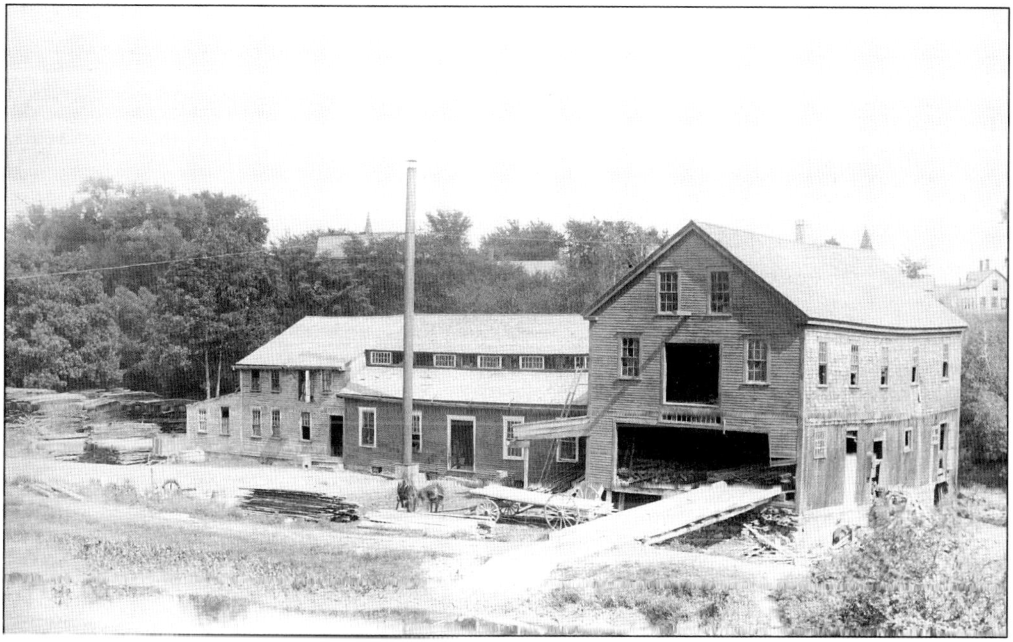

THE GOODWIN & TRASK BOX SHOP. The firm of Goodwin, Trask & Co., manufacturer of wooden and paper boxes, was formed in 1888. It was one of the many manufacturers that availed itself of the excellent waterpower of the Cocheco River. This business was purchased by Archie Fownes in 1910 and was later operated by M.B. Claff & Sons.

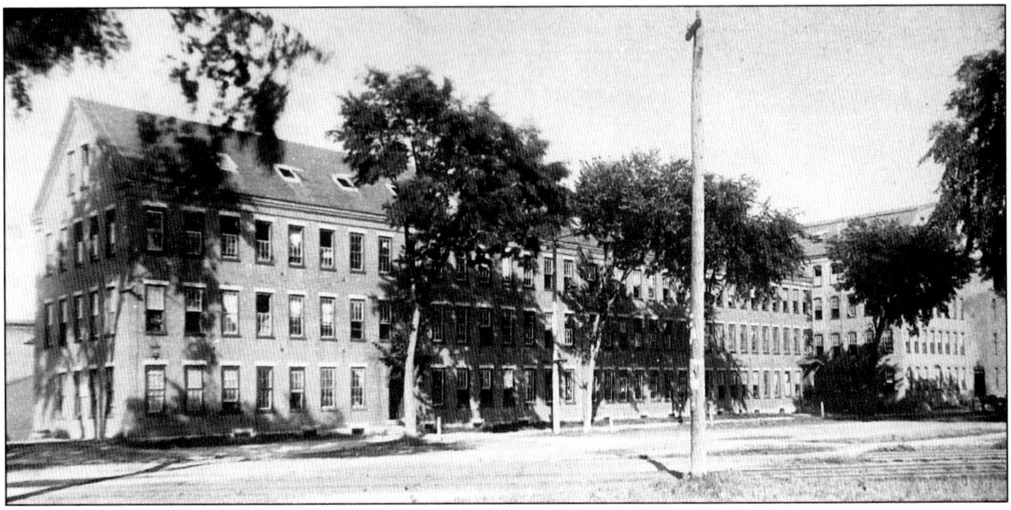

THE WALLACE SHOE FACTORY. The firm of E.G. & E. Wallace was formed in 1858 by twin brothers Ebenezer and Edwin Wallace. At first the partners were engaged in tanning leather only, but at the beginning of the Civil War the Wallace brothers found themselves with a surplus of leather and decided to make boots. In a few years they became the largest shoe factory in the state. Their businesses occupied 5 acres of land and employed about 600 people.

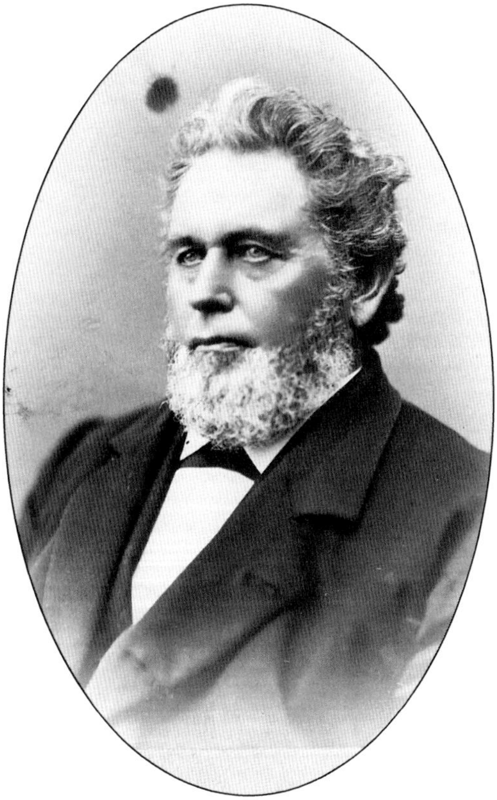

EBENEZER WALLACE (1823–1893).

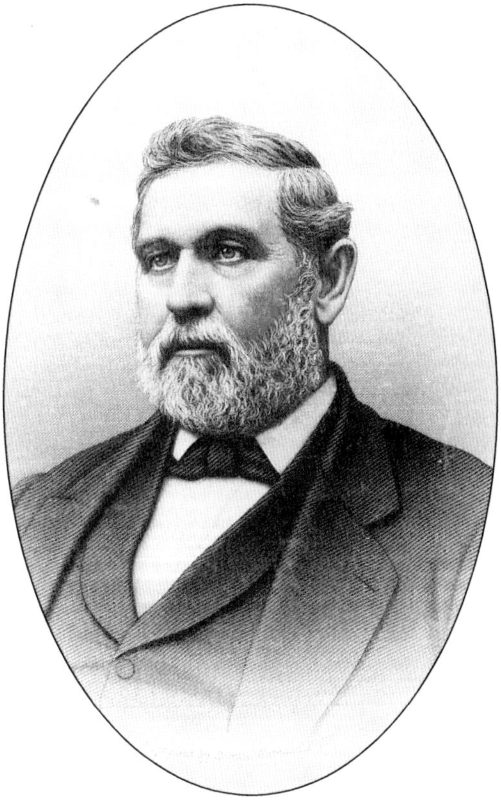

EDWIN WALLACE (1823–1894).

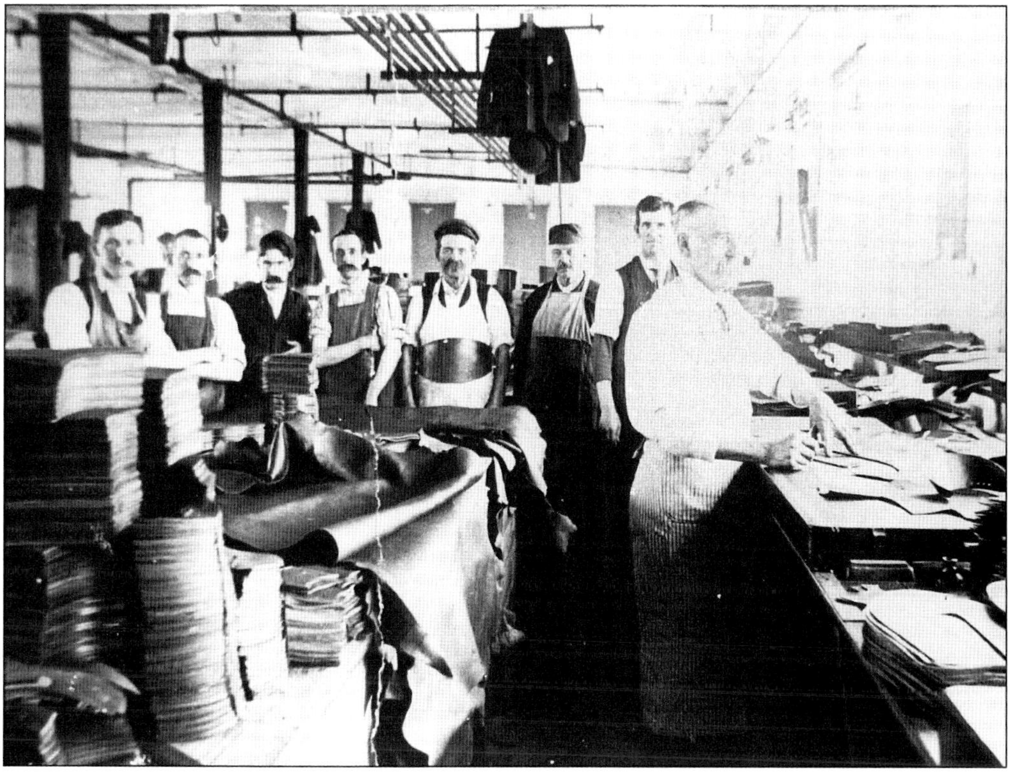

WORKMEN AT THE WALLACE SHOP. This view takes us inside the cutting room of Wallace Shoe, *c.* 1900. Notice the white shirts and leather aprons.

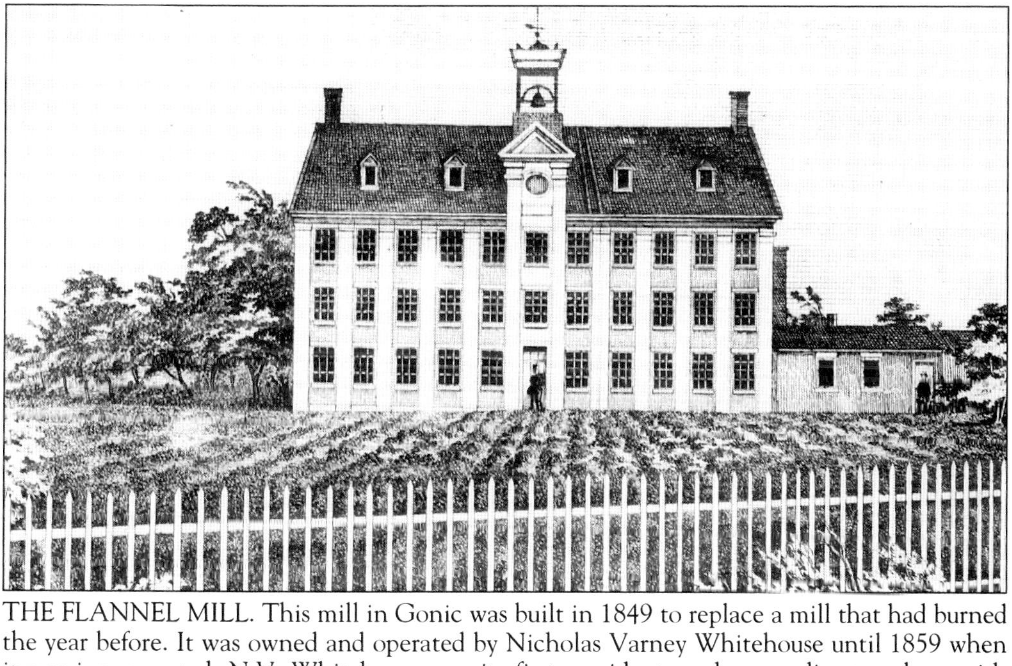

THE FLANNEL MILL. This mill in Gonic was built in 1849 to replace a mill that had burned the year before. It was owned and operated by Nicholas Varney Whitehouse until 1859 when it was incorporated. N.V. Whitehouse was its first president, and was a director along with Samuel B. Rindge and Marshall P. Wilder.

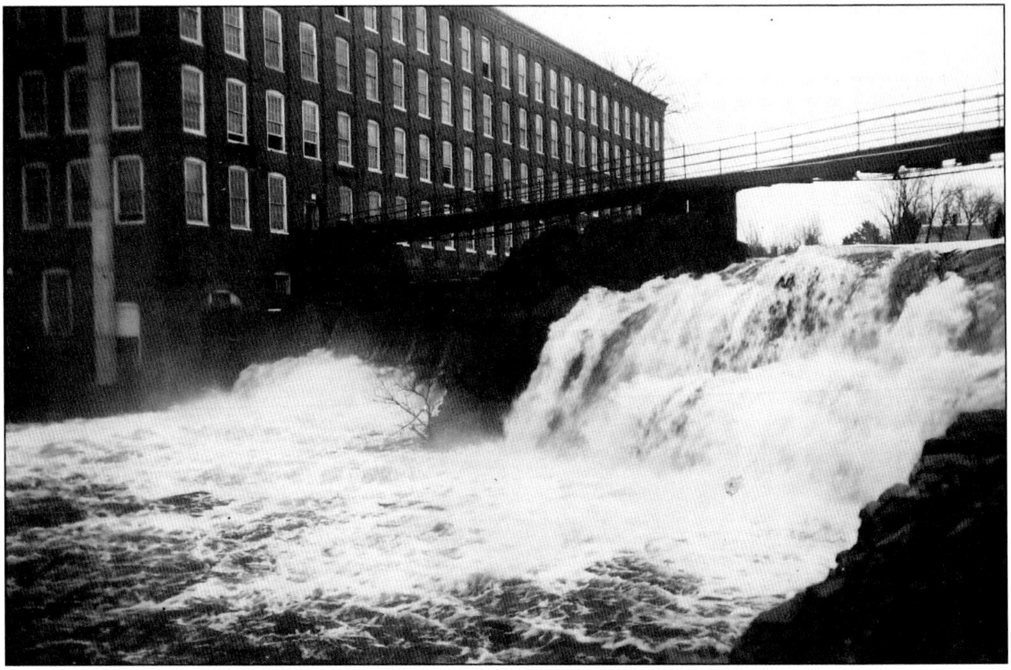

THE GONIC MILL DAM. A new channel below the falls was dug in 1861 which increased the drop of water by 3 feet. A new woolen mill under the name of the Gonic Manufacturing Co. was built in 1864 and was connected to the old mill by a wing.

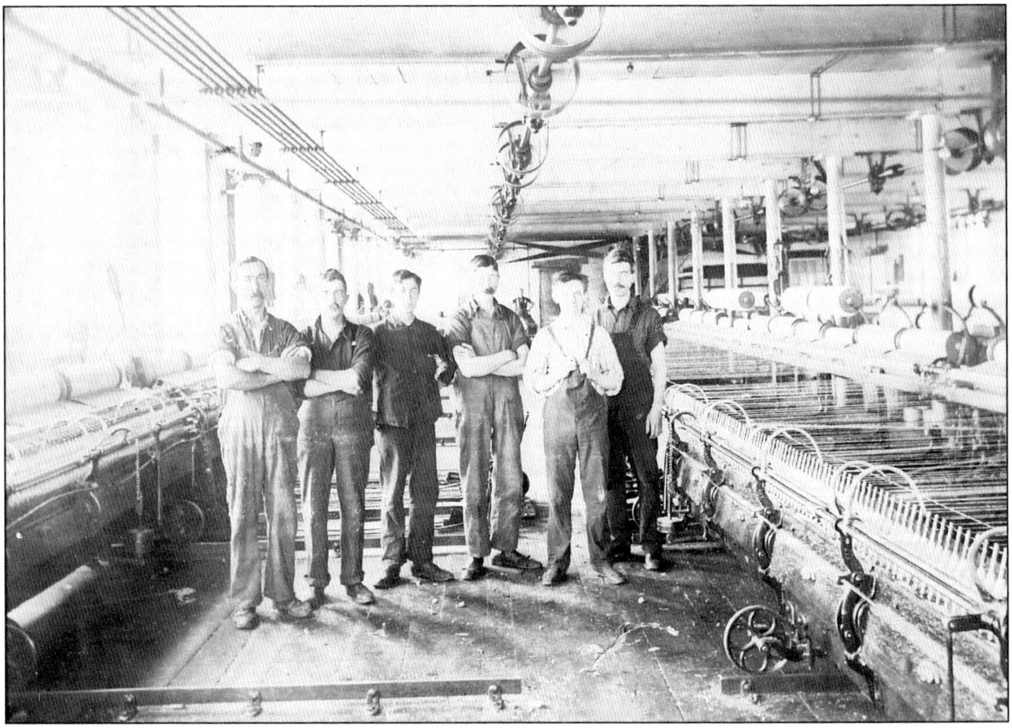

A SPINNING ROOM OF THE GONIC MILL. Employees of the lower spinning room pose for a photographer, c. 1886.

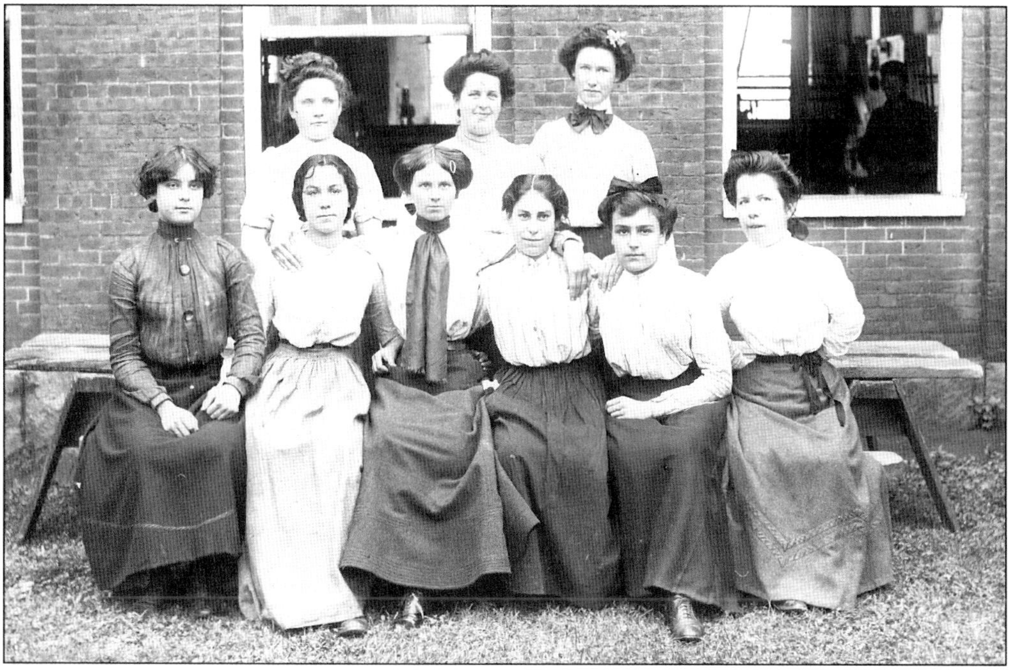

GONIC MILL GIRLS, c. 1900. Pictured are, from left to right, Edith Worcestor, Leah Osborne, Blanche Osborne, Jennie D'Anjou, Albertine Stone, Sadie Foss, Valerie Beauhill, Ellen Gagnon, and Mabel Harrison.

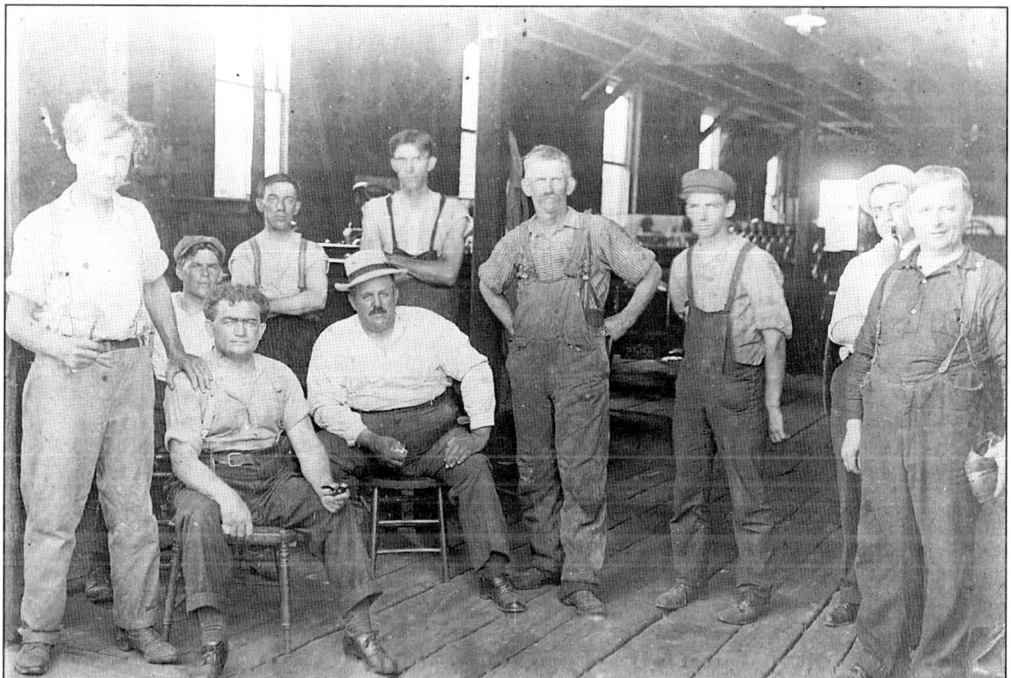

INSIDE SHAW'S GARAGE. This group of men posed in the garage on North Main Street prior to 1913. The first man on the left is John Perreault, next is Gilbert Shaw, and the last man on the right is Oral Boardman.

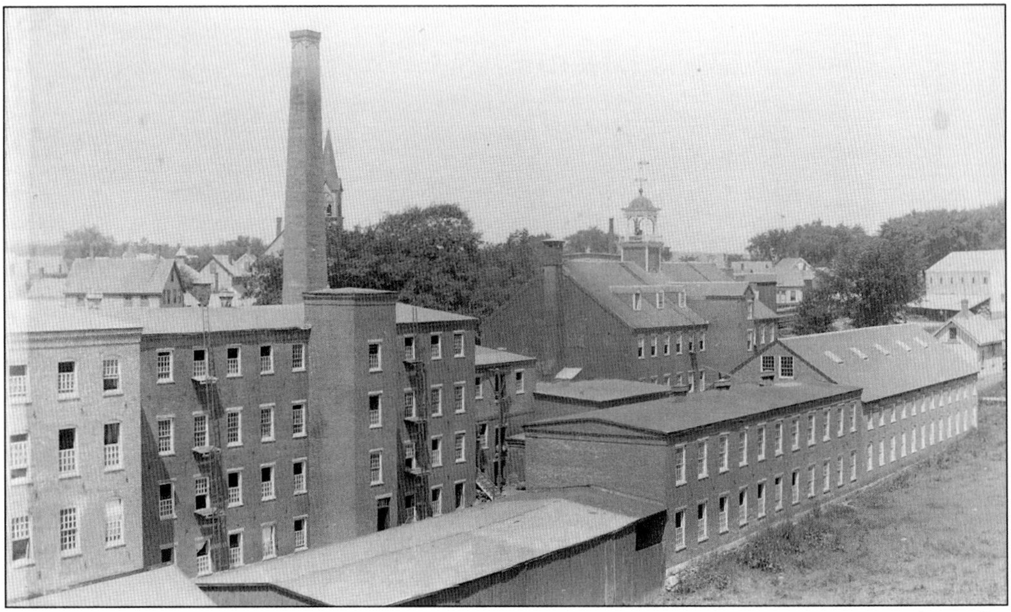

THE NORWAY PLAINS COMPANY. The Norway Plains Company, succeeding the Mechanics Manufacturing Co., was chartered in 1846. It was set up in a group of wooden buildings, but at the end of twenty years all but the storage house had been replaced by brick buildings. The mill last operated under the name Wyandotte.

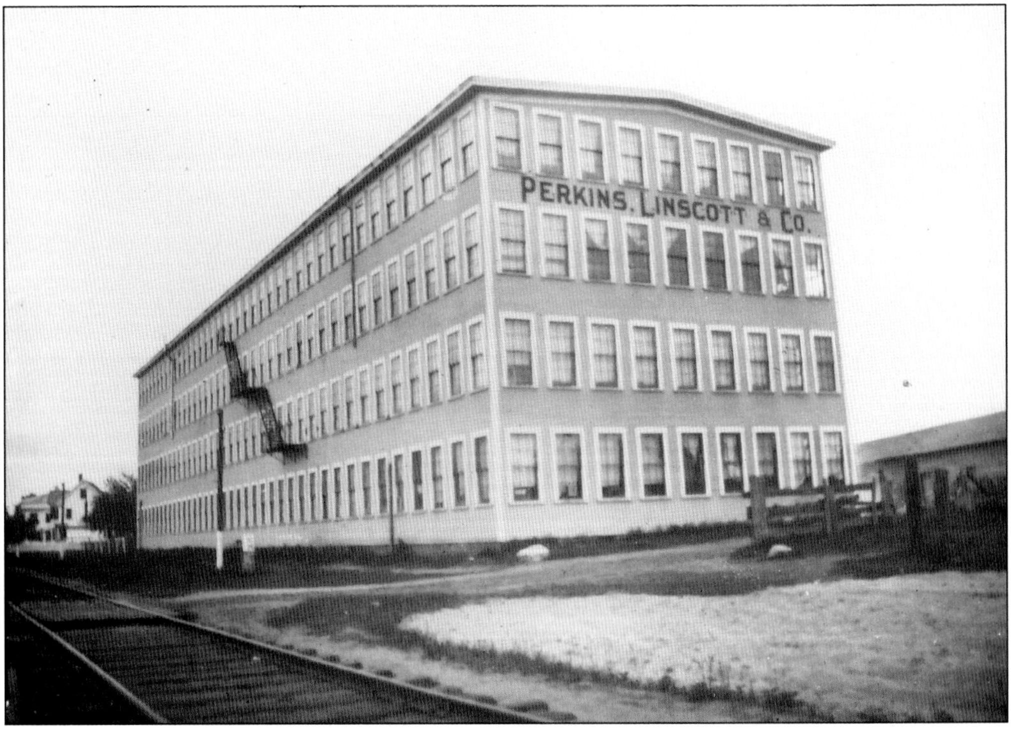

THE LINSCOTT SHOE FACTORY. Perkins & Jones of Springvale, Maine, began a shoe factory here in 1895, with Albert Linscott as superintendent. After two years, Jones dropped out and Linscott became a partner. Today, Encore Shoe is in this building.

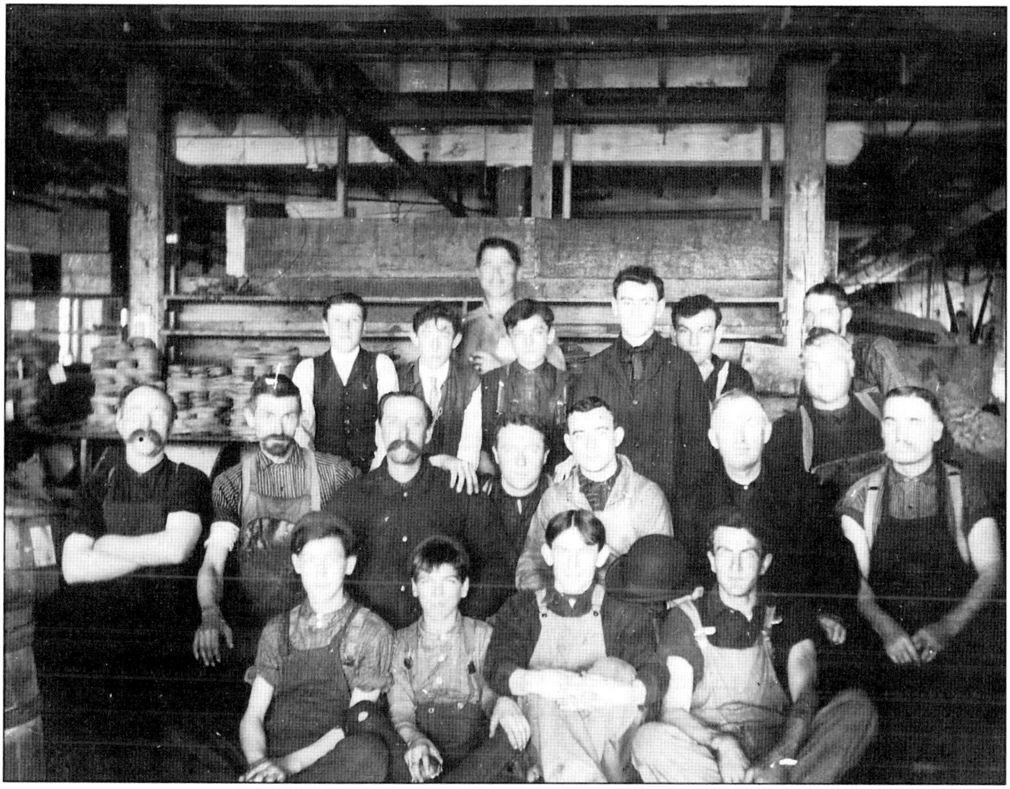

WORKERS AT HUBBARD SHOE. The Linscott Shoe Shop was purchased by Hubbard Shoe in May of 1932. Hubbard had started another shop in East Rochester a few years earlier. This group was employed in the sole leather room in Rochester. Third from the right in the back row is Walter Young.

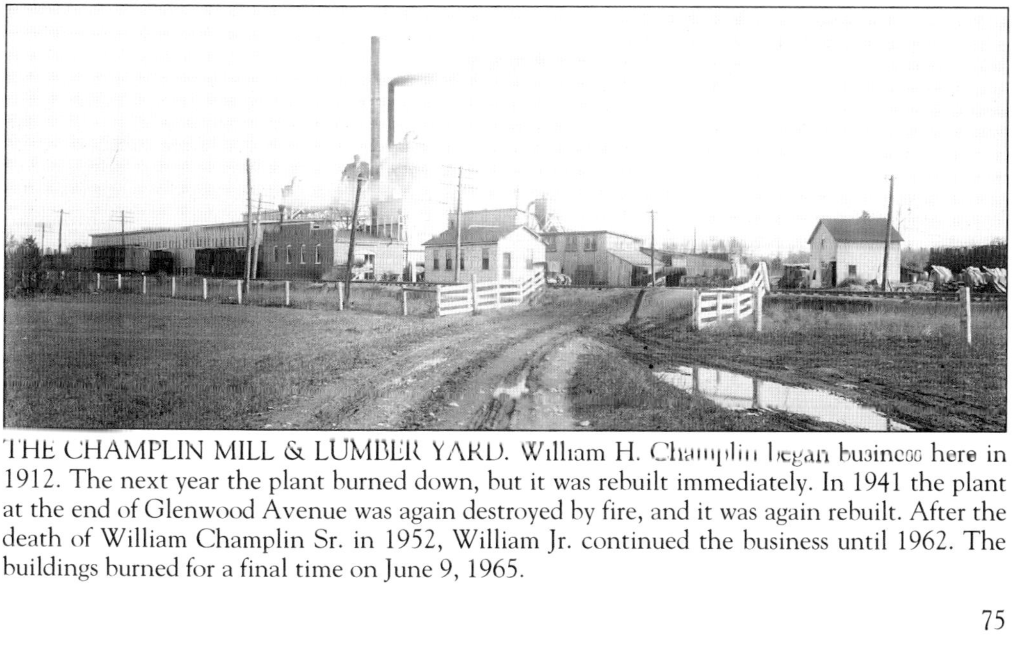

THE CHAMPLIN MILL & LUMBER YARD. William H. Champlin began business here in 1912. The next year the plant burned down, but it was rebuilt immediately. In 1941 the plant at the end of Glenwood Avenue was again destroyed by fire, and it was again rebuilt. After the death of William Champlin Sr. in 1952, William Jr. continued the business until 1962. The buildings burned for a final time on June 9, 1965.

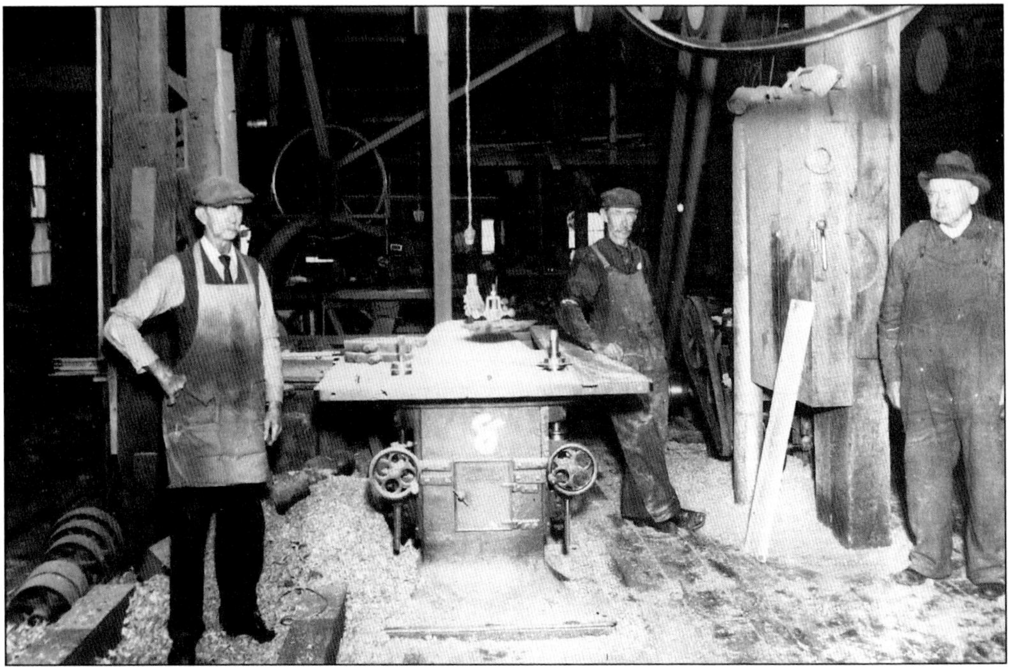

THE ROCHESTER LUMBER COMPANY. The Rochester Lumber Company was located on Autumn Street opposite Union Station in 1900. This business, managed by P.B. Preston, manufactured shingles, clapboards, doors, windows, blinds, moldings, and other building woodwork.

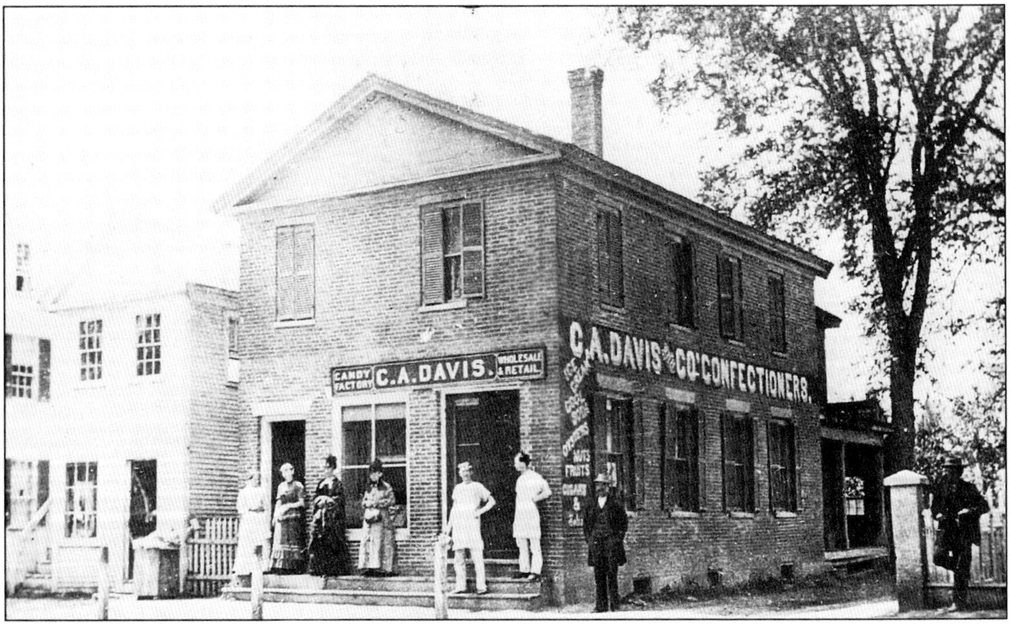

THE DAVIS CANDY FACTORY. Charles A. Davis, who had conducted a successful candy business in Portland, Maine, moved to Rochester in 1877 and opened a candy store. With the help of four employees, he manufactured candies and ice cream which he sold both wholesale and retail.

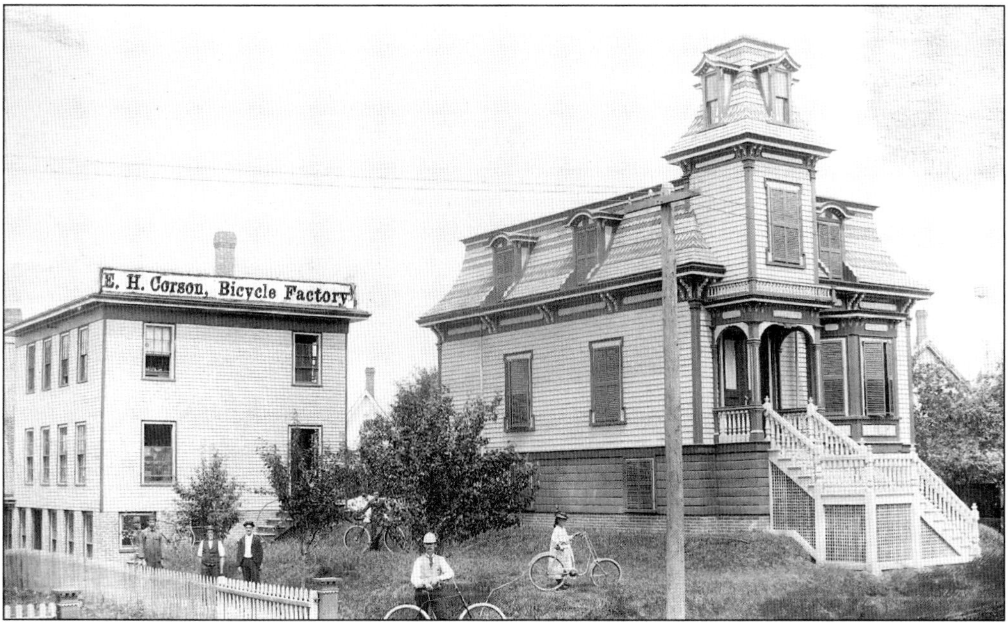

CORSON'S BICYCLE FACTORY. The E.H. Corson Bicycle Factory was located on Pleasant Street in East Rochester. It was at the rear of the home of Elbridge Corson, who became famous for coasting down Mt. Washington on a bicycle. He manufactured and repaired bicycles and typewriters.

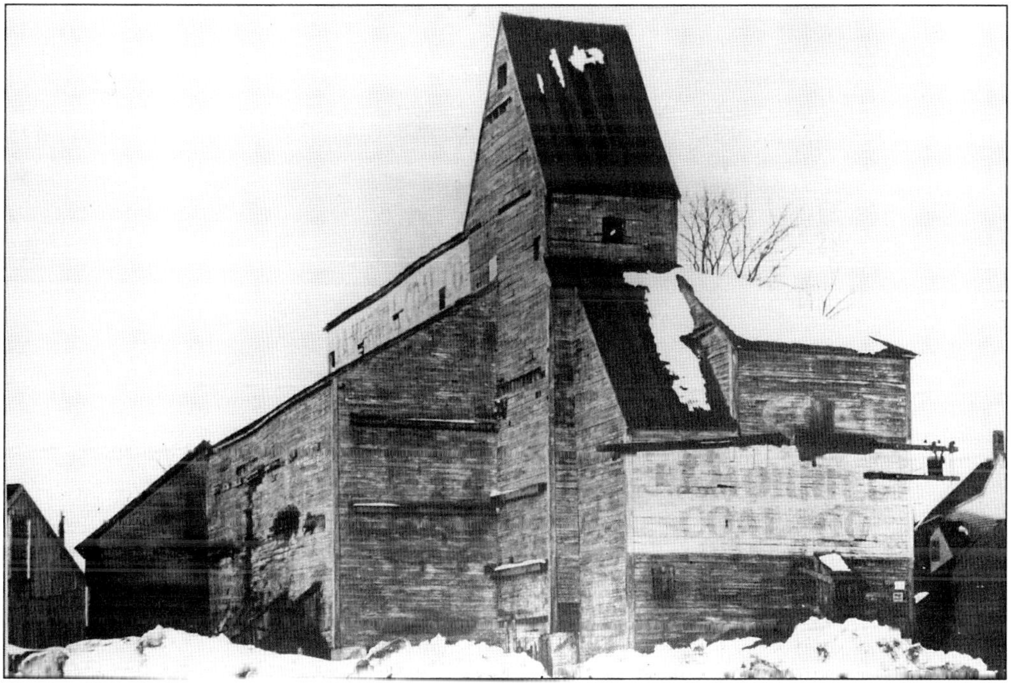

MORRILL'S COAL SHEDS. Charles W. Bradley built these coal sheds northeast of the tracks near Winter Street in 1913. Sometime after he retired in the 1920s he sold the property to Jedediah Morrill, who conducted a coal and ice business here for many years. These buildings were demolished in 1971.

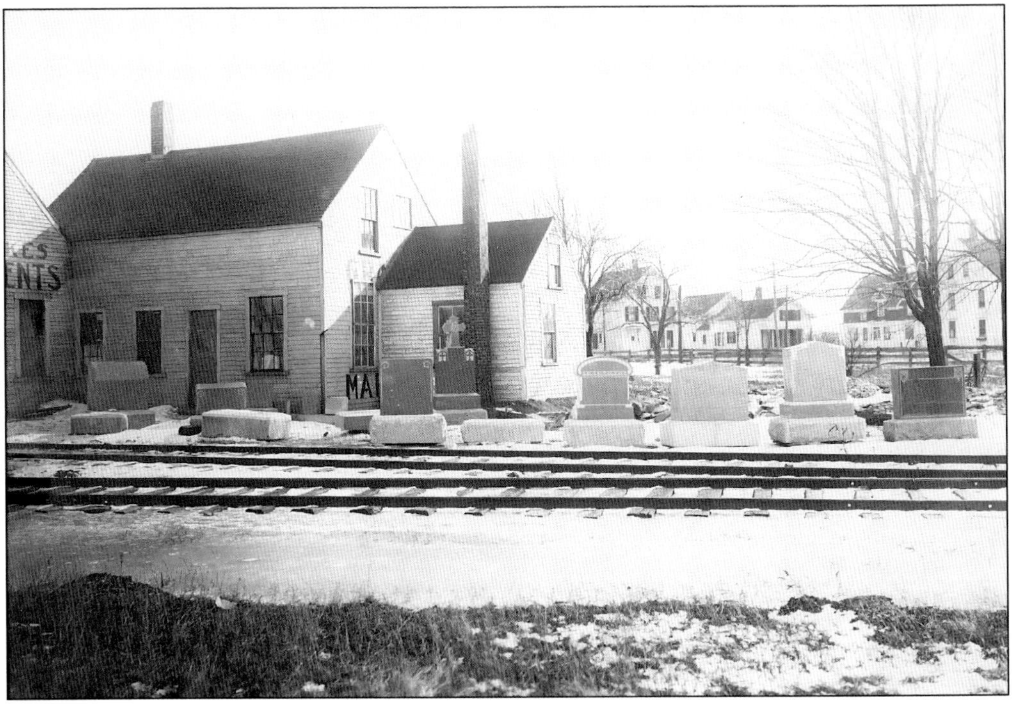

EZRA HAWKS' STONE WORKS. Ezra Hawks' granite and coal business was on Winter Street at the corner of Carr Court.

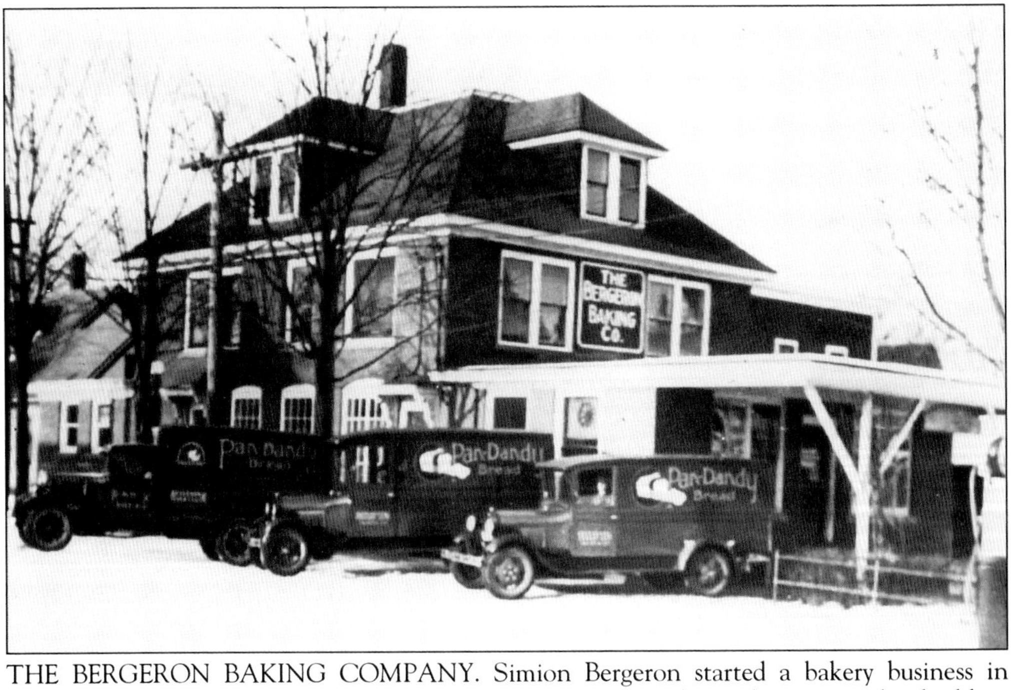

THE BERGERON BAKING COMPANY. Simion Bergeron started a bakery business in Rochester in 1881. Later he was joined by his two sons, Emilio and Louis, at this building located at 5 Waldron Avenue. The bakery was famous for its Pan Dandy Bread.

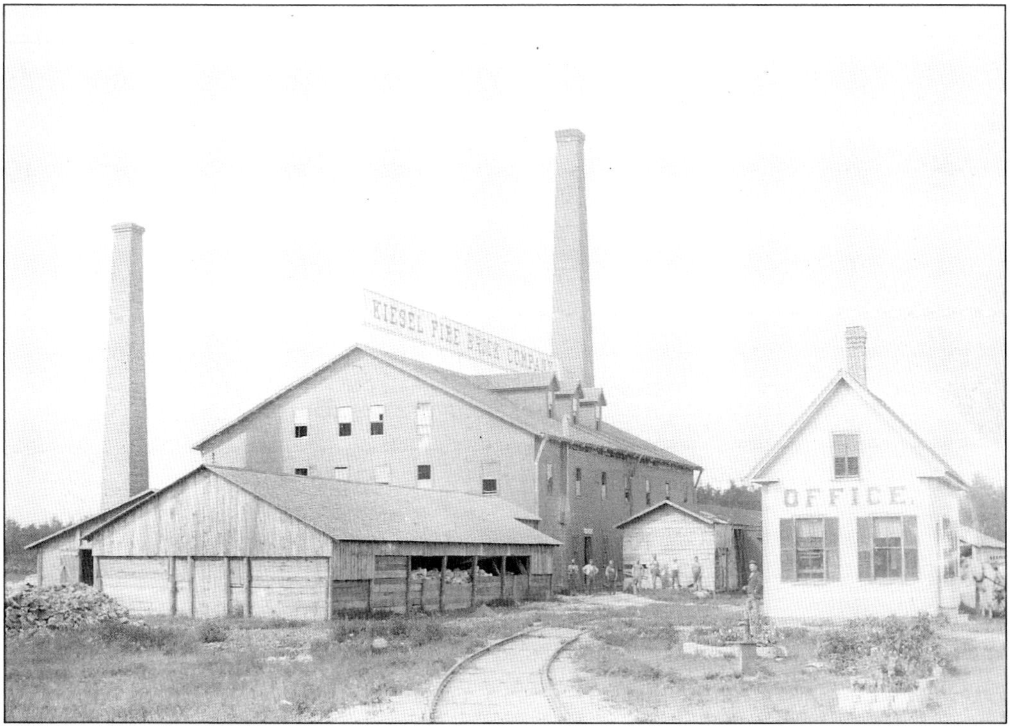

KEISEL FIRE BRICK. The Keisel Fire Brick Company was located at the end of Glenwood Avenue in 1889. It manufactured fire brick and tiles for boilers, forges, ovens, and furnaces from silica mined at Blue Job. In 1906 it was completely destroyed by a fire started by train sparks, but by June of the next year it had been rebuilt and was once more in operation.

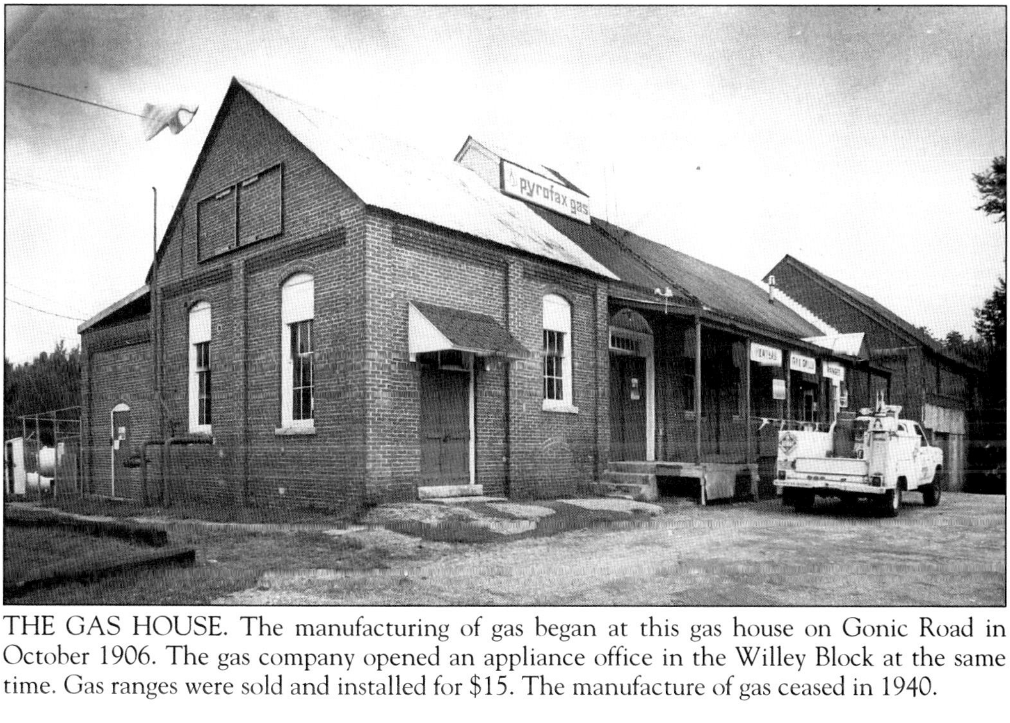

THE GAS HOUSE. The manufacturing of gas began at this gas house on Gonic Road in October 1906. The gas company opened an appliance office in the Willey Block at the same time. Gas ranges were sold and installed for $15. The manufacture of gas ceased in 1940.

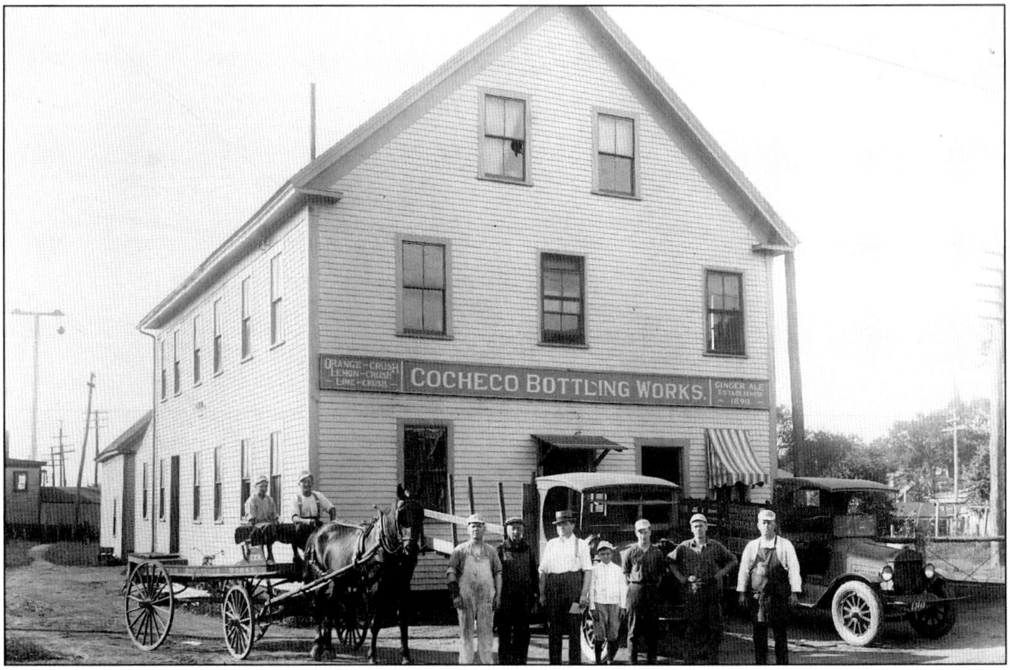

THE COCHECO BOTTLING WORKS. Eugene Emerson opened the Emerson Bottling Company in 1890. Emerson was succeeded in March of 1904 by James Lucey, who renamed the business the Cocheco Bottling Works. Alfred Lagasse purchased the company in 1917 and operated it with his sons.

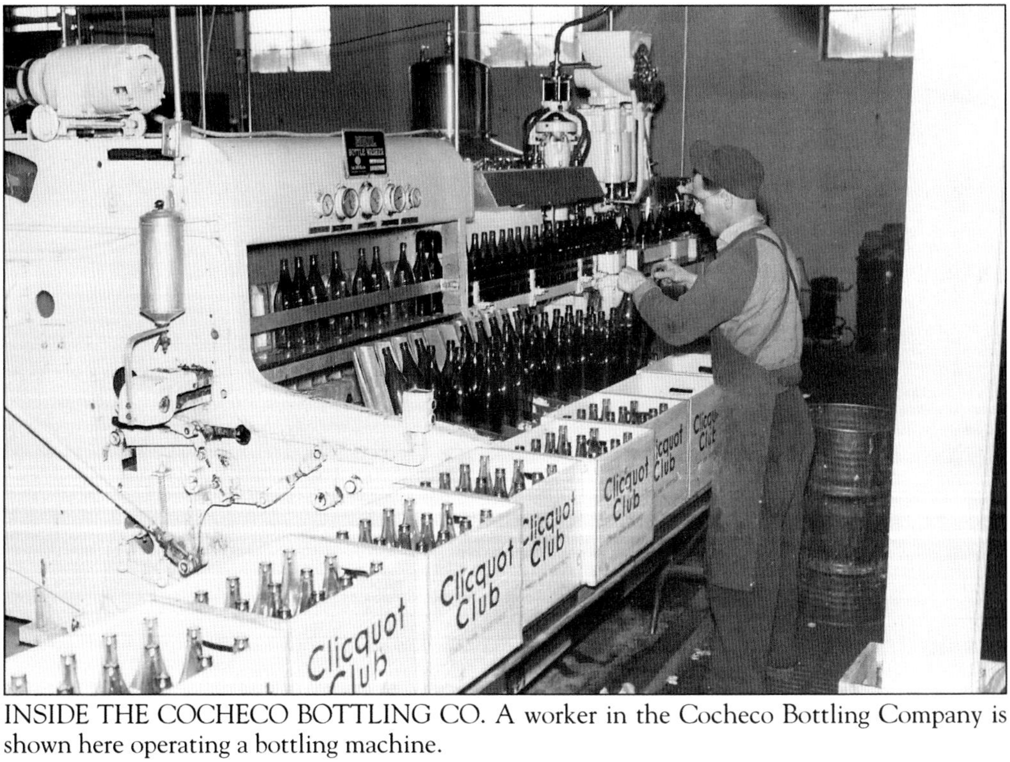

INSIDE THE COCHECO BOTTLING CO. A worker in the Cocheco Bottling Company is shown here operating a bottling machine.

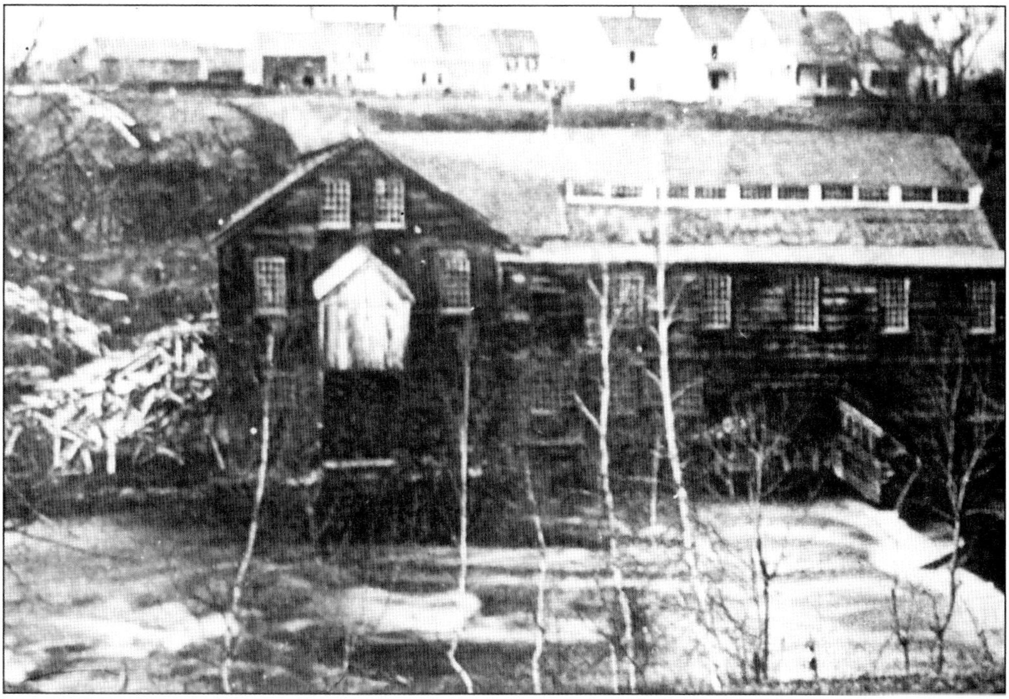

BARKER'S MILL. An early saw and gristmill built by Benjamin Barker on the banks of the Cocheco River was owned by John Hanscom and George McDuffee from 1876 to 1888. They changed the up-and-down saw to a circular saw in June of 1880 and the new saw delivered 8,000 feet of lumber a day in contrast to 3,000 feet from the old saw.

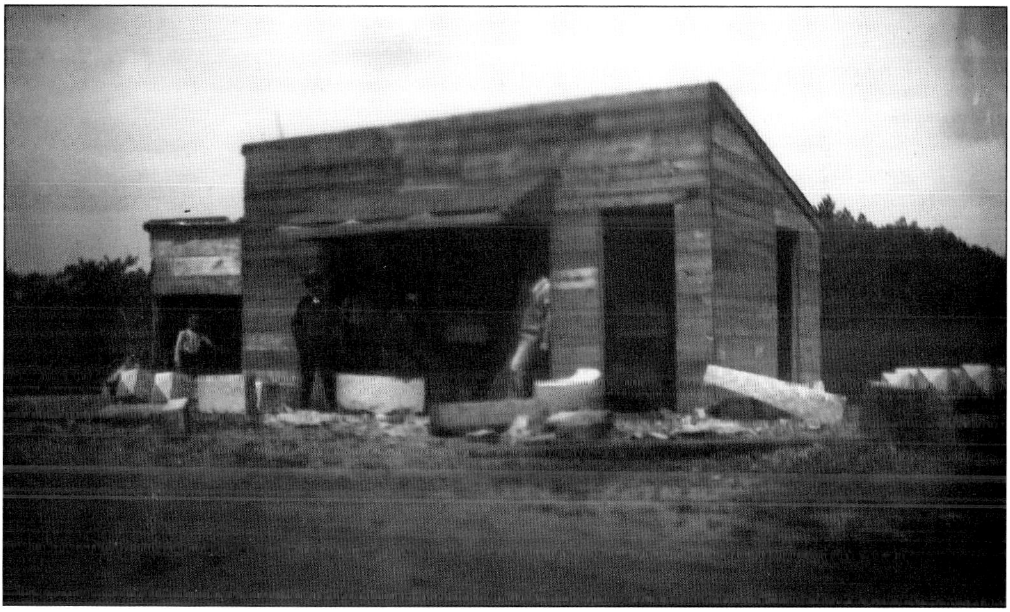

HUSSEY'S STONE SHED. Silas Hussey's stone shed was located at Sheridan Avenue and Granite Street. Hussey was an expert at all kinds of granite work. He did much cemetery work and building construction, built the stone arch bridge over the Cocheco River, and worked on the soldiers monument on the Rochester Common.

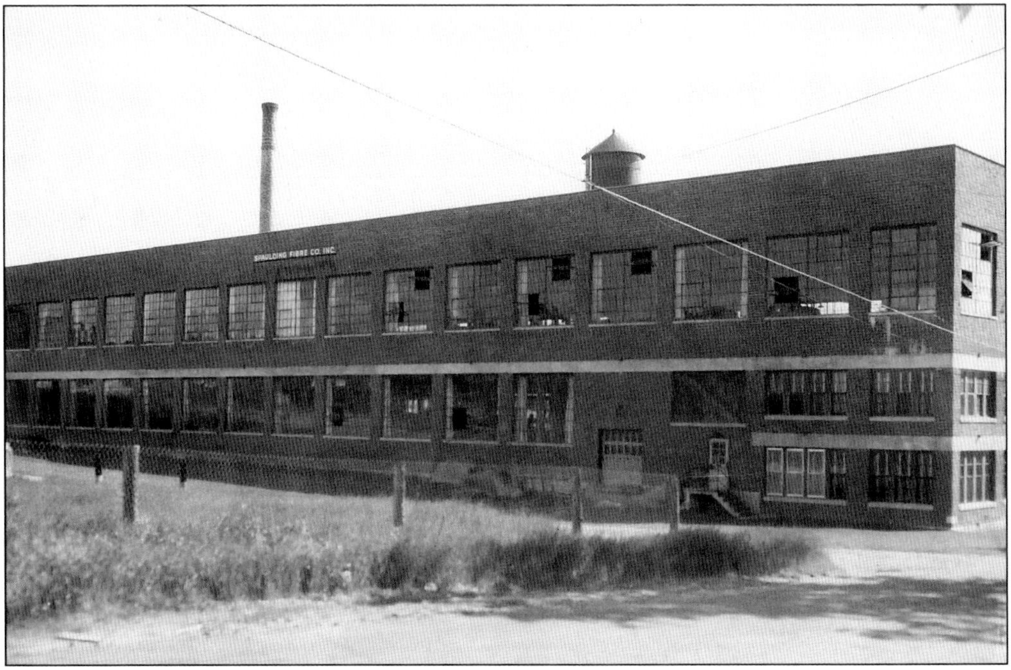

THE SPAULDING LEATHERBOARD AND COUNTER FACTORY. When Jonas Spaulding first came to the area he leased a building of the Wyandotte Mill in Rochester until he found a suitable place to build in North Rochester. Before constructing this mill in 1899, Jonas Spaulding built a dam and a canal for a water wheel. The building itself was 52-by-200 feet and four stories high.

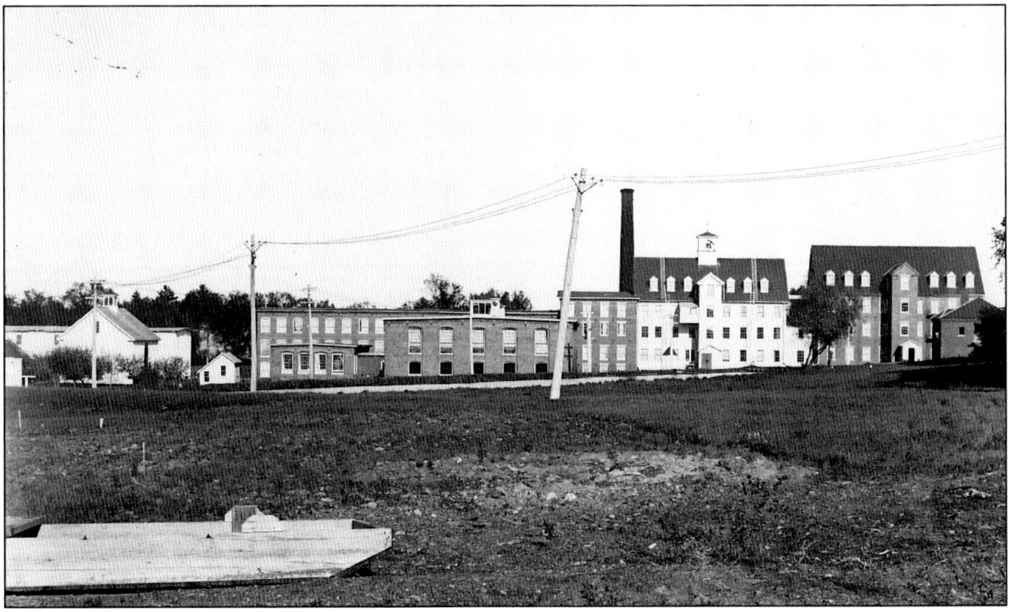

THE COCHECO WOOLEN MANUFACTURING COMPANY. John Hall began manufacturing woolen goods in East Rochester in 1862. Soon the industry was incorporated under the name of the Cocheco Woolen Manufacturing Company. The works covered 10 acres on the Salmon Falls River.

Eight

Homes

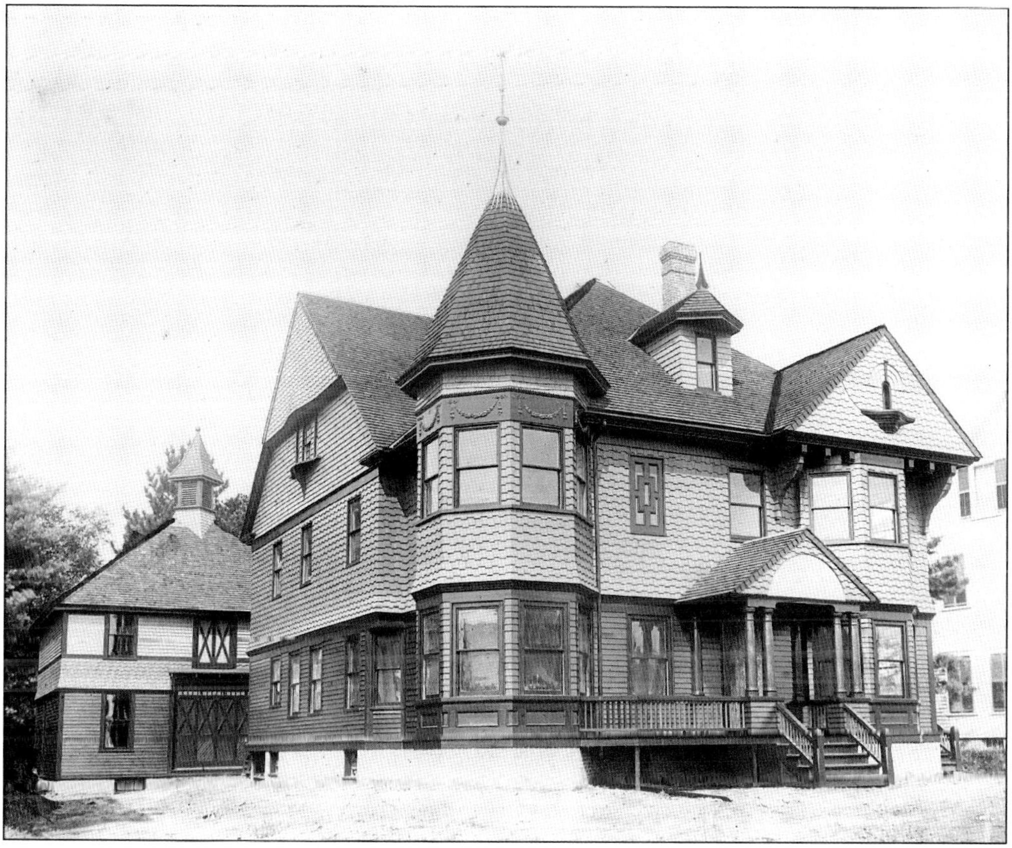

THE WILDER NEAL HOUSE. Wilder Neal built this house on Charles Street *c.* 1900. Neal came here from Farmington and opened the Globe Crockery Store on Market Street.

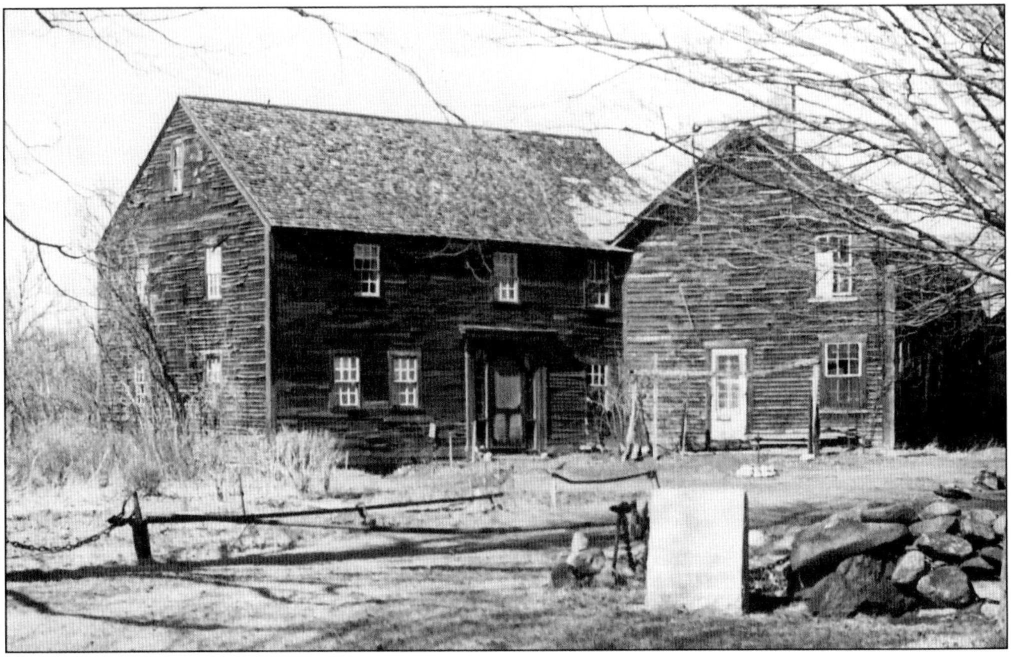

THE OLD DAME HOMESTEAD. Jabez Dame built this house on Rochester Hill in 1758. The barn was added in the late 1800s by Charles Dame, a descendant of the builder. In 1974 the home was sold to Arnold Skrome and transported to Moline, Illinois. Although Mr. Skrome planned to rebuild it, he never did, and he later sold it to Steve Figlmiller, who moved it to Balsam Lake, Wisconsin.

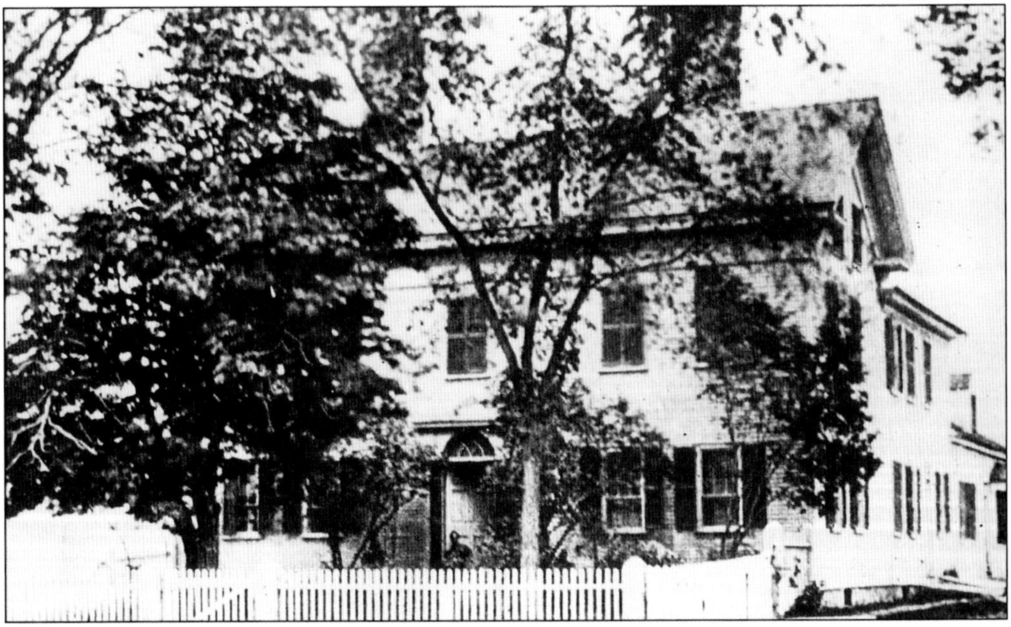

THE JOHN P. HALE HOUSE. John P. Hale was born in this house on North Main Street on March 31, 1806. Young Hale became a lawyer and began practicing law in Dover in 1830. From the time he became a lawyer he was interested in politics. He eventually became a resident of Dover and was elected to the U.S. House of Representatives and later the Senate.

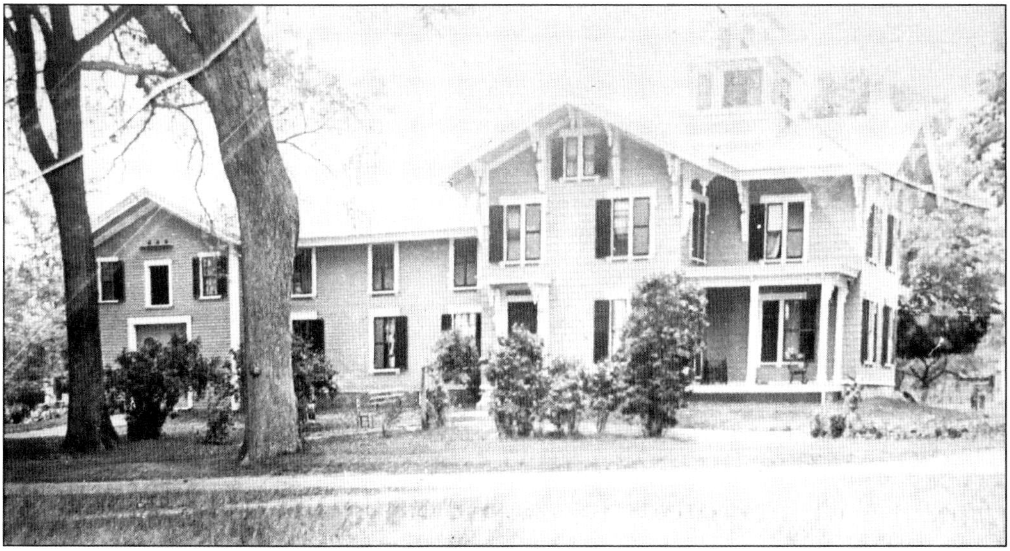

THE LEGRO HOUSE. John Legro built this house sometime before 1871. It later became part of the St. Charles Children's Home complex and served as a home for the caretaker and his family. This house was razed in 1972 and a Getty service station was built on the site.

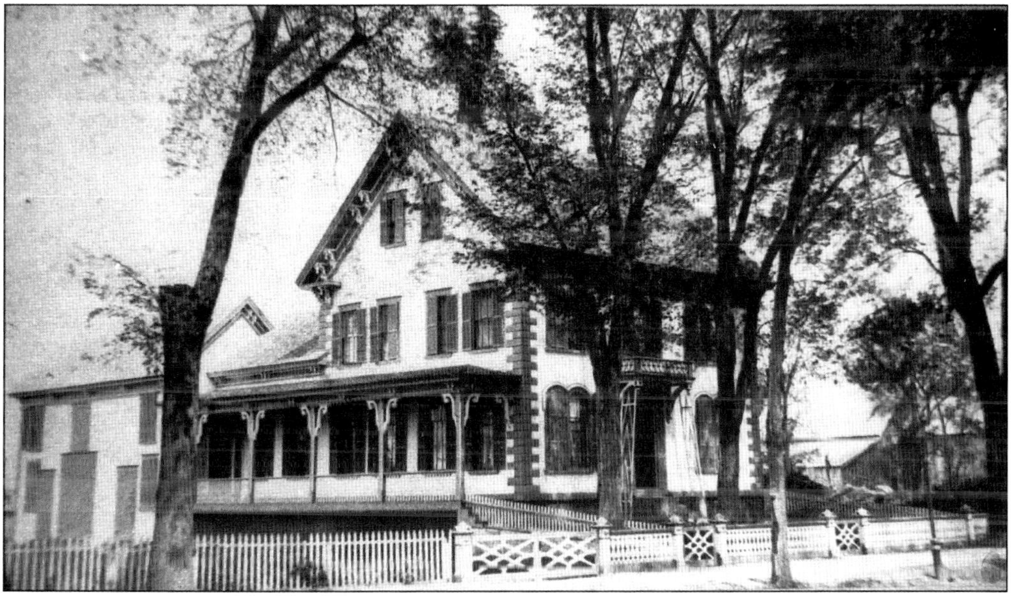

THE SPRINGFIELD HOUSE. Isaac W. Springfield, owner and operator of the textile mill in East Rochester, built this house before 1871. Dr. Walter Roberts and Nurse Minnie Eagle operated the Eagle Hospital in this building from 1918 to 1922. In 1922 the house was moved to the back of the lot and the telephone exchange building was erected on the front of the lot on Main Street.

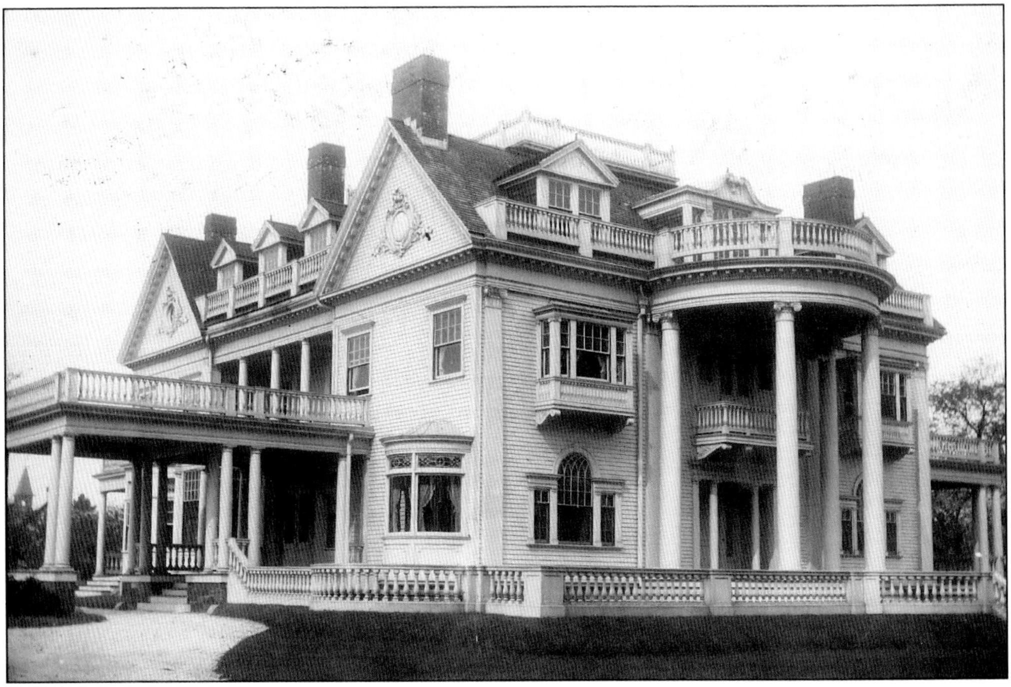

THE SUMNER WALLACE HOUSE. Sumner Wallace had this magnificent home built in 1901 at a cost of $75,000. One of the most beautiful houses in New Hampshire, it had twenty large rooms and a ballroom that covered the entire top floor. It became the state headquarters of the Ku Klux Klan and they occupied the building, with a fiery cross on the roof, from 1924 to 1927. The mansion was razed in 1932.

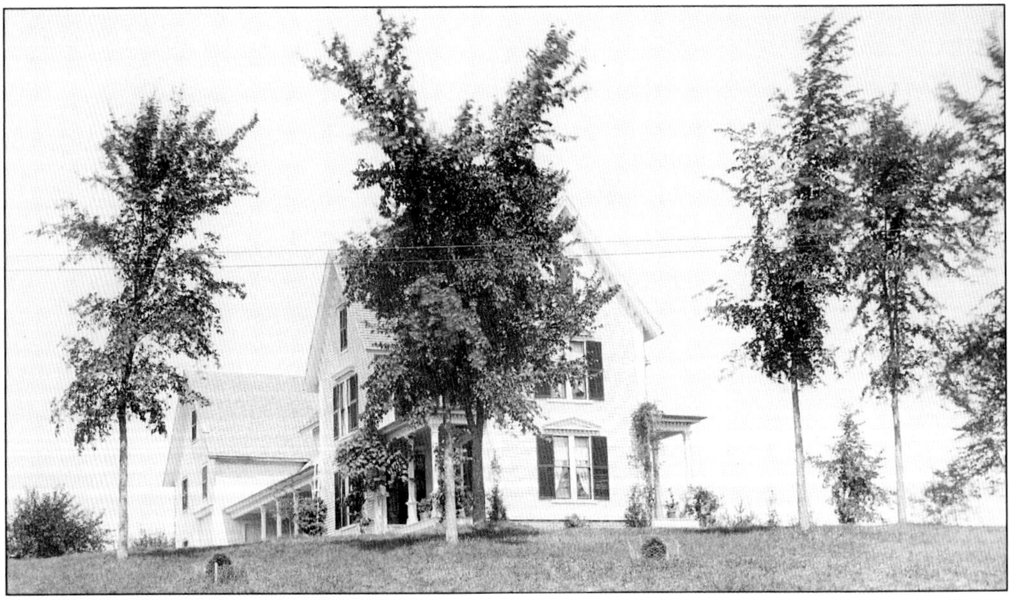

CAPTAIN SMITH'S HOUSE. Smith was the proprietor of a handle factory on Wadleigh Brook (later the Axehandle Brook), which was behind his house on Gonic Road. The business, started in 1853 by his father-in-law, Warren Wadleigh, produced quality wood handles and shipped them all over the country.

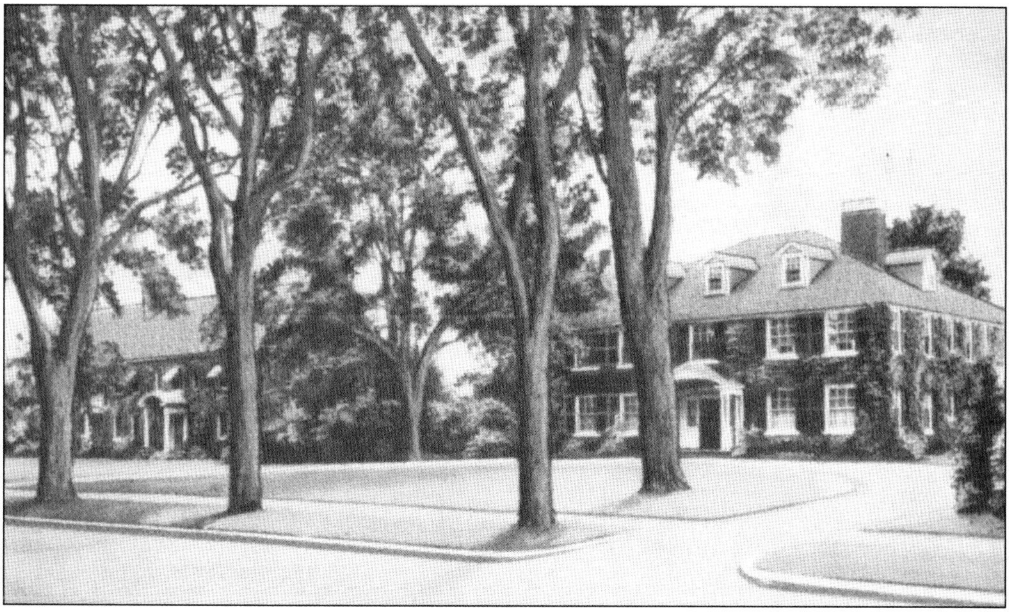

THE SPAULDING HOMES. These houses side by side on Wakefield Street were the homes of two Spaulding brothers. Rolland H. Spaulding owned the home at 76 Wakefield Street. He was governor of New Hampshire from 1915 to 1917. The Huntley M. Spaulding home was at 78 Wakefield Street. He was governor of New Hampshire from 1927 to 1929.

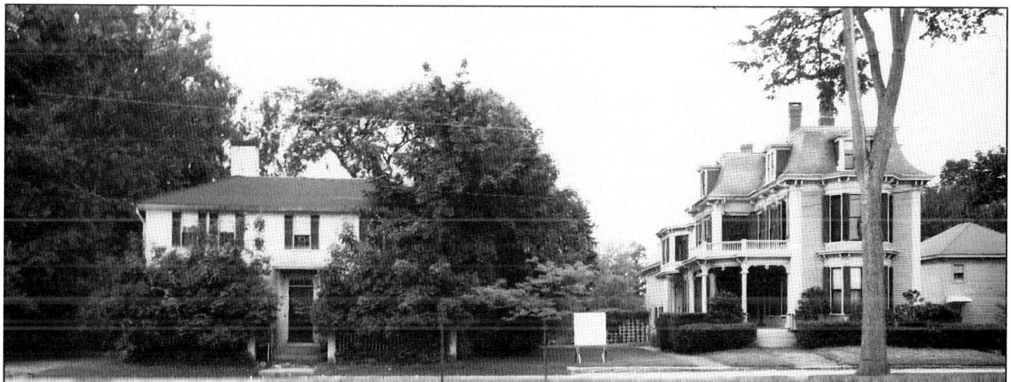

THE DENNETT AND WALLACE HOUSES. These two houses were torn down in 1976 and replaced by Friendly's Restaurant. The smaller house was built in 1813 by Charles Dennett, cabinet maker, who with his wife Abigail raised nine children and celebrated their golden wedding anniversary in the house. On the right is the Ebenezer Wallace house, built in 1876 by Wallace, a co-owner of the Wallace Shoe Company.

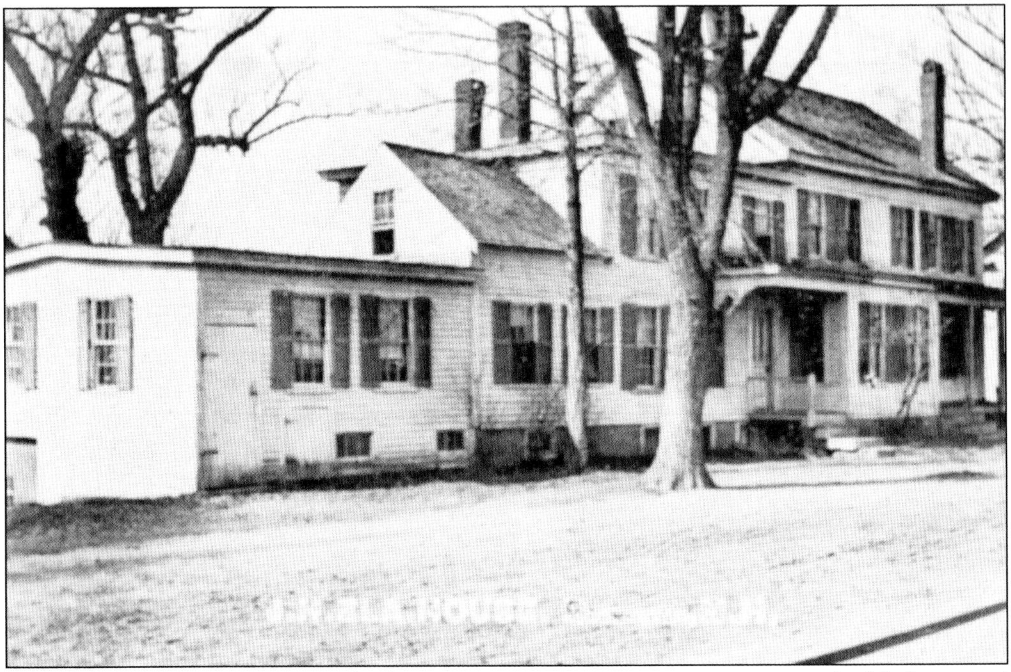

JACOB ELA'S HOUSE. Jacob Ela's house on Congress Street was a station in the Underground Railroad during the Civil War. Ela joined an anti-slavery society as a teenager and became an active abolitionist. He was elected representative to Congress in 1867.

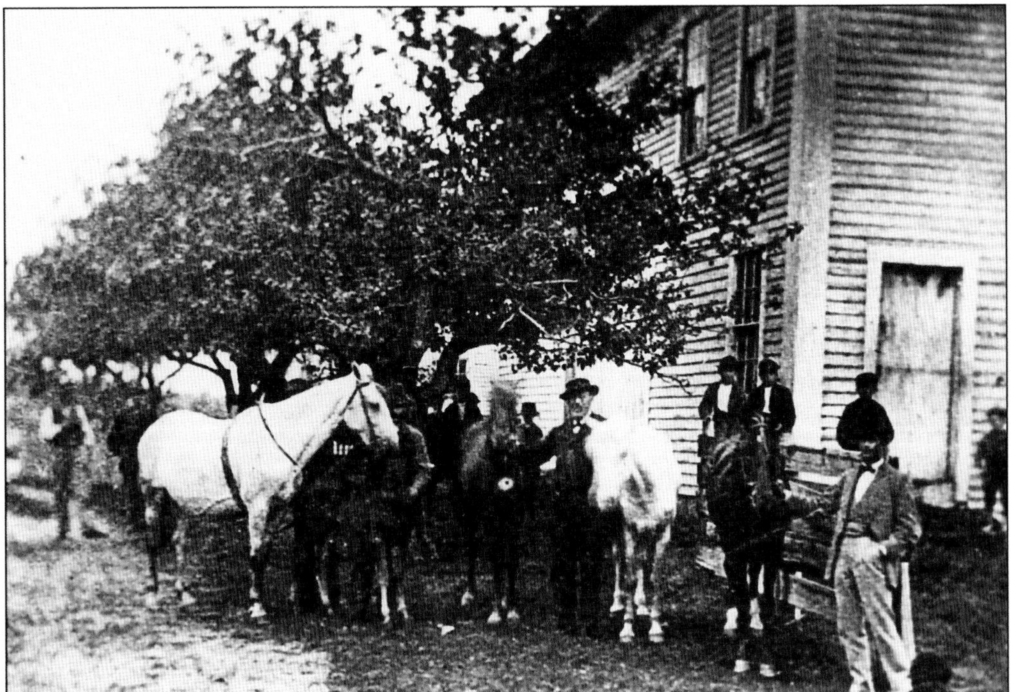

JACOB ELA'S BARN. Jacob Ela was a lover of horses, and he kept a horse while he was in Washington and rode nearly every day. This barn housed escaping slaves as well as horses.

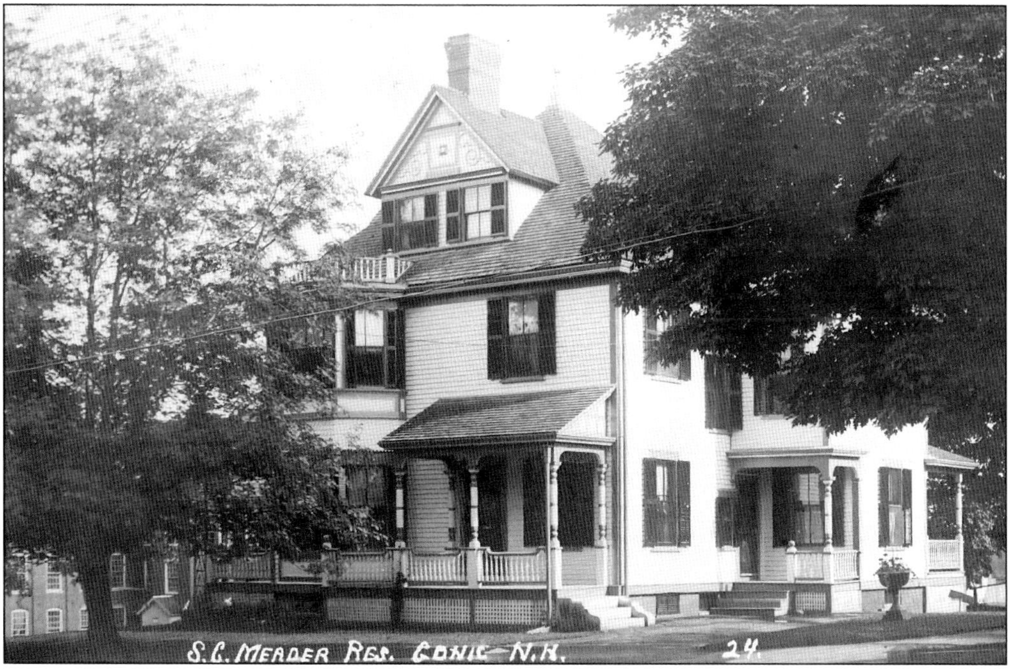

STEPHEN MEADER'S HOUSE. The Stephen Meader house was next to the residence of Charles S. Whitehouse in Gonic. After finishing school in 1861, Stephen Meader worked in the mill of N.V. Whitehouse. He learned all about the industry and received many promotions. In 1881 he became agent.

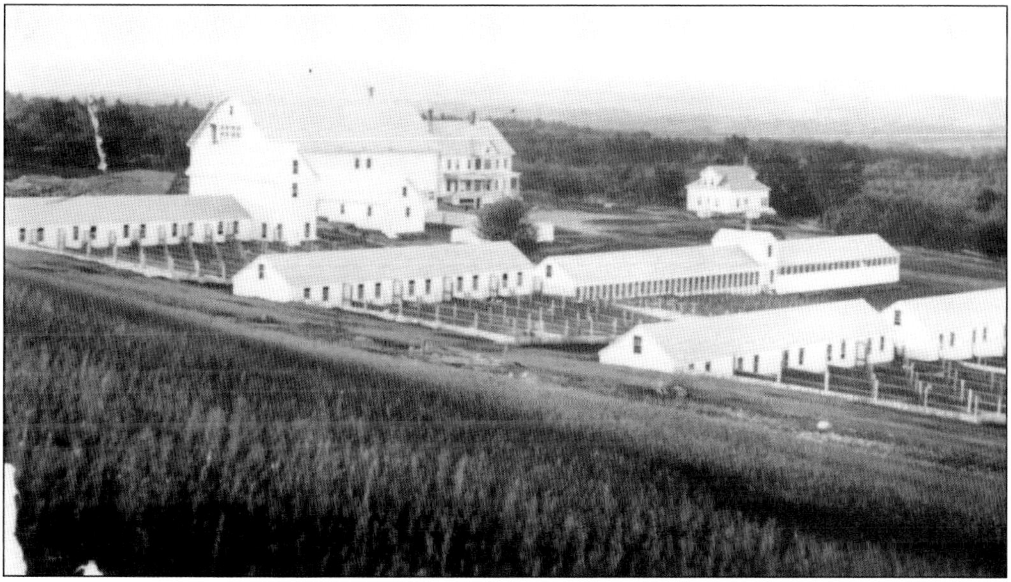

BROADVIEW FARM. George Wallace, son of Edwin Wallace, built Broadview Farm on 185 acres on Ten Rod Road. Barn timbers were 30–40 feet long and were brought to Rochester on flat cars. They were moved from the station to the farm by ten to fifteen yoke of oxen.

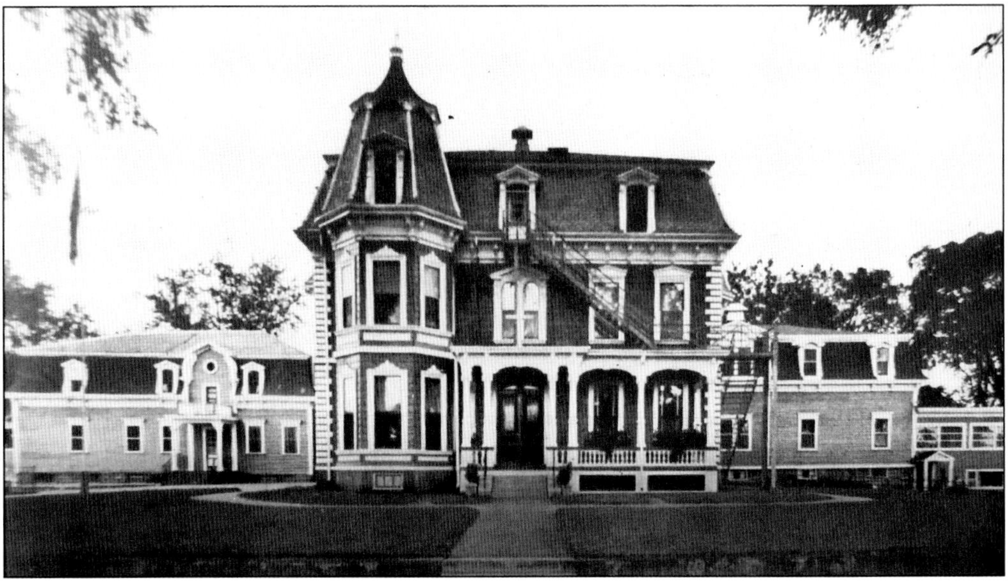

THE EDWIN WALLACE HOUSE. Edwin Wallace, a co-owner of the Wallace Shoe Company, built this house in 1878. In 1914 the property was sold to the Catholic bishop of Manchester and it was converted into a children's home. It is still serving children today as the St. Charles Children's Home on Grant Street.

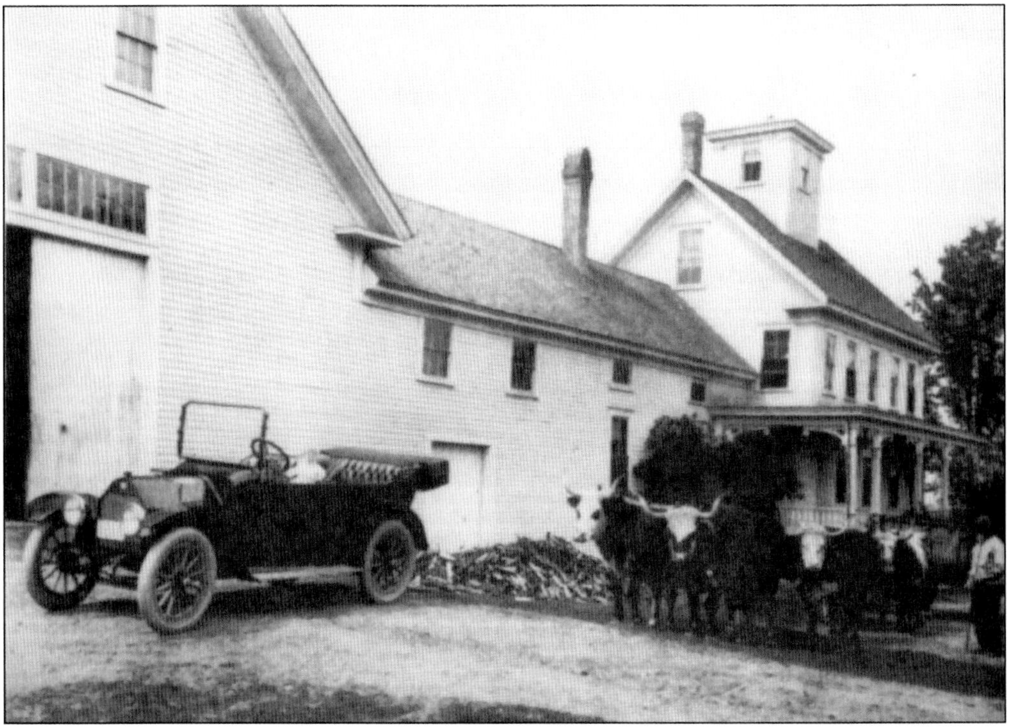

THE JAMES CORSON HOUSE. James Corson built this house on Adams Corner after the Civil War. It was here that Harry Thaw, murderer of Stanford White, ran out of gas while fleeing to Canada. Mr. Corson gave him a ride to town and later testified in the trial in New York.

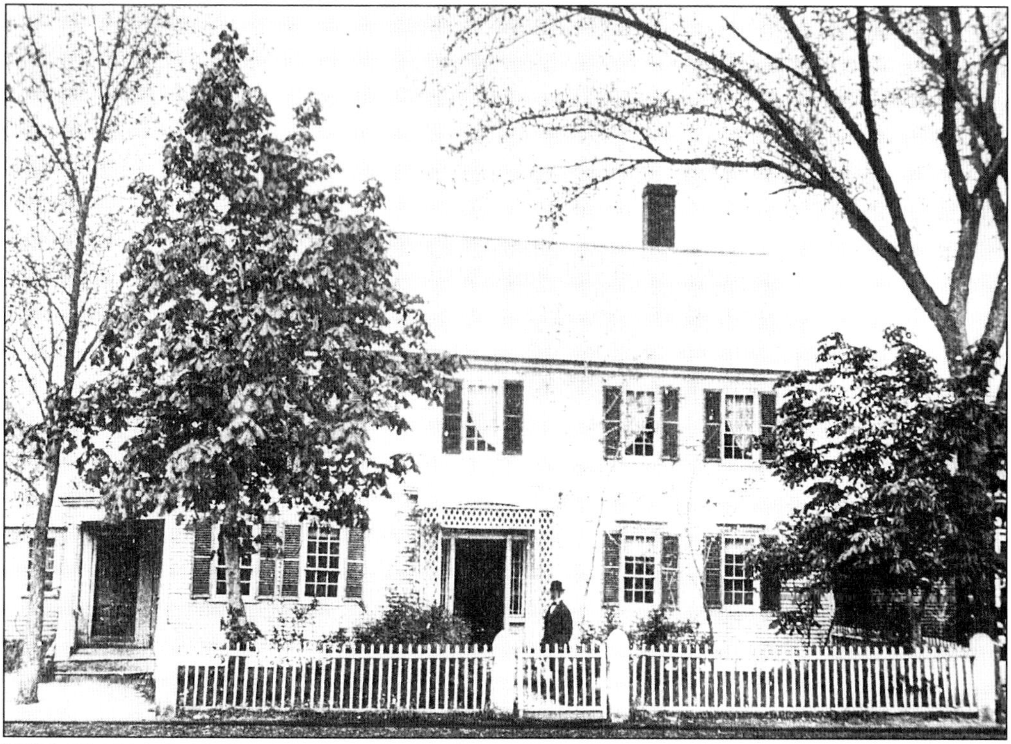

THE SIMON CHASE HOUSE. Simon Chase bought an early tavern kept by Levi Dearborn on Main Street and added another story to make it his home. In 1878 he sold the land to A.W. Hayes and moved his house to Congress Street.

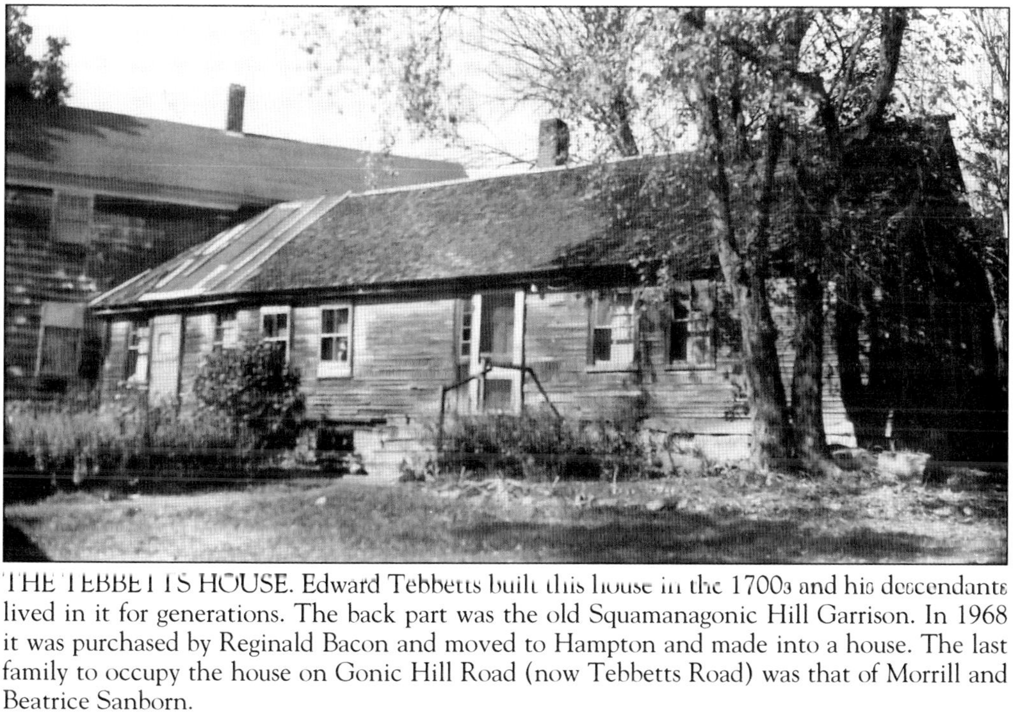

THE TEBBETTS HOUSE. Edward Tebbetts built this house in the 1700s and his descendants lived in it for generations. The back part was the old Squamanagonic Hill Garrison. In 1968 it was purchased by Reginald Bacon and moved to Hampton and made into a house. The last family to occupy the house on Gonic Hill Road (now Tebbetts Road) was that of Morrill and Beatrice Sanborn.

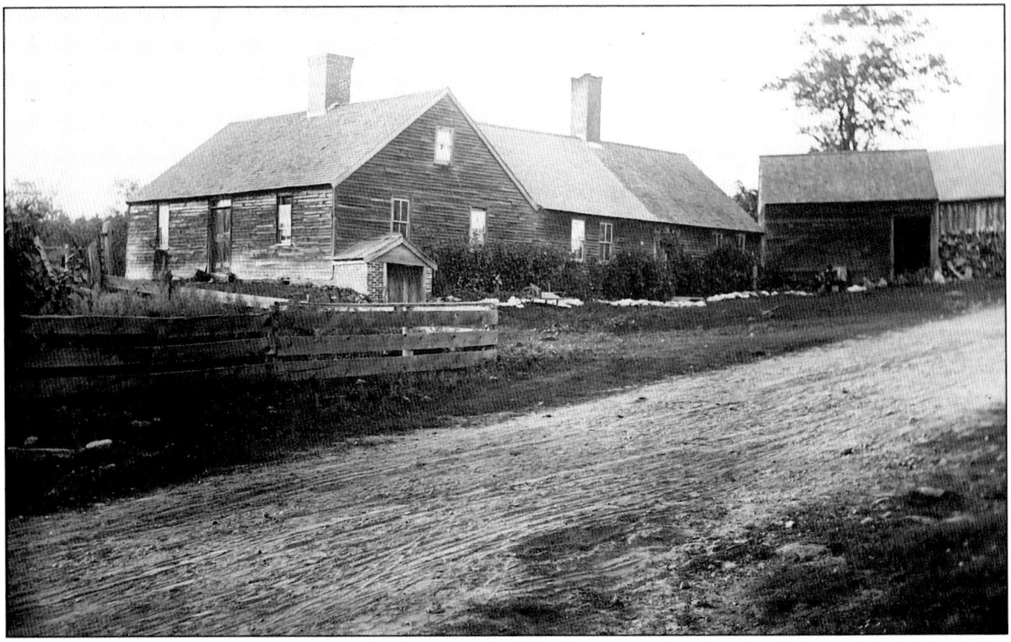

THE SIMON TORR HOUSE. Simon Torr built this house on Chestnut Hills Road in 1775. It is now one of the oldest houses in the city, and is still in the Torr family.

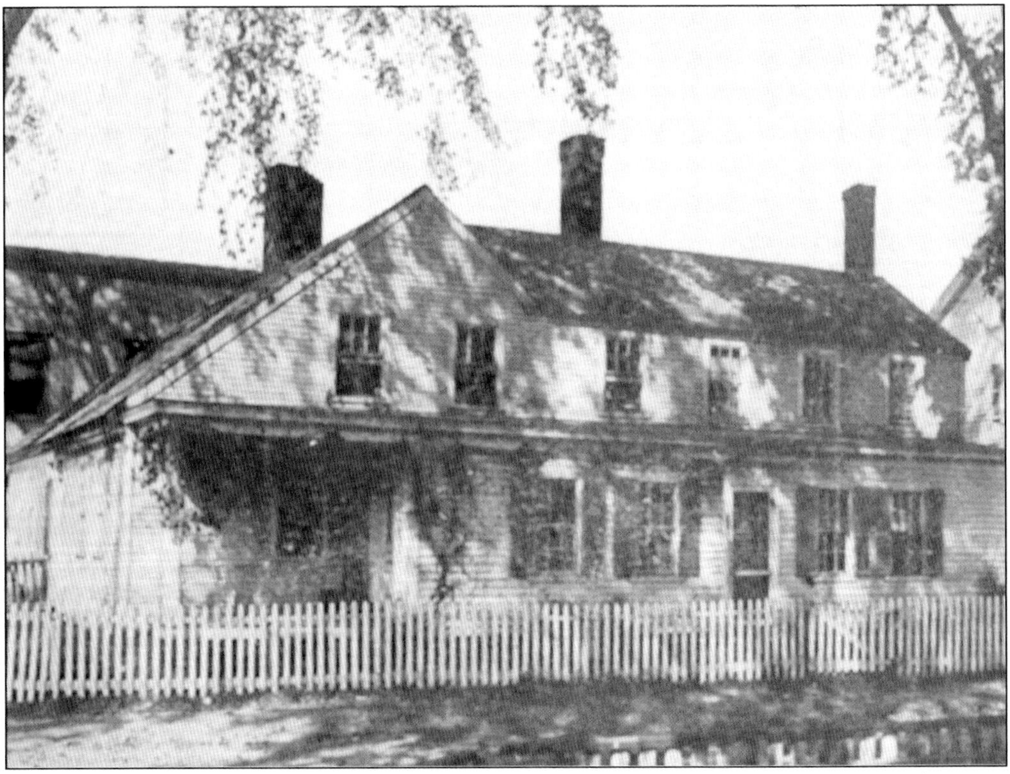

THE CALEB DAME HOUSE. The Caleb Dame house at the corner of Market and Union Streets was the first Methodist meeting place in the village in 1808.

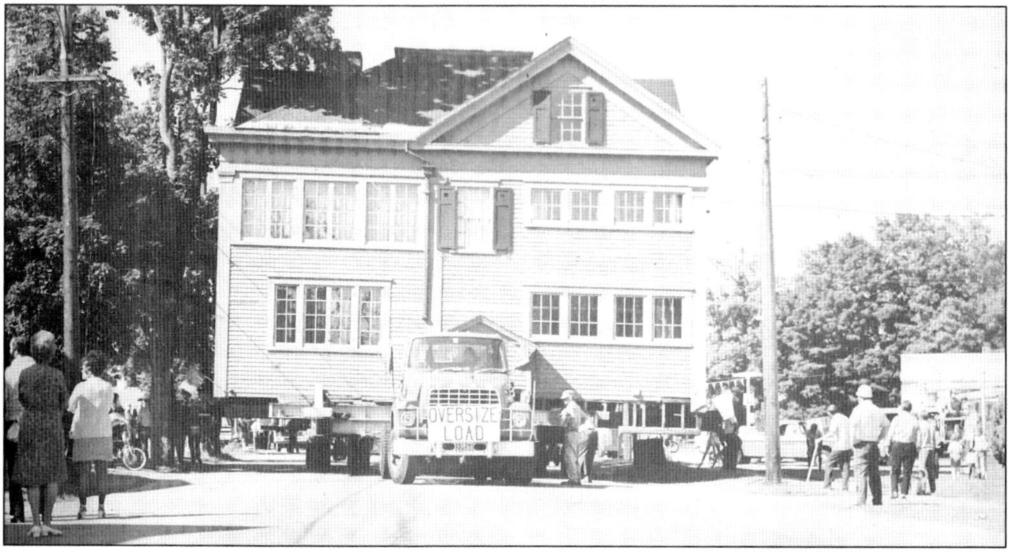

MOVING THE MCDUFFEE HOUSE. This house was occupied by Charles Chase and Abbie McDuffee, who were married in 1876. Abbie left the house on Wakefield Street to her nephew, Willis McDuffee, and he lived there with his wife Dora. The house was purchased by George Lovejoy in 1972 and moved to the end of Eastern Avenue.

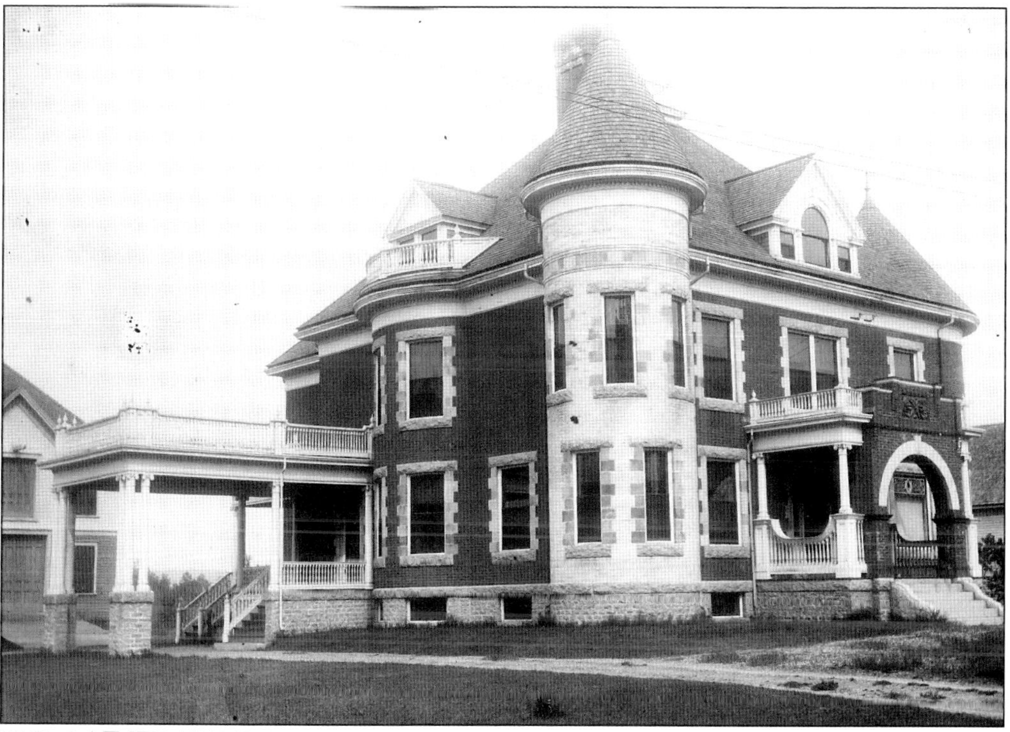

THE GAFNEY HOME. Judge Charles B. Gafney built this house in 1897. When he died a year later he left a will appointing several friends as trustees of his estate and instructing that they care for sickly Mrs. Gafney until her death, at which time they were to choose a charitable purpose for the house. Mrs. Gafney died in 1900 and the trustees decided that a home for aged women was a suitable use for the home. The Gafney Home opened on September 12, 1904.

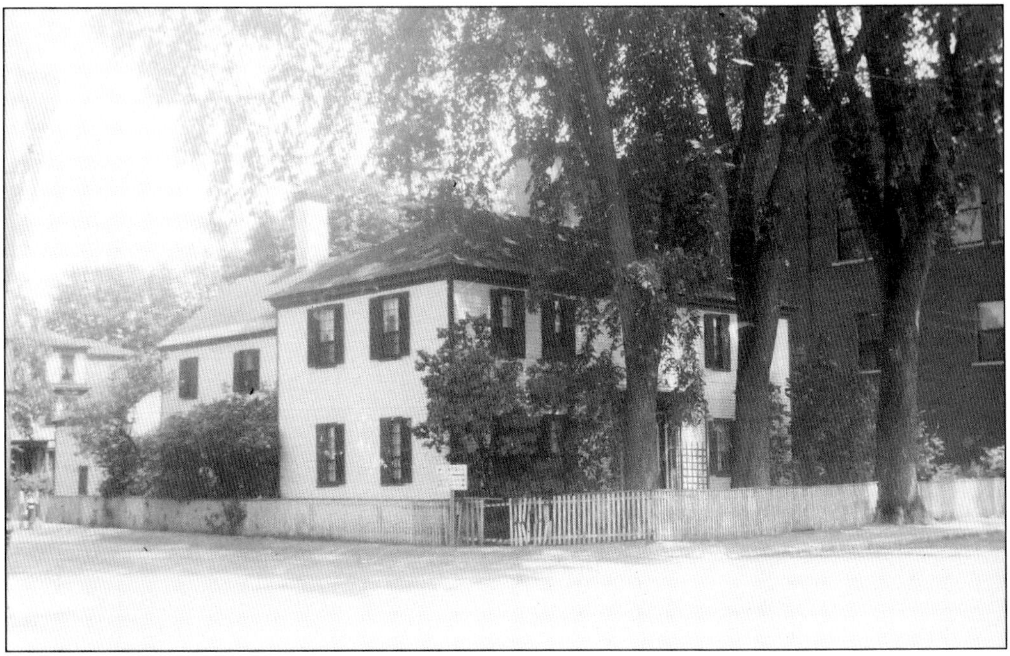

THE BICKFORD HOUSE. The house on the corner of Union and Main Streets was the home of Mayor Charles Bickford and his wife, Mary Louise, who died in 1903. Bickford's second wife and widow Frances Hussey Bickford died in 1948 and the house was sold to Joseph Michael. The old house was purchased by Harry Bullock and moved to Alfred, Maine, and a W.T. Grant store was built on the site.

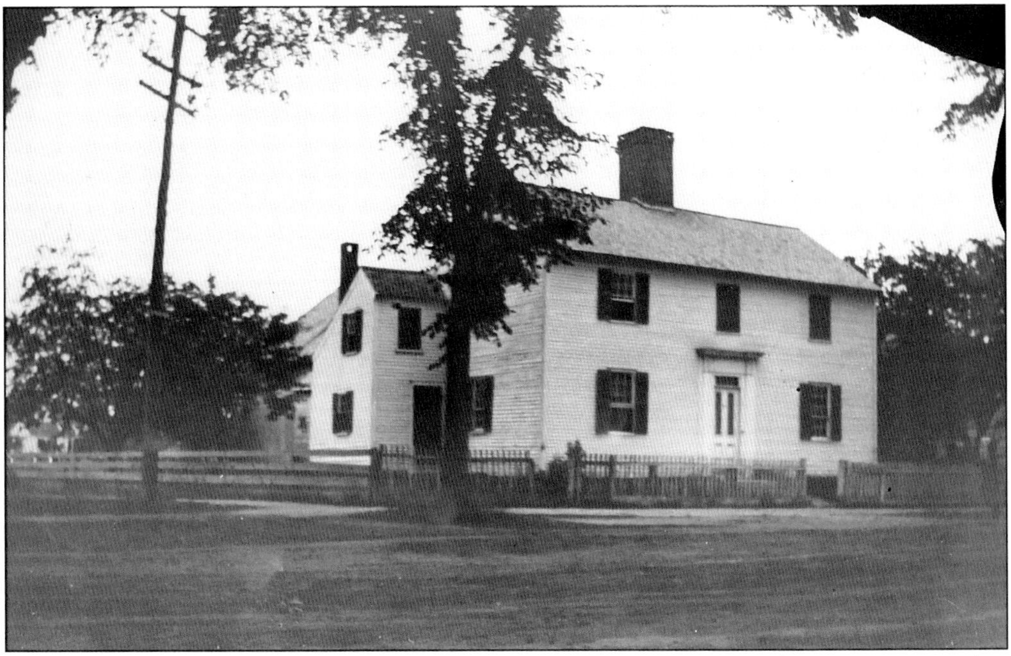

THE SOLOMON EVANS HOUSE. In 1901 this house at 35 Wakefield Street was moved to Milton Road. The Rochester High School was built on the lot that same year. The Church of the Redeemer occupies the site today.

Nine

Churches and Schools

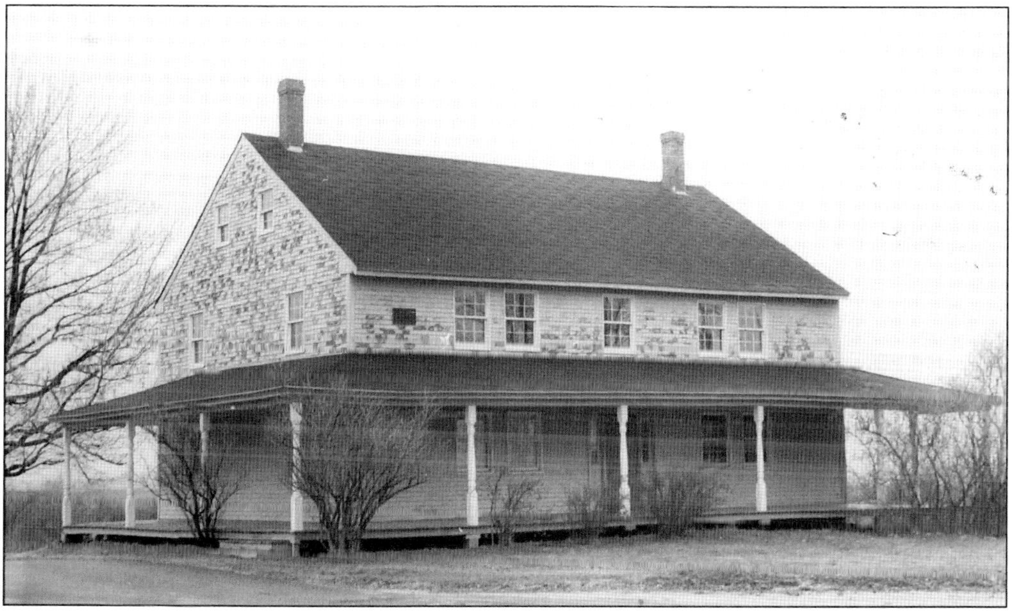

THE HAVEN HILL PARSONAGE. This parsonage was named for Joseph Haven, who served as pastor for forty-nine years. The building was later privately owned and a piazza was added in 1901 by John Quinlan. The building still stands on the top of the hill.

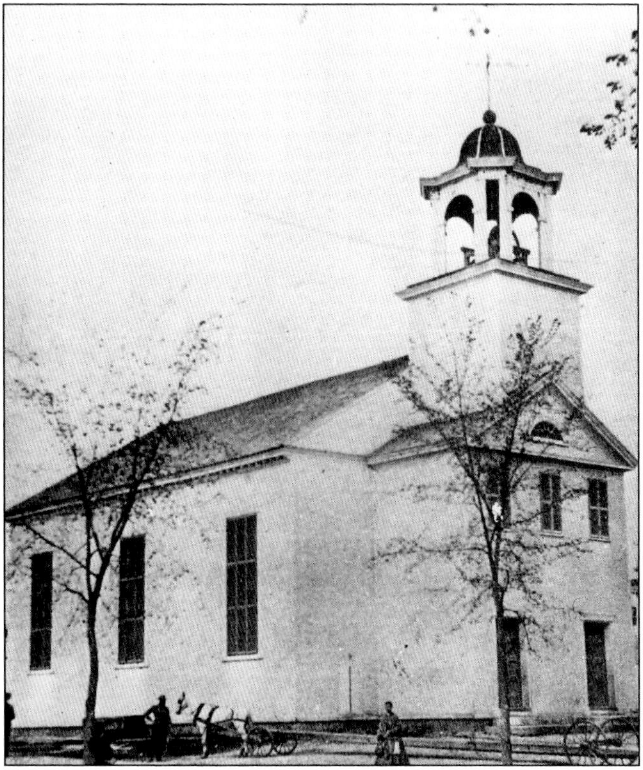

THE FIRST CHURCH. The first meetinghouse was built at the top of Rochester Hill in 1731. The meetinghouse was taken down in 1842 and rebuilt on the Common. Using what could be salvaged from the old building and repairing with new materials, the church was enlarged by the addition of twenty pews. In 1872 it was moved to the corner of Liberty Street and raised, adding a new lower story for a small vestry and storage room.

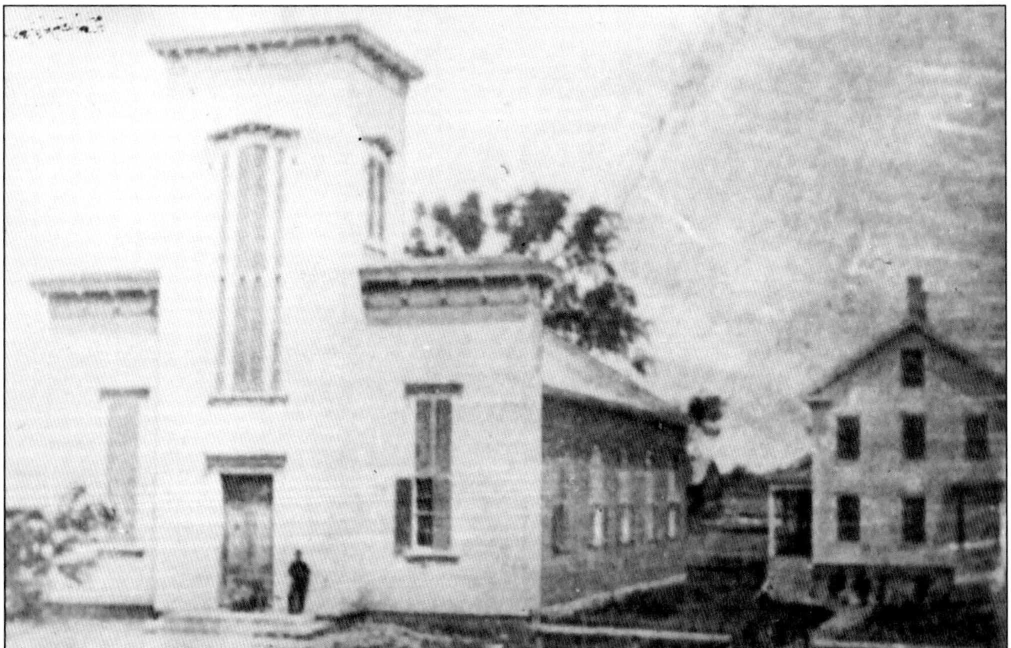

THE METHODIST CHURCH. This is the Methodist church, built in 1825 on the site formerly occupied by Barker's Tavern on Main Street. It measured 42-by-55 feet and cost $1,923. The parsonage was built in 1828.

THE NEW METHODIST CHURCH. A new church was built on the site of the old one in 1868, at the same time the McDuffee Block was going up on the other side of Main Street. It was built with two small spires below the steeple. One spire was struck by lightning in June 1895 and badly damaged. Instead of repairing the damage, both spires were removed.

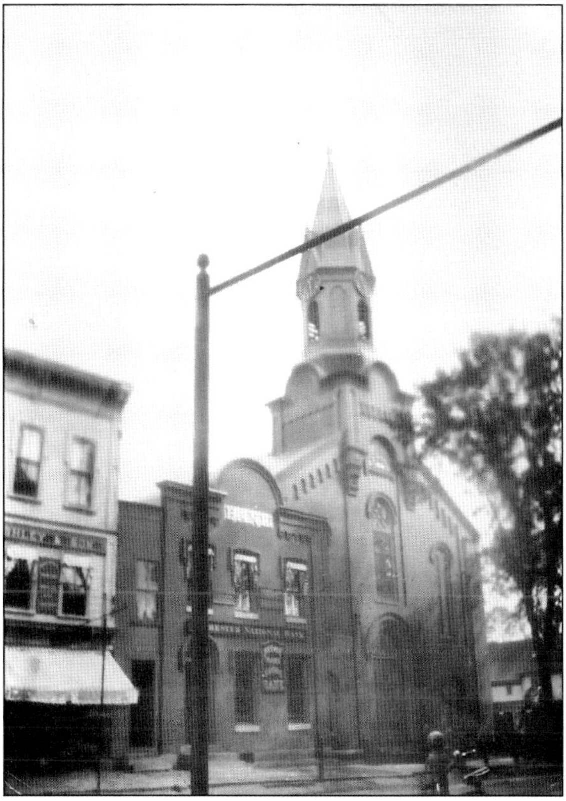

A LAWN PARTY AT THE METHODIST CHURCH. On July 3, 1896, the day of the dedication of the Parson Main statue in Central Square, a lawn party was held at the Methodist church.

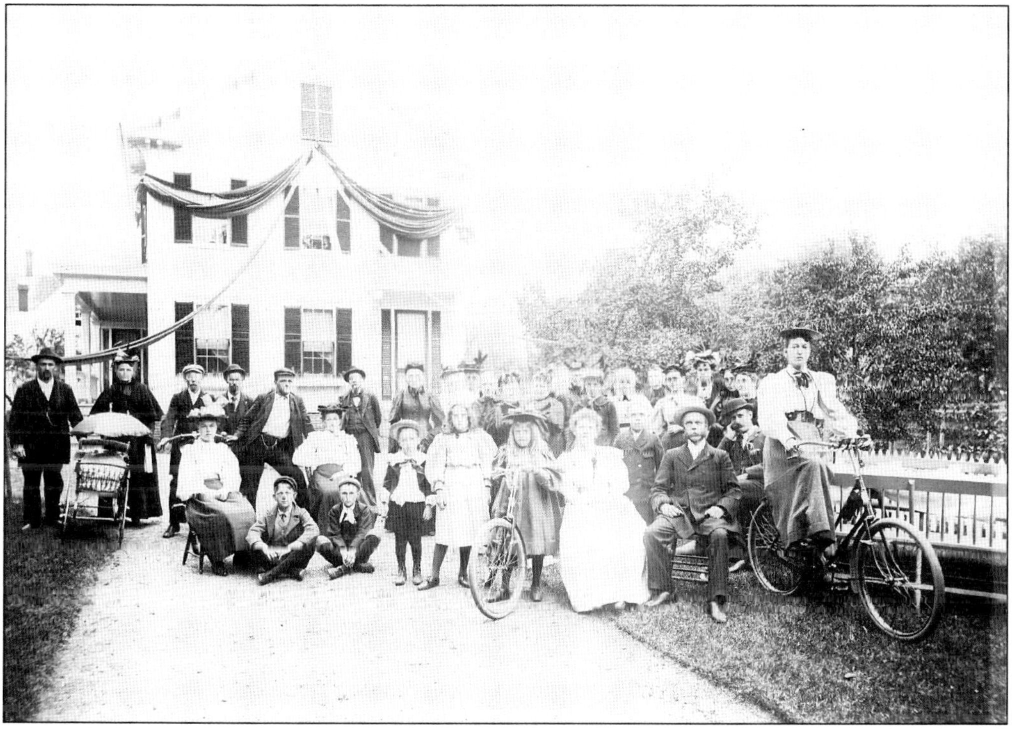

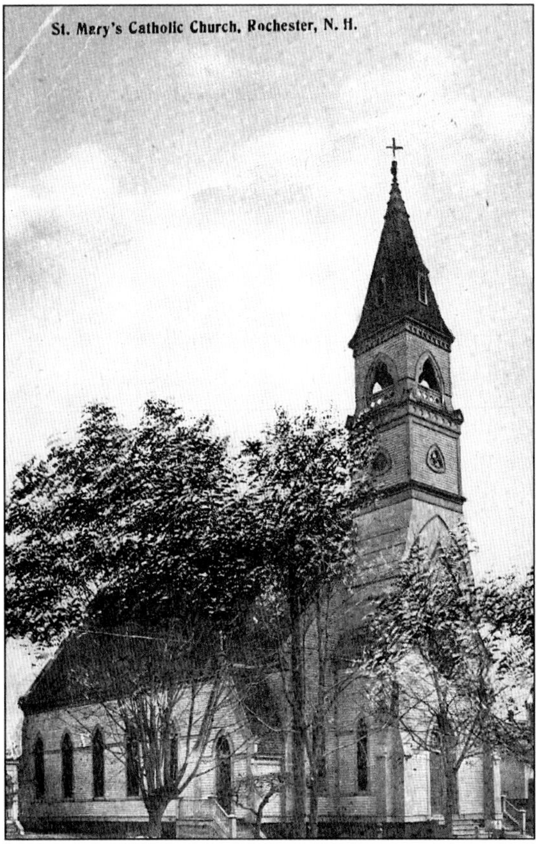

ST. MARY'S CHURCH. The St. Mary's congregation eventually outgrew their little church on Hancock Street. This new church on Charles Street seated 400 when the first Mass was celebrated on December 25, 1886, by Bishop Brady of Manchester.

THE HOLY ROSARY CHURCH. The first Holy Rosary Church was built on Bridge Street in 1883. Work on the 450-seat church was completed in time for celebration of Mass on Christmas Day. A new church, seating 936, was opened on North Main Street in June 1963. The old church was razed that same year.

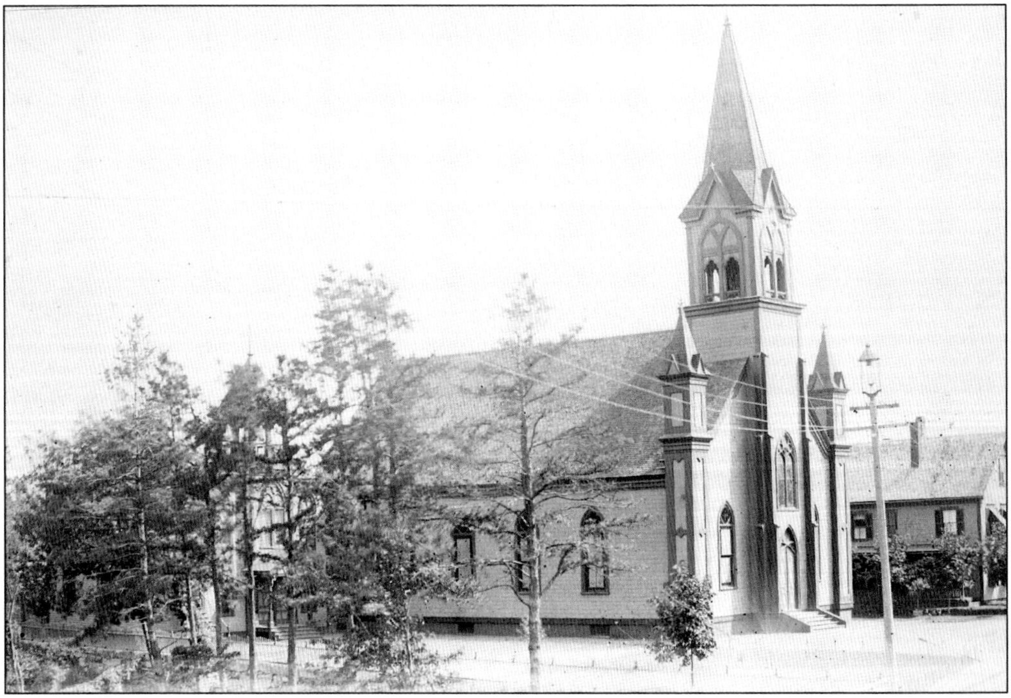

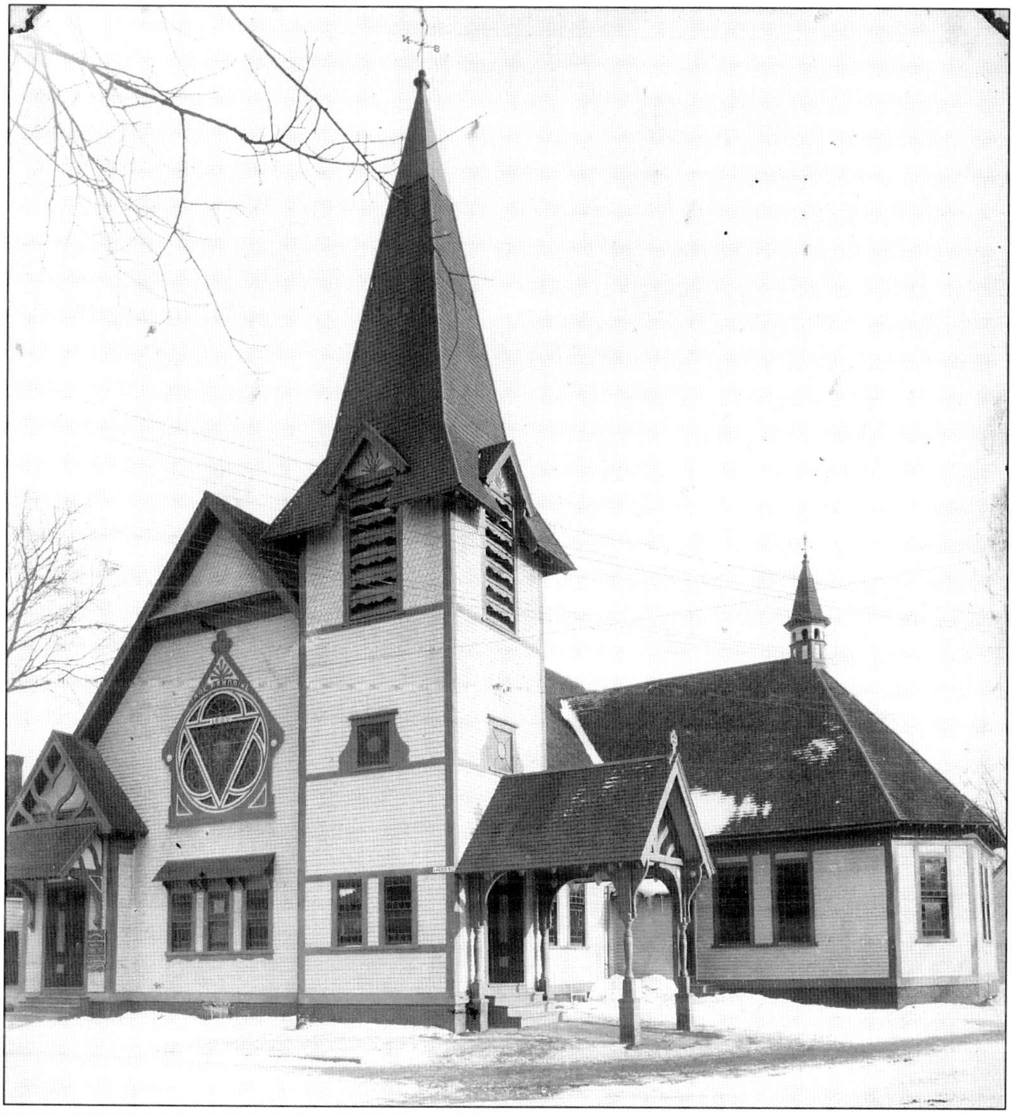

THE TRUE MEMORIAL BAPTIST CHURCH. The True Memorial Church dedicated on January 23, 1884, was named in honor of Ezekiel True, the founder and first pastor of the Free Will Baptist Church in Rochester. This building was destroyed by fire on March 13, 1961, and the next year it was replaced by a new building on Ten Rod Road.

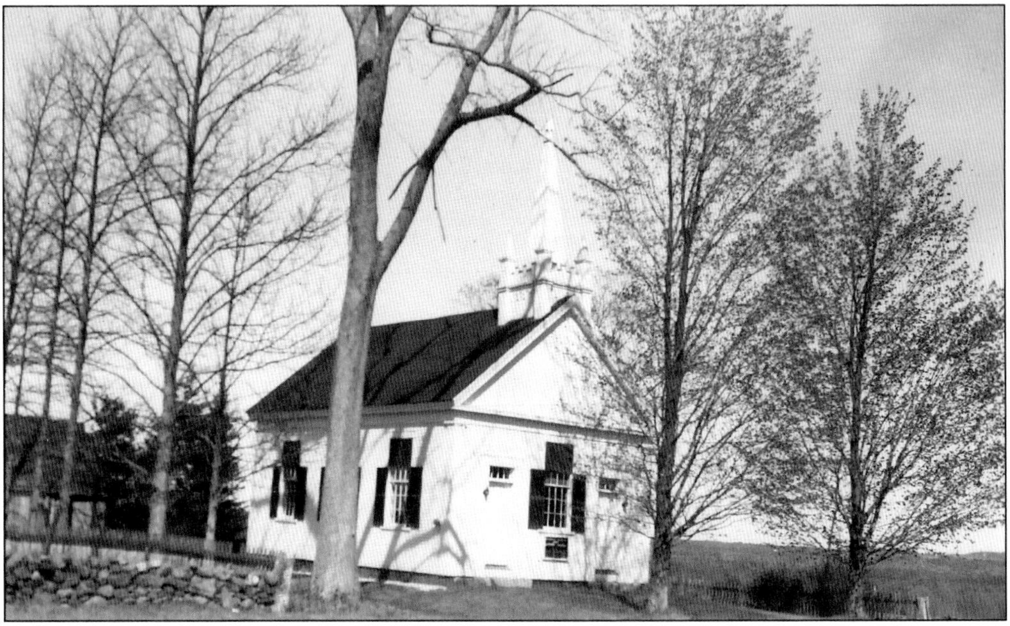

THE WALNUT GROVE CHURCH. The Walnut Grove Church was dedicated on February 27, 1868. It was built as a chapel with eighteen pews at the cost of $1,500. It remained without a pastor for four years until Reverend Plummer Chesley became its first pastor on January 1, 1872.

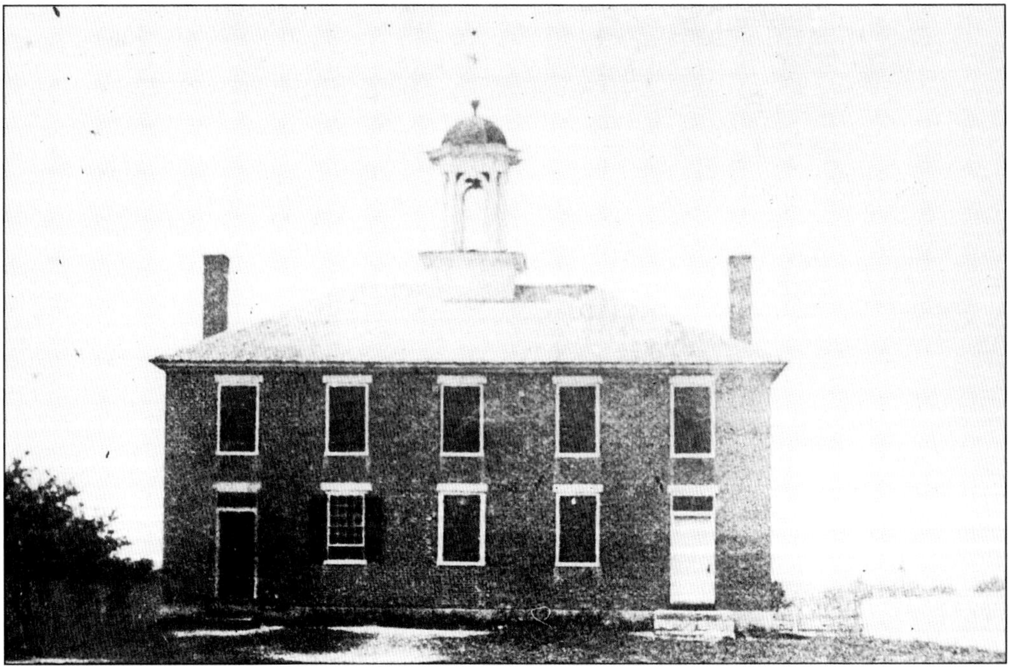

THE ROCHESTER ACADEMY. The Newmarket Wesleyan Academy moved to Rochester on October 31, 1828. It was renamed the Rochester Academy and located in this building until it closed in 1849. The building was used as a private school by Miss Caroline Knight until 1872. Miss Knight shared the building with the IOOF. This building is still at 4 Academy Street.

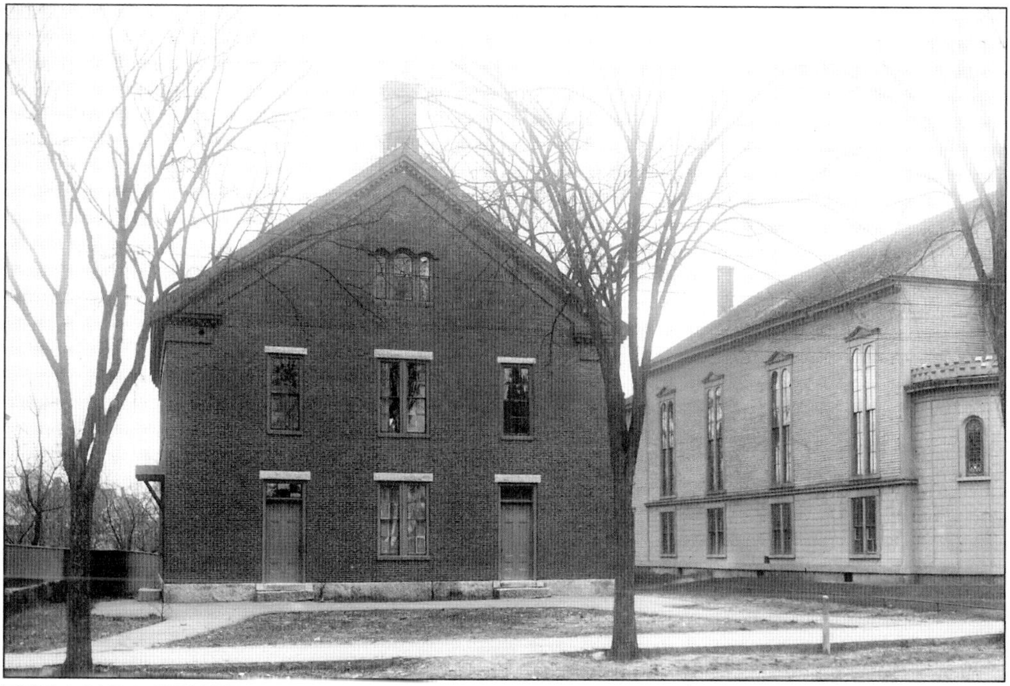

THE MAIN STREET SCHOOL. The Main Street School, built in 1856, was used as a high school as well as an elementary school. It was razed and replaced with the Rochester Public Library.

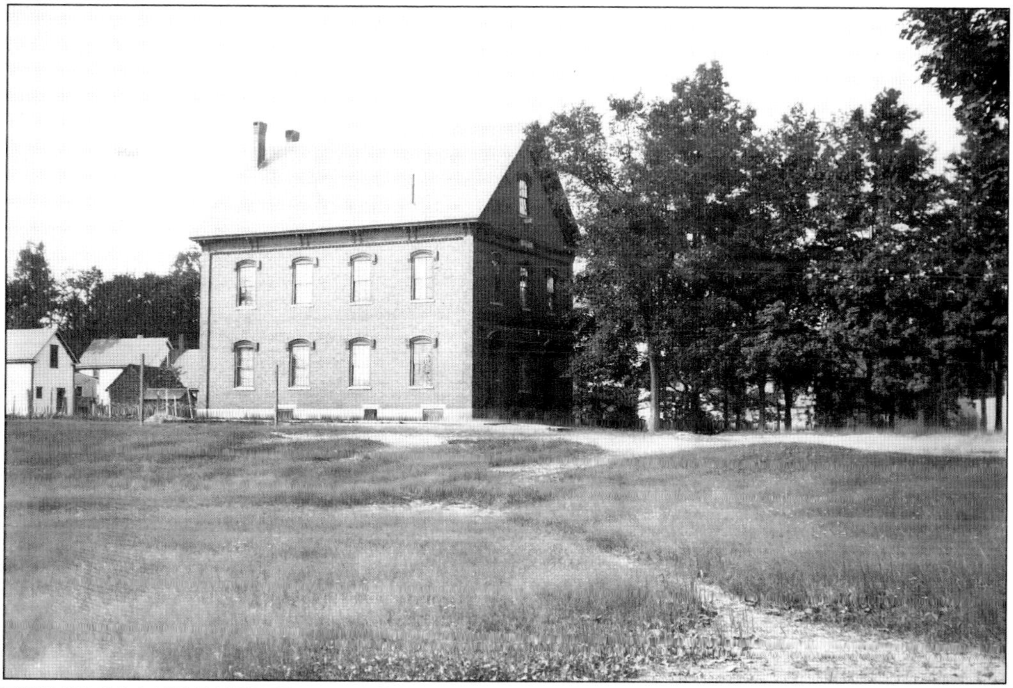

THE OLD MAPLE STREET SCHOOL. The old Maple Street School was built in 1875 after a school on North Main Street was closed. The entire second floor was used for the high school, while the elementary classes were held on the first floor.

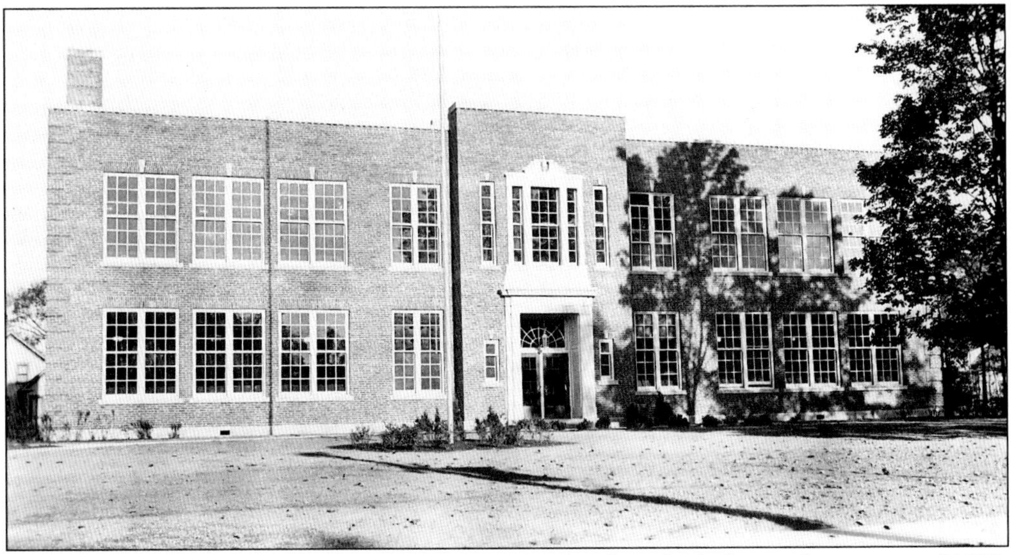

THE NEW MAPLE STREET SCHOOL. The new school was built during the summer of 1931. Classes were held in the old school until the end of the 1930–31 school year. By the next year, the old school was gone and the new school was completed in time for the opening day of classes, September 8, 1931.

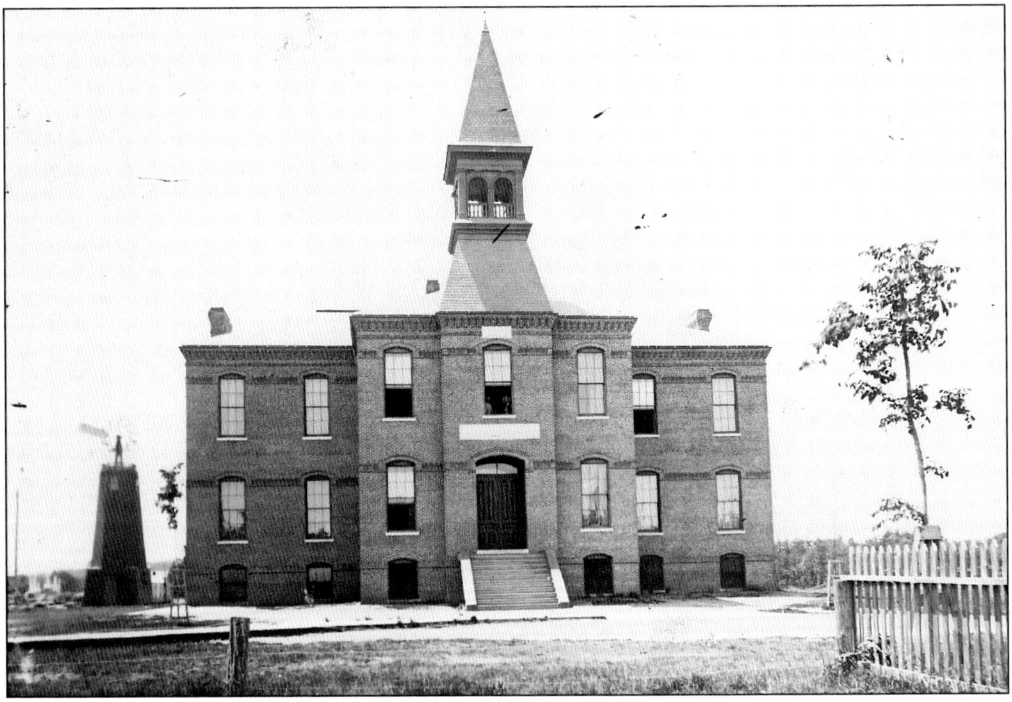

THE OLD ALLEN SCHOOL. This school, on Granite Street, opened in 1884 as a high school. The high school classes were conducted on the second floor while elementary pupils were accommodated on the first floor. Professor William Allen (opposite page), principal of the school, died in 1894 at the age of thirty-seven. The school became an elementary school in 1901 and was called the "Old High School" until 1907, when it was named the Allen School in honor of Mr. Allen.

PROFESSOR WILLIAM ALLEN (1857–1894).

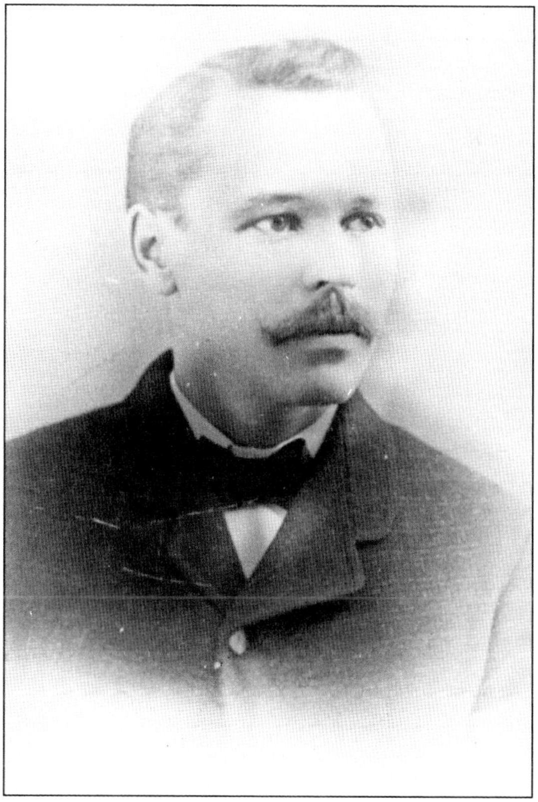

WILLIAM AND ANNA ALLEN. A group of teachers poses on the steps of the old high school on Granite Street, c. 1890. On the front left are William and Anna Allen, husband and wife and teachers at the school.

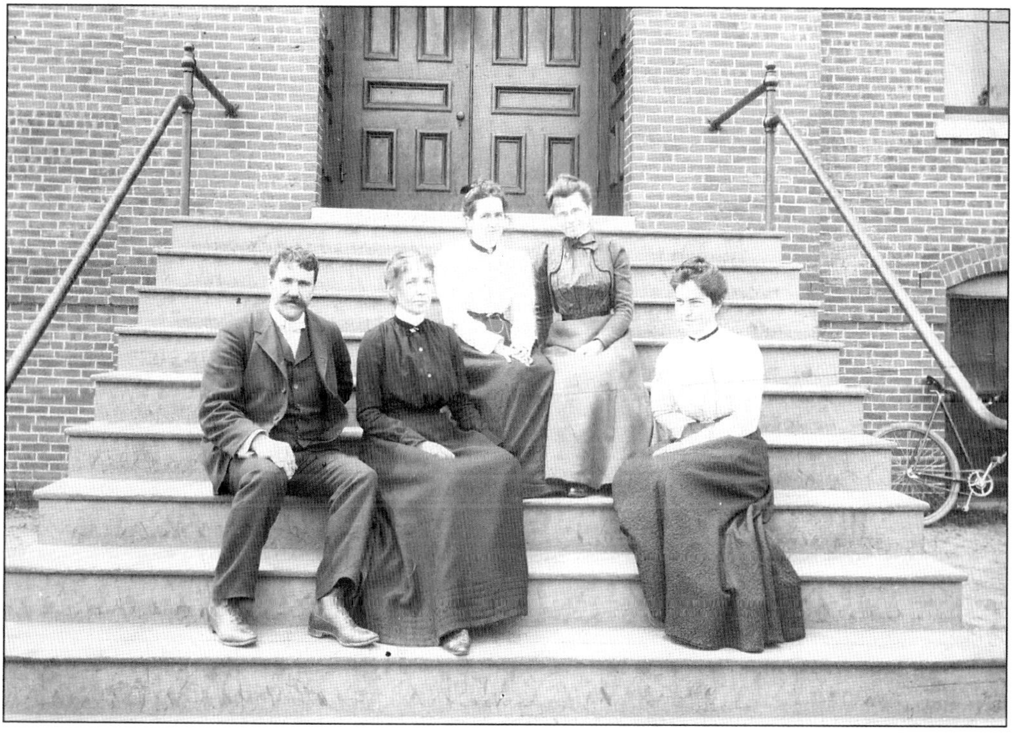

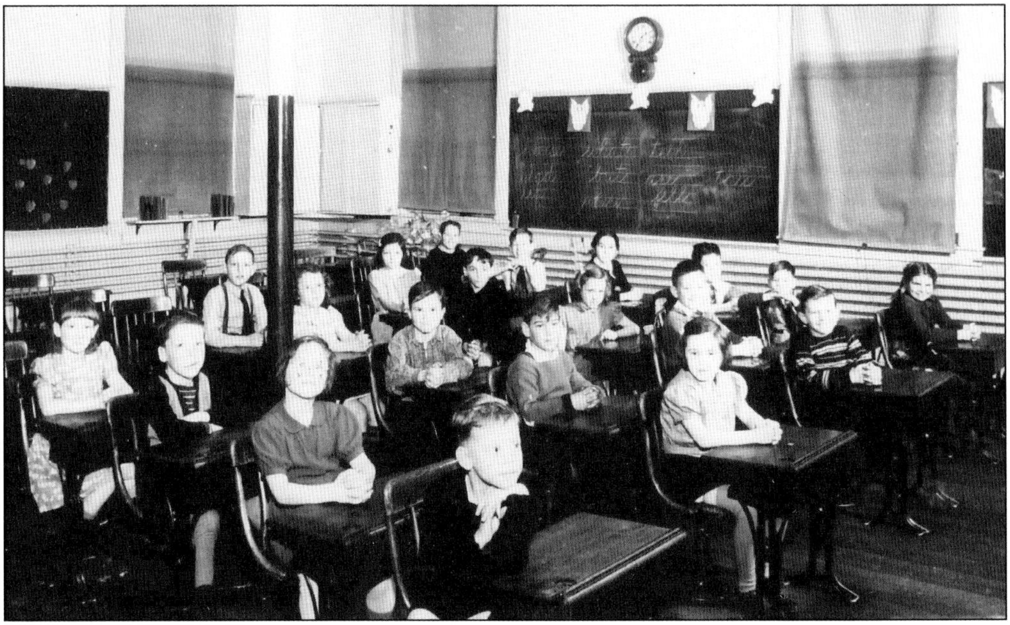

THE ALLEN SCHOOL SECOND-GRADE CLASS, 1941. Richard Welch, Marlene Rawley, James Maloney, Lillian Young, Etta Rodis, Donald Patch, Roger Balomenoes, Kenneth Beach, Shirley Horne, Charles Peroni, Marlene Beaudoin, Arthur Lambert, Paul Rosenberg, Pauline Kondrup, Robert Balomenoes, and Conrad Foss are in this group.

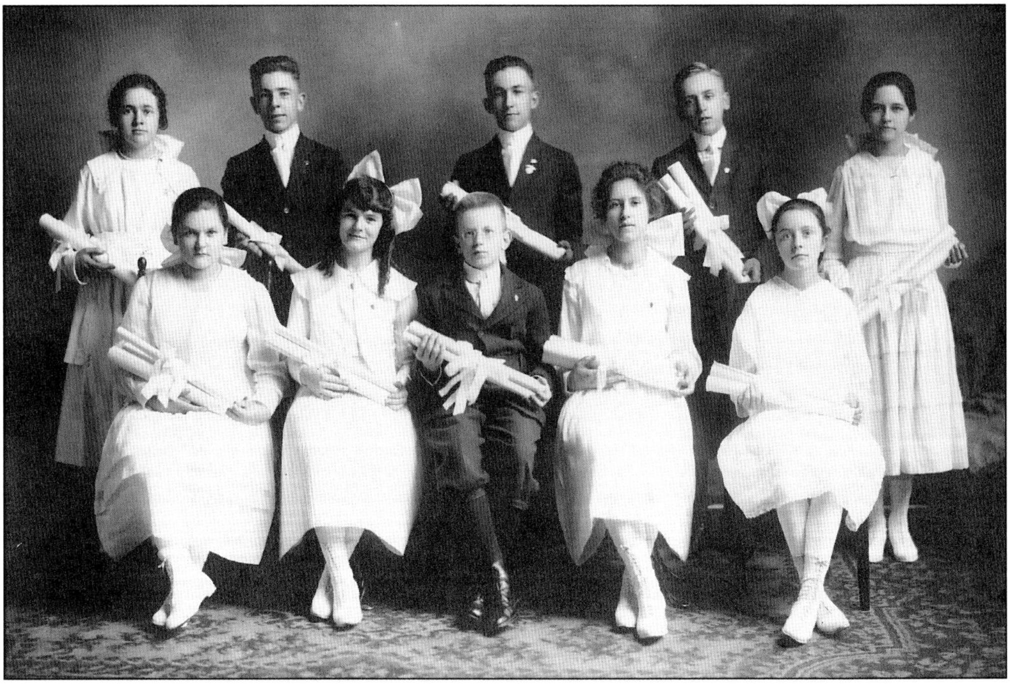

THE 1918 HOLY ROSARY GRADUATING CLASS. Students shown are as follows, from left to right: (front row) Amanda Trepenier, Beatrice Larochelle, Aime Lemire, Albertine Larochelle, and Juliette Ferland; (back row) Exilia Lessard, Leon Marquis, Raymond Marquis, Albert Turgeon, and Yvonne Grondin.

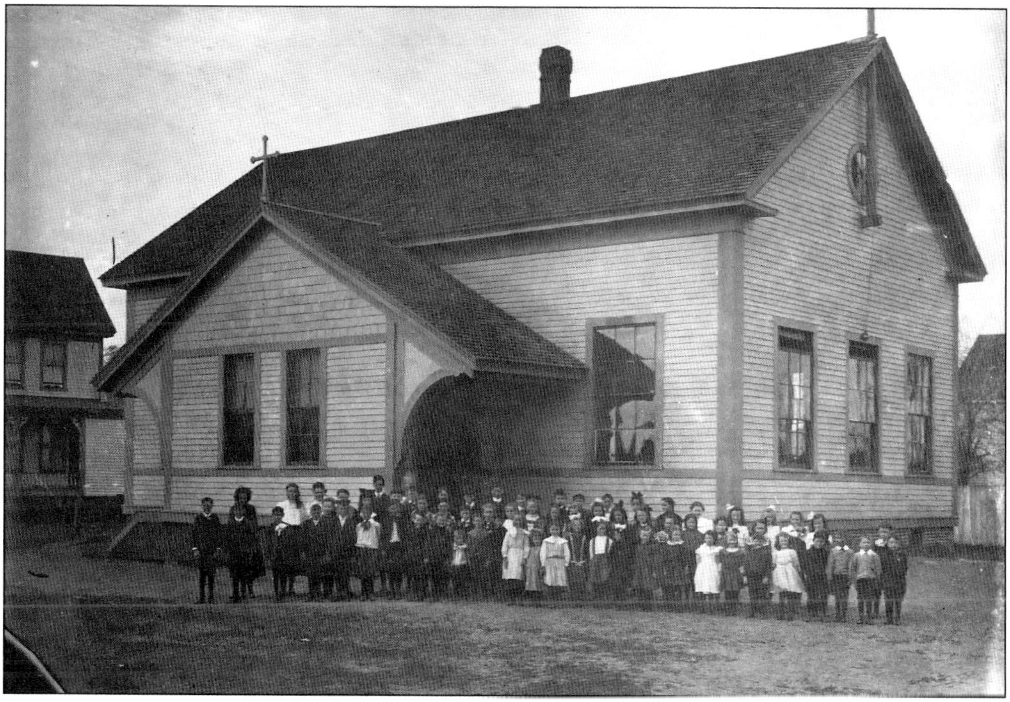

ST. MARY'S SCHOOL. The first St. Mary's church was built on Hancock Street in 1868. A new church was built on Charles Street and this building became a school in September 1891. It closed in 1952 when a new larger school opened on Charles Street.

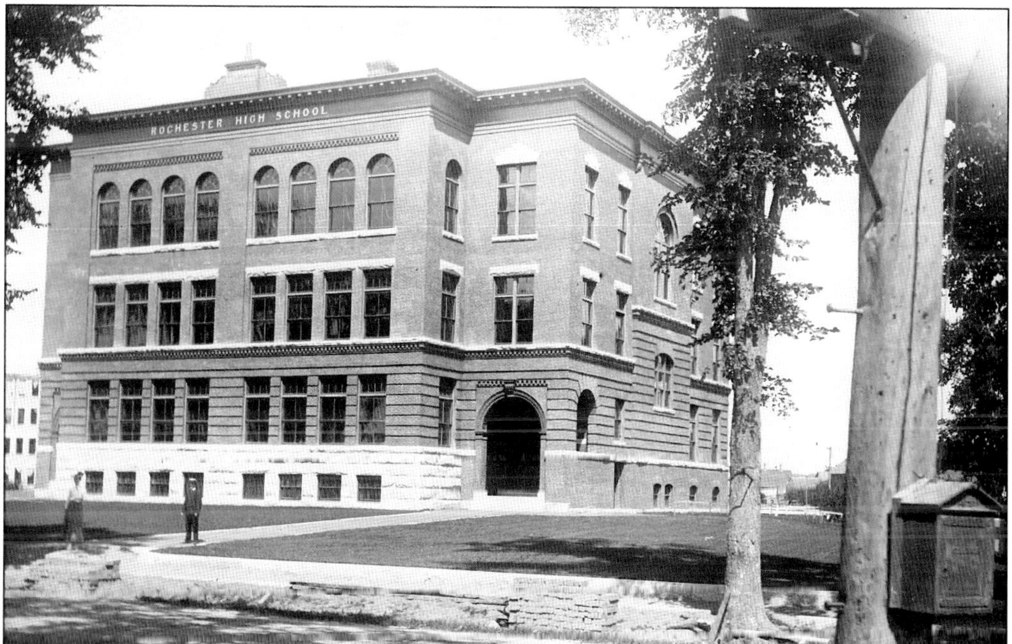

ROCHESTER HIGH SCHOOL ON WAKEFIELD STREET. The high school was built in 1901 on land purchased from the heirs of Solomon Evans. In less than thirty years, the building was much too crowded and the last class graduated here in 1939.

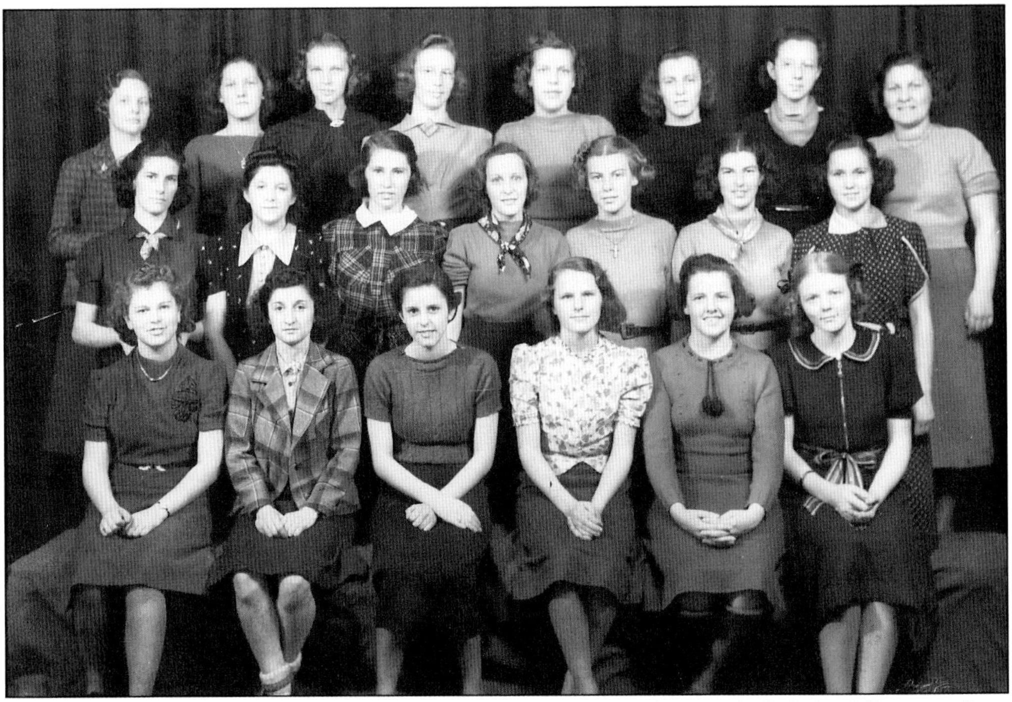

THE ROCHESTER HIGH TRI-HI-Y CLUB IN 1937. Members included the following, from left to right: (front row) Constance Snow, Arlene Wartelle, Beverly Brown, Alice Monroe, Mary Mitchell, and Betty Lucey; (middle row) Louise Baxter, Beatrice Owen, Mary Wallace, Alberta Massey, Isabelle Barber, Lorraine Baxter, and Jeanette Connor; (back row) Barbara Horne, Marion Otis, Meridith Goss, Janet Clark, Virginia Came, Georgia Clark, Betty Woodman, and Arlene Otis.

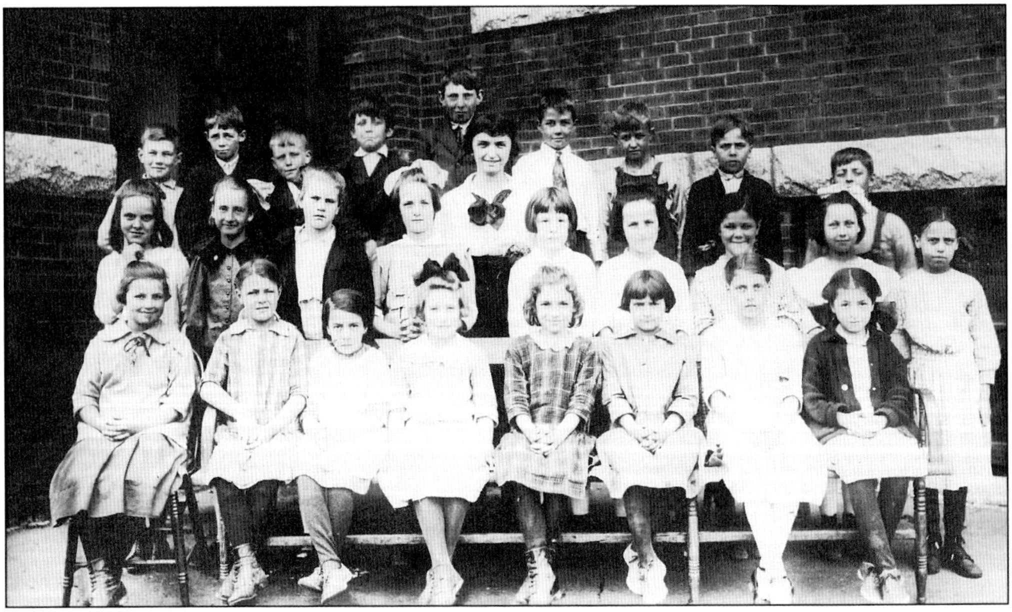

THE WAKEFIELD STREET SCHOOL GRADUATING CLASS IN 1922. The high school on Wakefield Street had an eighth-grade class until it became too crowded.

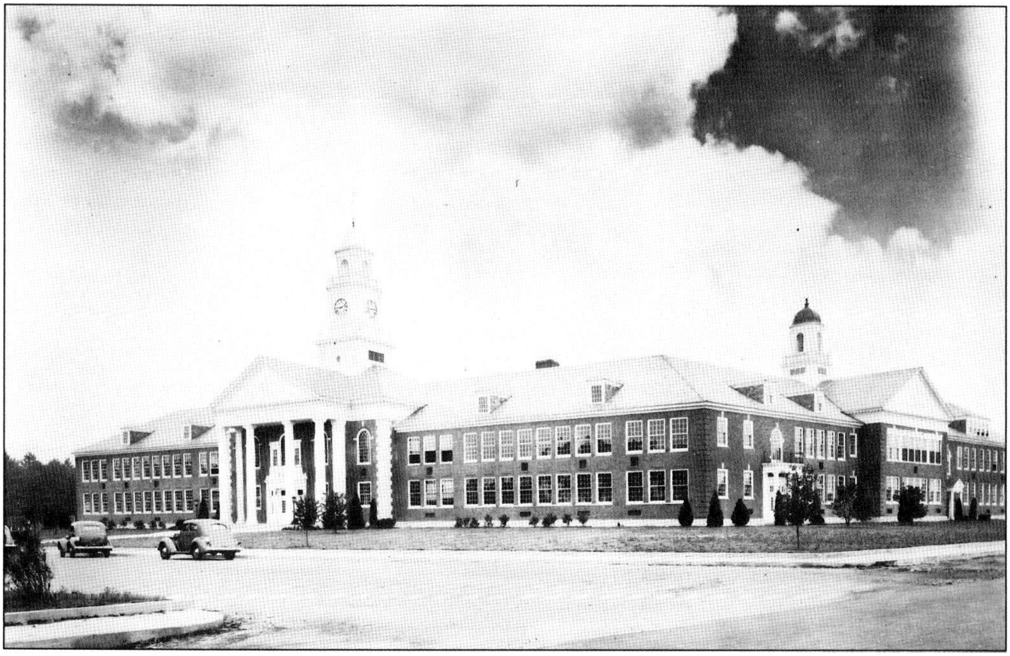

SPAULDING HIGH SCHOOL. This school was made possible by a gift of the Spaulding families of Rochester. Built on 33 acres on the triangle between Wakefield Street and Chestnut Hill Road, it opened in September of 1939.

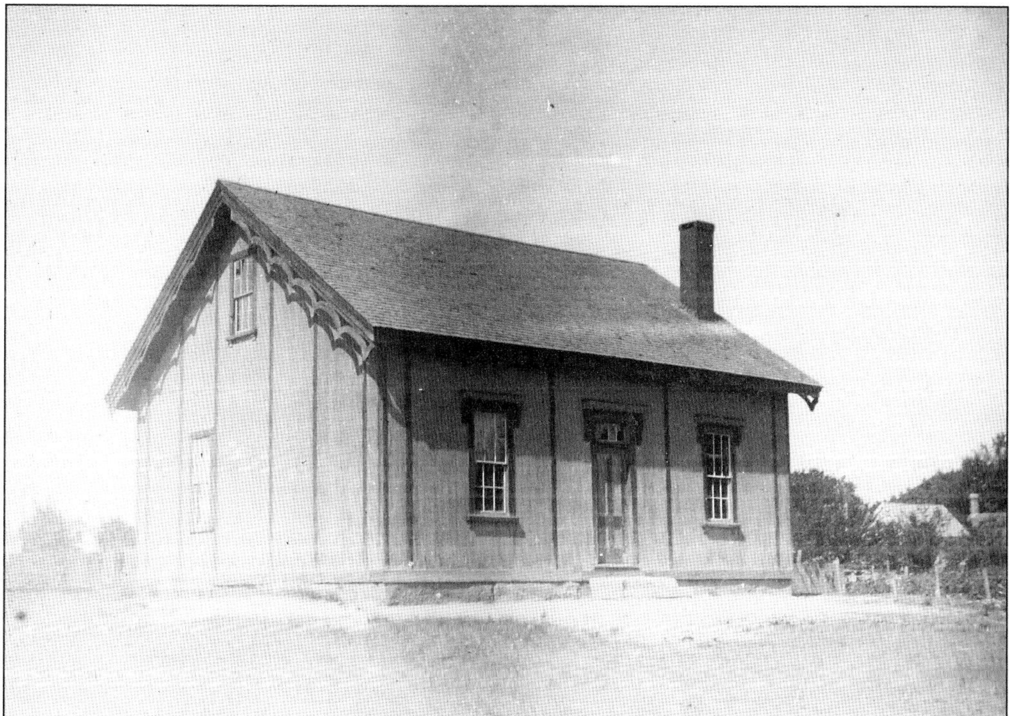

THE OLD SCHOOL STREET SCHOOL. This old school was built on North Main Street in 1856. It was moved to School Street in 1876 at the cost of $650, including repairs.

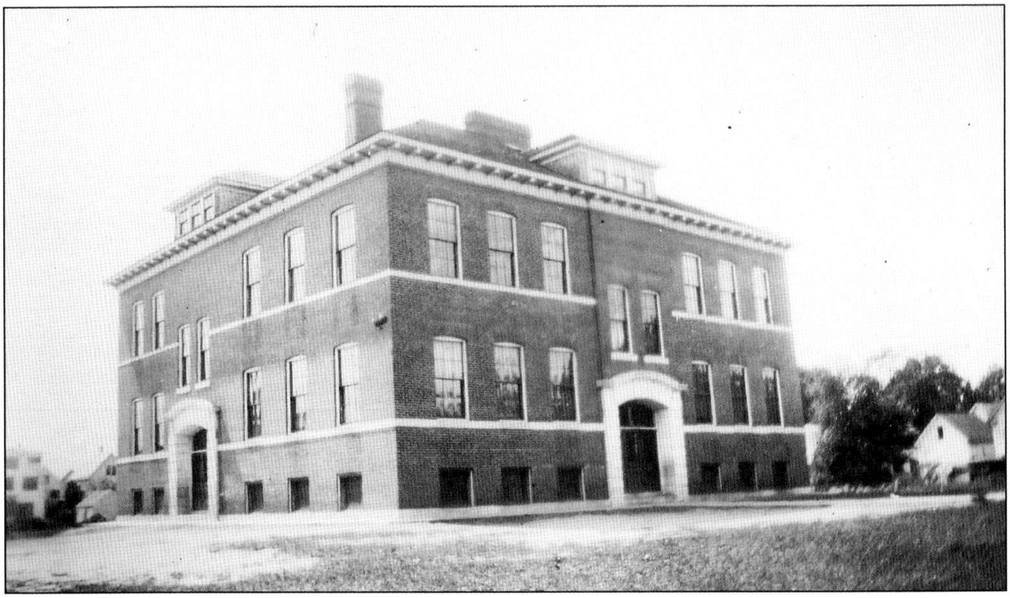

THE SCHOOL STREET SCHOOL. This structure was completed in 1911 at the cost of $17,091.40, just $91.40 over the appropriation. Principal Mary G. Collins taught grades seven and eight.

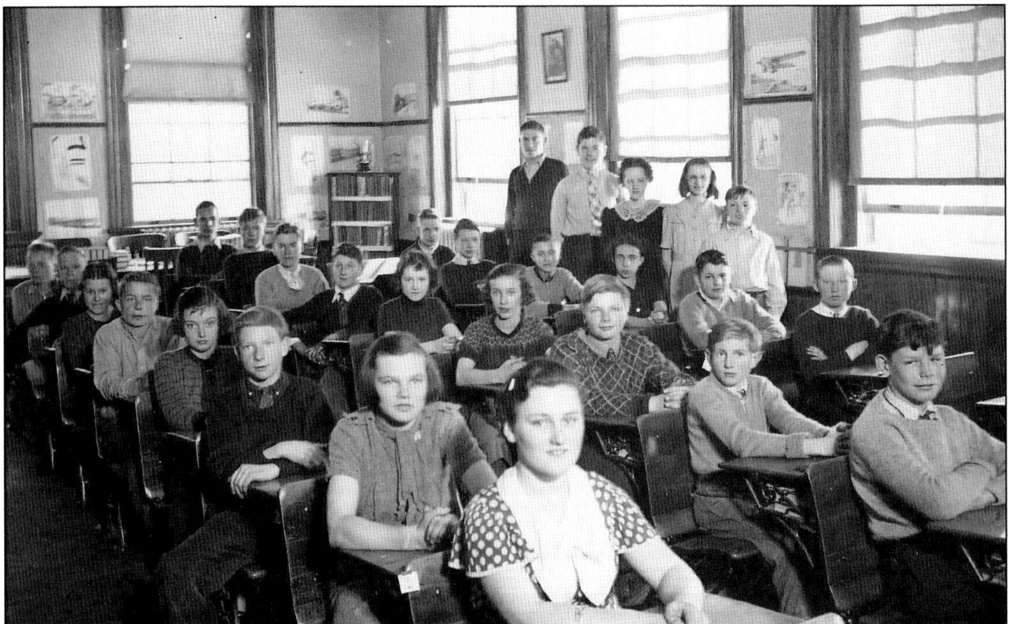

A CLASS AT THE SCHOOL STREET SCHOOL, 1935. These students include the following, listed from front to back: (left row) Bertha Norman, Gertrude Ellis, Clarence Hamilton, Eleanor Lamper, Malcolm Miller, Doris Edmond, Bruce Fowler, and Earl Harriman; (second row) Everett Canney, Charles Brown, Gerald Corson, Edith Herdt, Kathleen Baxter, Richard Weeks, Edwin Norwood, George Blackadar, and Laurent Autotte; (third row) Thomas Nesbitt, John Clark, Norma Schafer, Stanley Burns, Harvel Winkley, and Jerold Wiggen; (standing) Russell Littlefield, Betty Smith, Anna Amero, Wesley Page, and Nolan Avery.

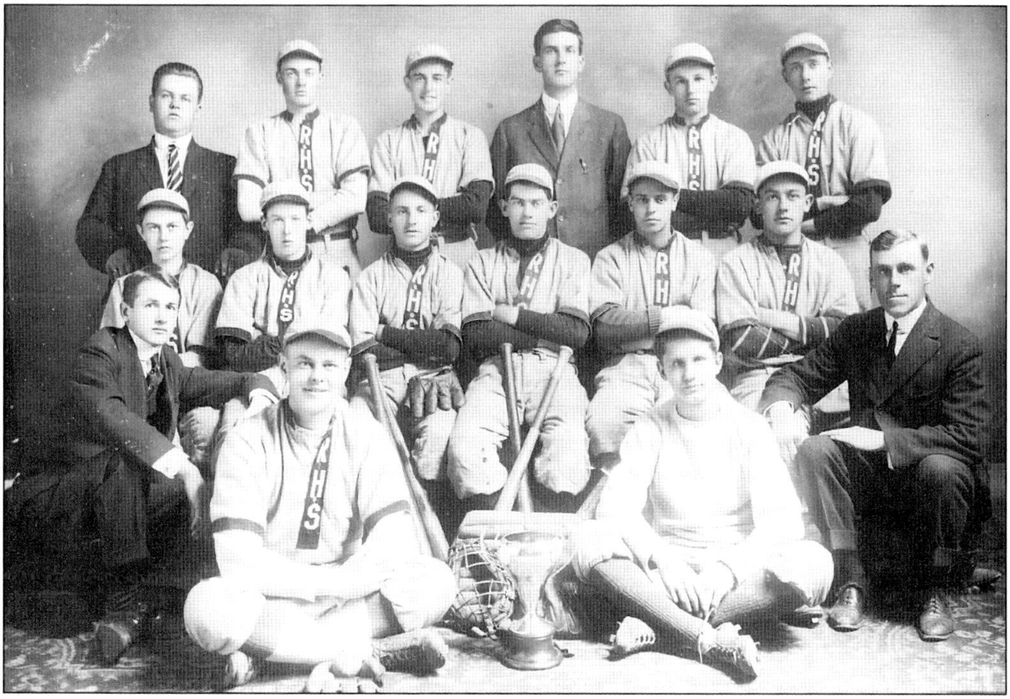

THE 1915 ROCHESTER HIGH BASEBALL TEAM. Players included the following, from left to right: (front row) Robert Foss, Eben Wallace, Raymond Beaudoin, and Roscoe Hersom; (middle row) Jack Fergerson, Downing Osborne, Henry Jacques, Capt. Murrey Collins, Kenneth Brock, and Kenneth Magoon; (back row) Cecil Morrison, John Hickey, Robert Sweet Jr., Ralph Whipple, Burton Sylvester, and Gordon Booth.

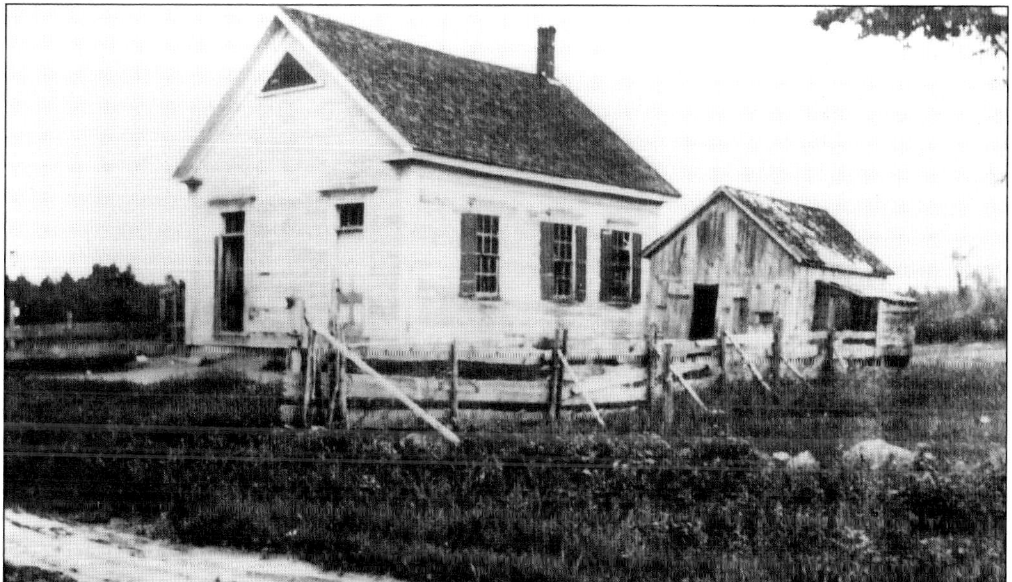

THE JENNESS SCHOOL. District #4's school was the Pickering Crossing or Jenness School, across the road from the Noah Jenness farm. In 1859 the teacher was Martha Jenness. The school was on the property that later became the Great Elm Farms.

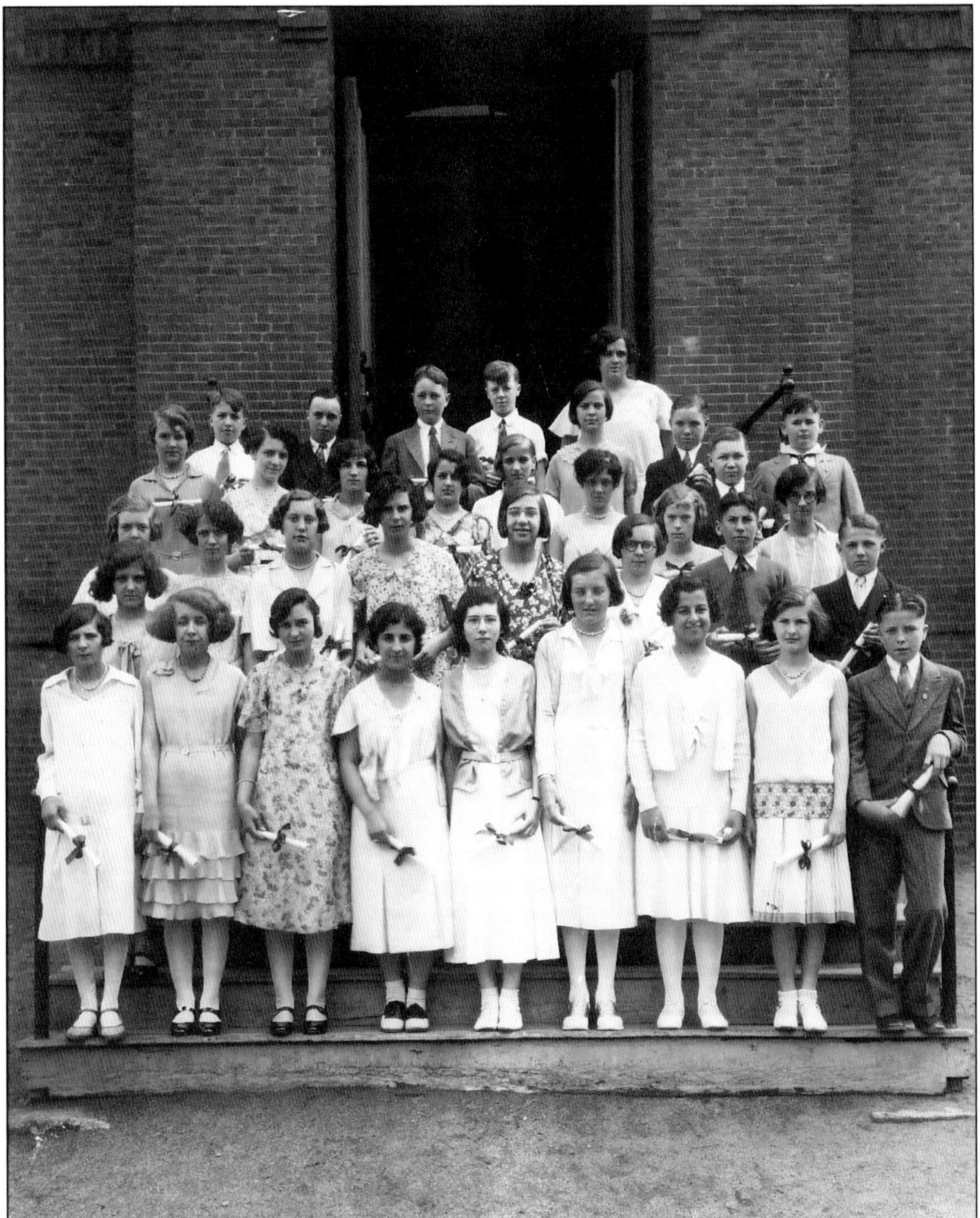

ALLEN SCHOOL GRADUATES, 1931. The following individuals are shown here at graduation: (front row) Marian Boudreau, Charlotte Teel, Priscilla Sylvain, Nagella Richards, Bertha Feineman, Alice Fisher, Evelyn Michael, Mary Louise Hayes, and Franklin Lord; (second row) Eva Alimi, Elsie Cassidy, Priscilla Houle, Helen Rutstein, Barbara Buker, Florence Allen, Arthur Veno, Ruth Wood, and Edgar Seavey; (third row) Elizabeth Pray, Betty Ham, Pauline Longly, Eva Forcier, Ruth Bond, Mary Hatch, Lena Lavoie, Agnes Weymouth, Leland Wormwood, and Bradley Corson; (back row) Maxwell Campbell, Edgar Edgerly, Sanford Wilcox, Edwin Steadman, Blanche Stanton, William McDuffee, and teacher Charlotte Leighton.

Ten

People

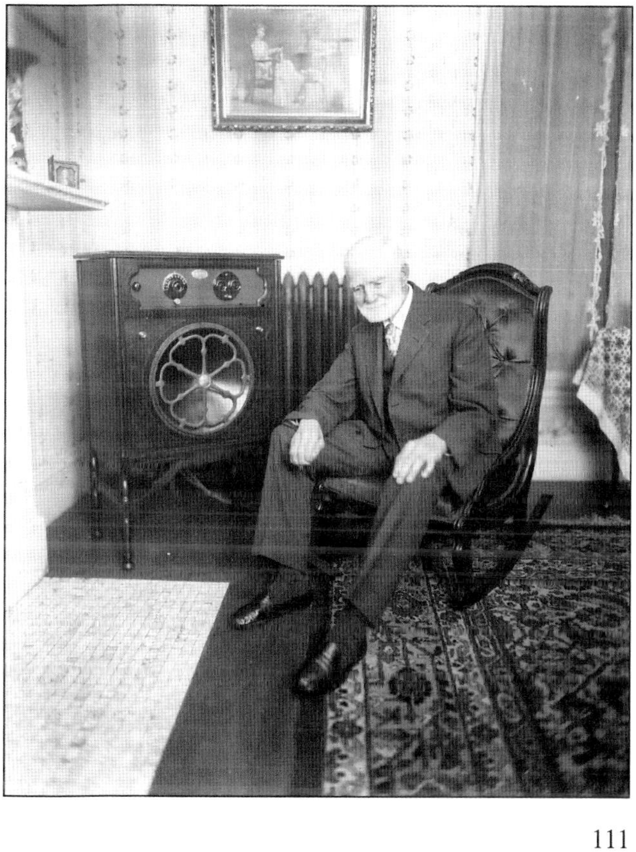

CHARLES BRADLEY. Charles Bradley bought one of the first radios in the city. Lothrop and Farnums, who sold it to him, had this picture taken to use in advertising. Bradley was named Charles Coexter when he came from England. He changed his name to please Alice Felker, who would not marry him until he did so. He died on January 12, 1930, at the age of 101.

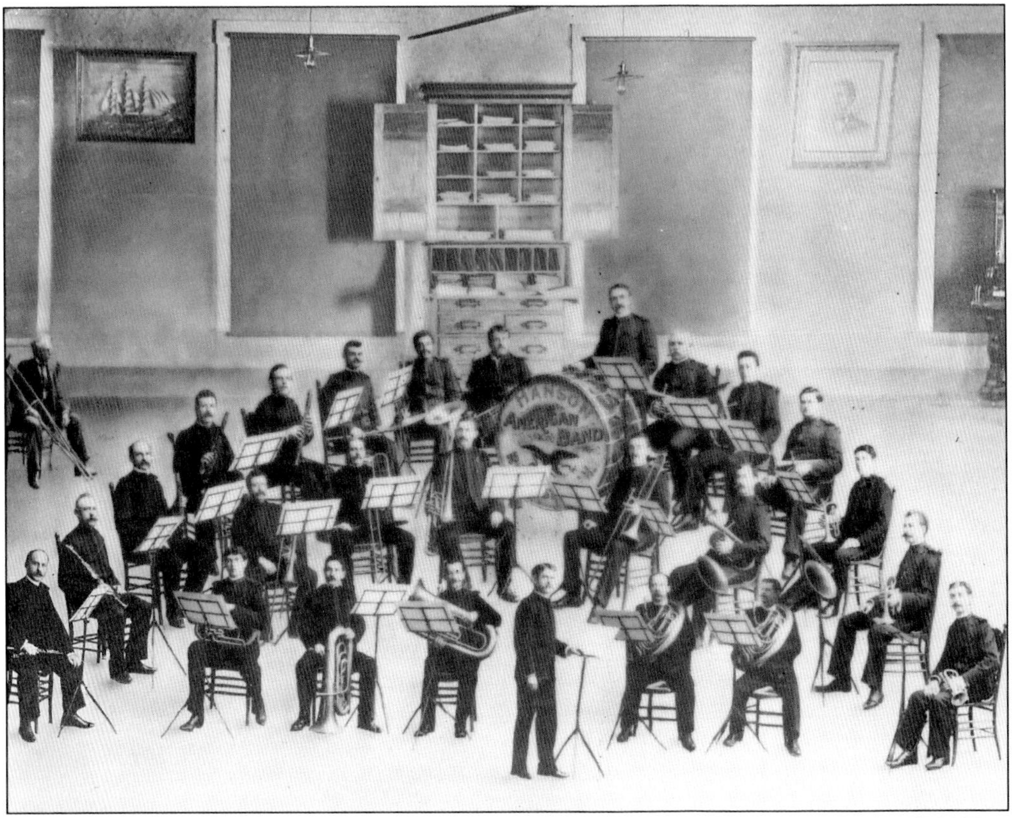

HANSON'S AMERICAN BAND. Tony Manning was a popular leader of this band, considered the best in the state. Here, Mr. Manning is leading a practice session in a hall on Hanson Street furnished by Charles Hanson. Mr. Hanson is seated in the background.

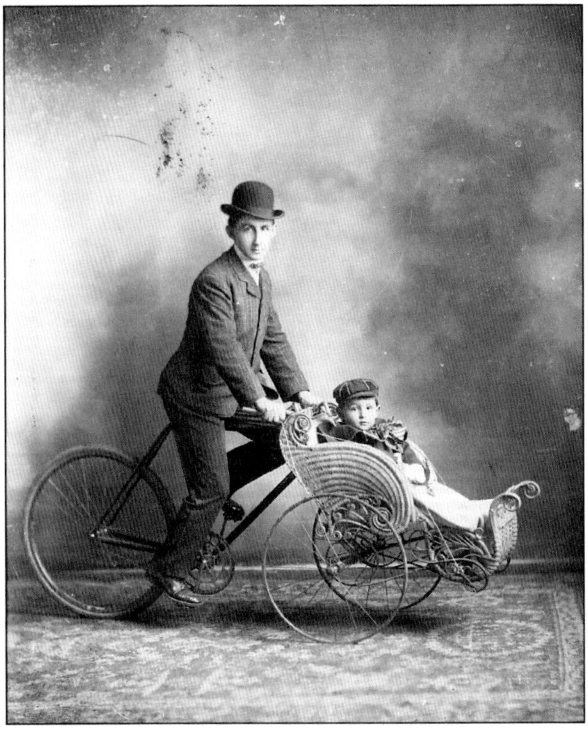

JOSEPH RUEL AND SON. Joseph Ruel attached his son Arthur's baby carriage to his bicycle in 1904. Arthur was born on June 12, 1902, and died on December 4, 1995, at the age of ninety-three.

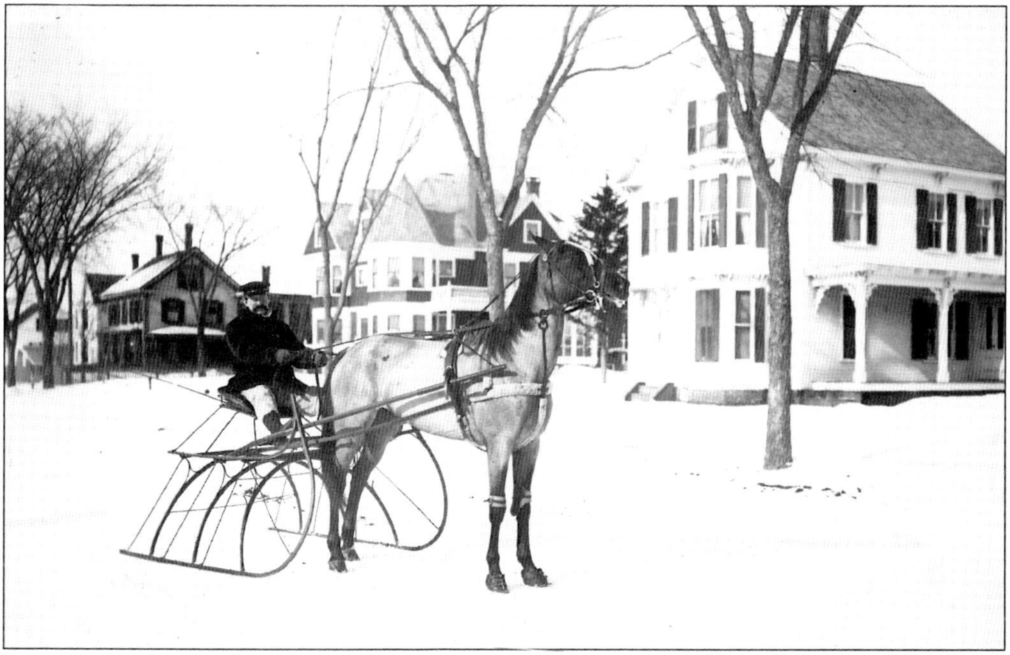

WILLIAM BRADLEY RACING ON NORTH MAIN STREET. Horse racing was very popular at the turn of the century. Williata Bradley, a seven-term mayor of Rochester, owned this horse, Gagnaught. On Saturday afternoons, part of North Main Street was closed for racing and five or six horses would race at a time.

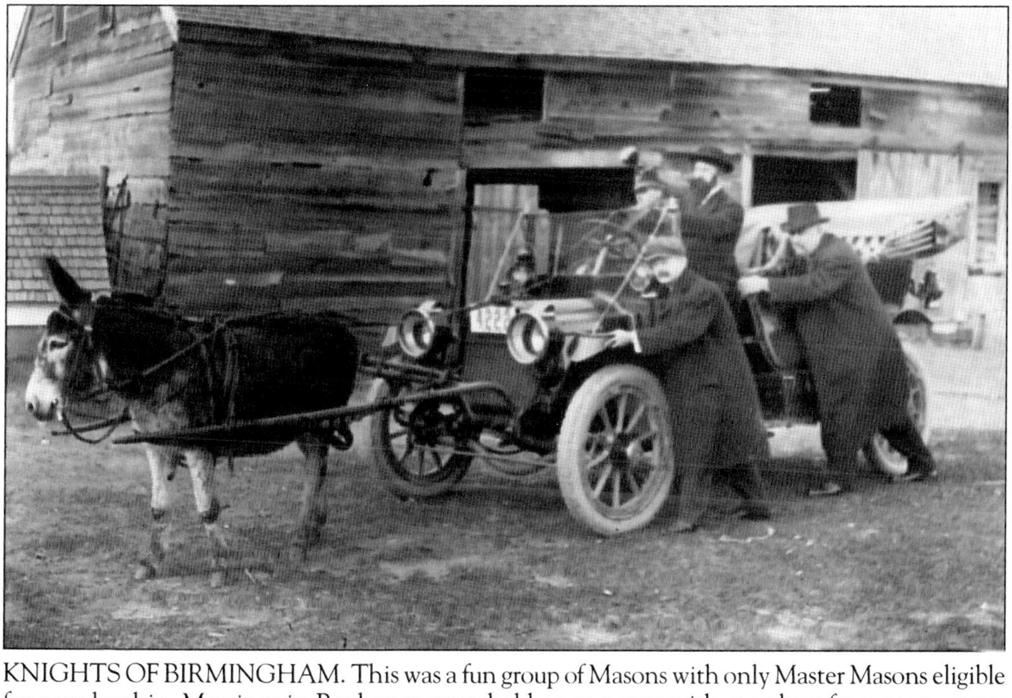

KNIGHTS OF BIRMINGHAM. This was a fun group of Masons with only Master Masons eligible for membership. Meetings in Rochester were held once a year with members from many states attending. The mascot donkey was prominent at such affairs. The group disbanded in 1912.

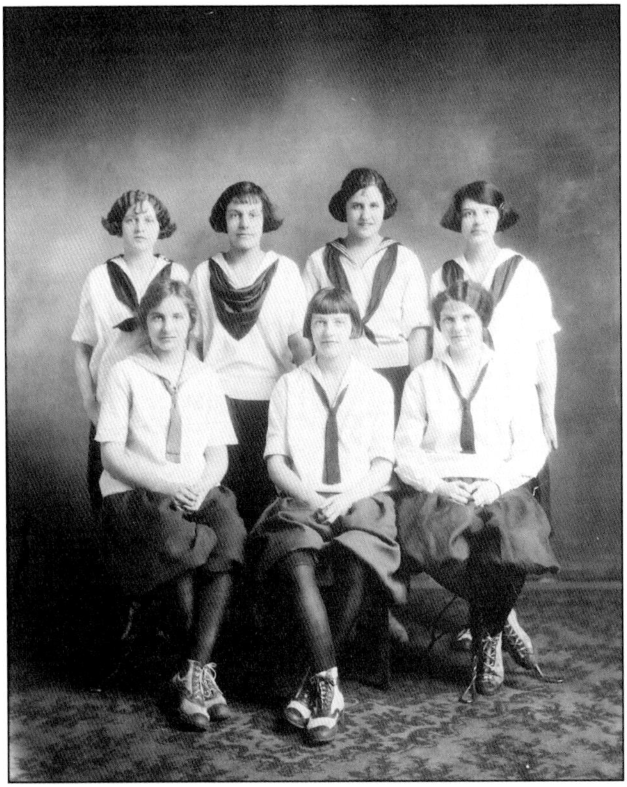

A GIRLS' BASKETBALL TEAM. Members of the 1923 Rochester High School girls basketball team included the following: (front) Dallas Fraser, Betty Carnegie, and Bernice Crosby; (back) Zelma Libby, Dorothy Seavey, Arline Shaw, and Pauline Lagasse.

THREE MEN AND AN AUTO. Louis McDuffee and Dr. John Neal are riding with Gustav Andreas, a cigar maker and owner of the Maxwell car.

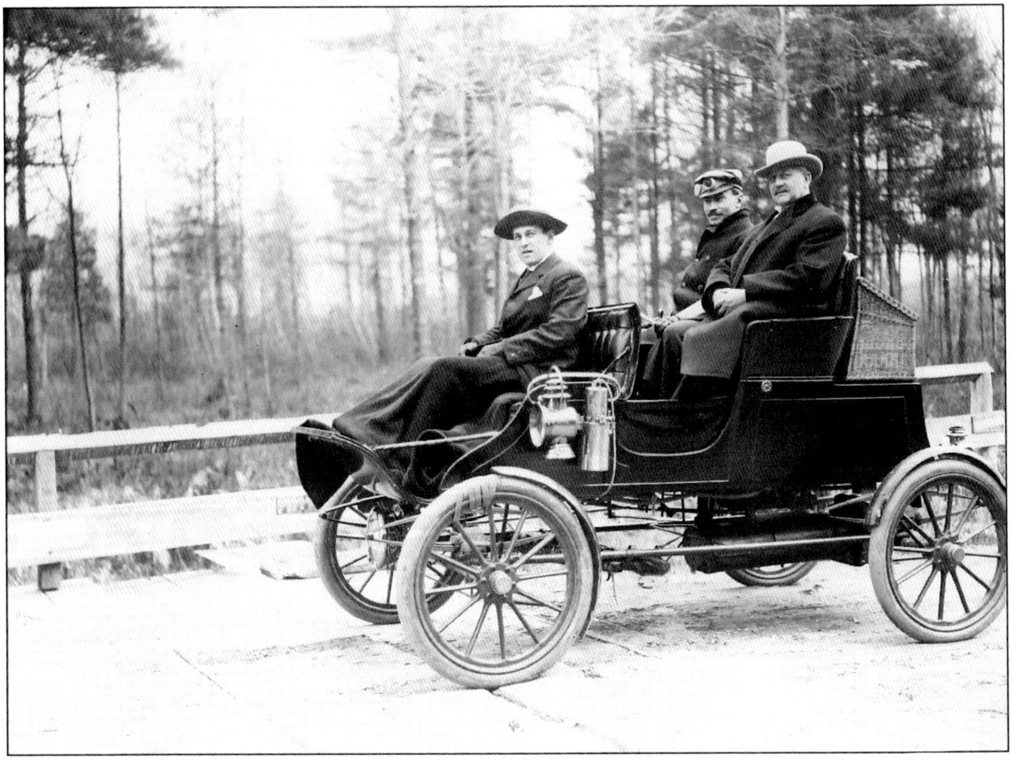

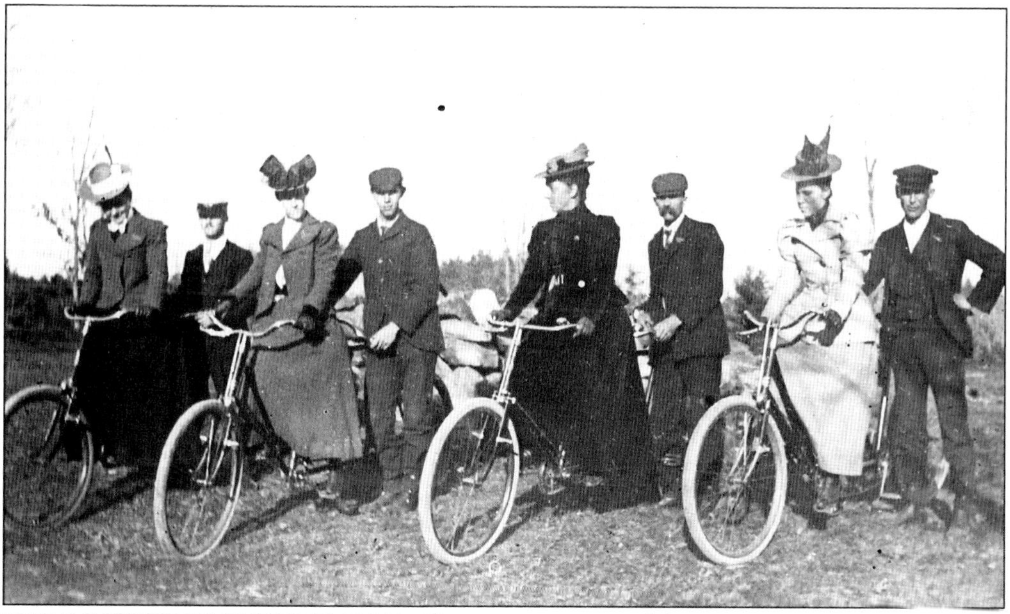

THE ROCHESTER BICYCLE CLUB. This group was one of the most popular organizations in the city when this photograph was taken in Farmington in 1898. They had a clubhouse in the old three-story Chase house on Congress Street.

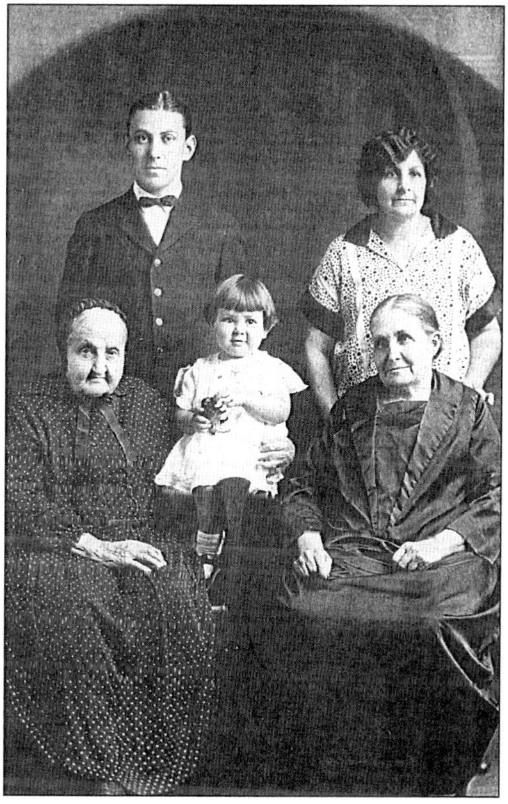

THE SYLVAIN FAMILY IN 1925. Members included the following: (front) Caroline Sylvain (age ninety-three), Phyllis Seavey (age two), and Delema Ruel (age seventy-three); (standing) Ernest Seavey and Mary Ruel Seavey.

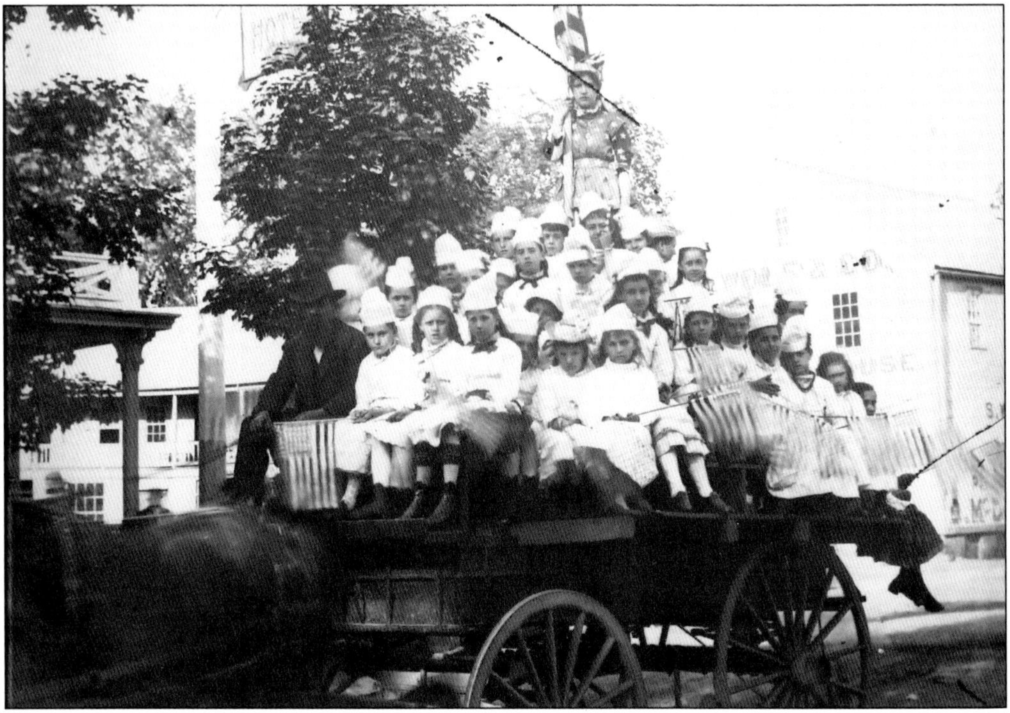

A WAGONLOAD OF GIRLS. These young women are on their way to the dedication of the Soldiers' Monument on the Common on September 5, 1872.

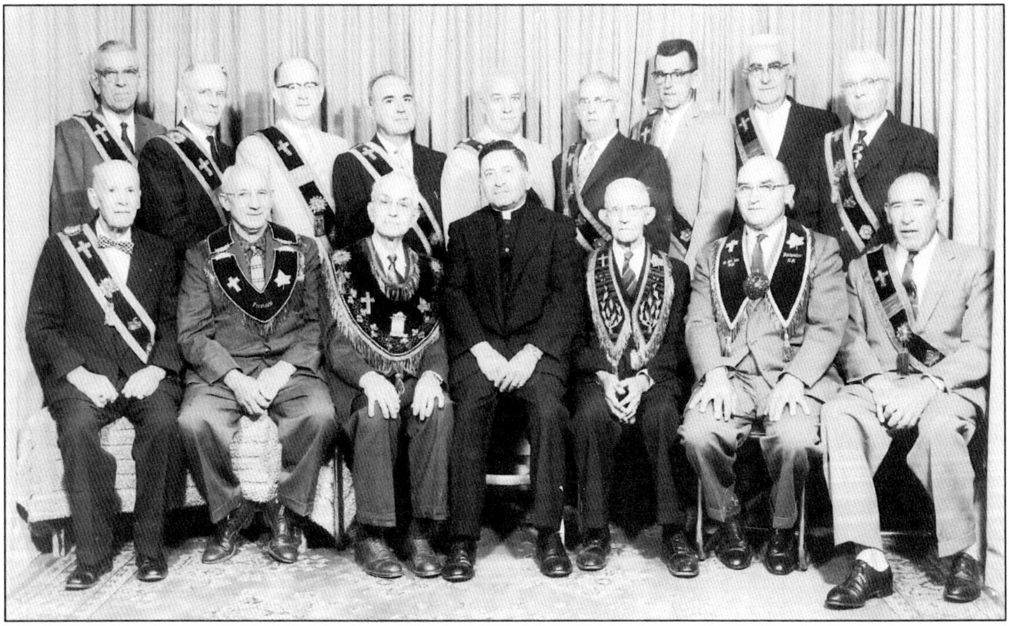

THE SOCIETY OF ST. JEAN-BAPTIST. Those pictured include the following: (front row) Alfred Landry, Val Blanchard, Archie Sylvain, Fr. Brunelle, Albert Grondin, Paul Lemay, and Donat Lafontaine; (back row) Albert Gagne, Henry Grondin, Raymond Grondin, Arthur Nadeau, Dr. Albert Barcomb, Dr. Wilfrid Roy, Raymond Gagne, Arthur Sylvain, and Joseph Huppe.

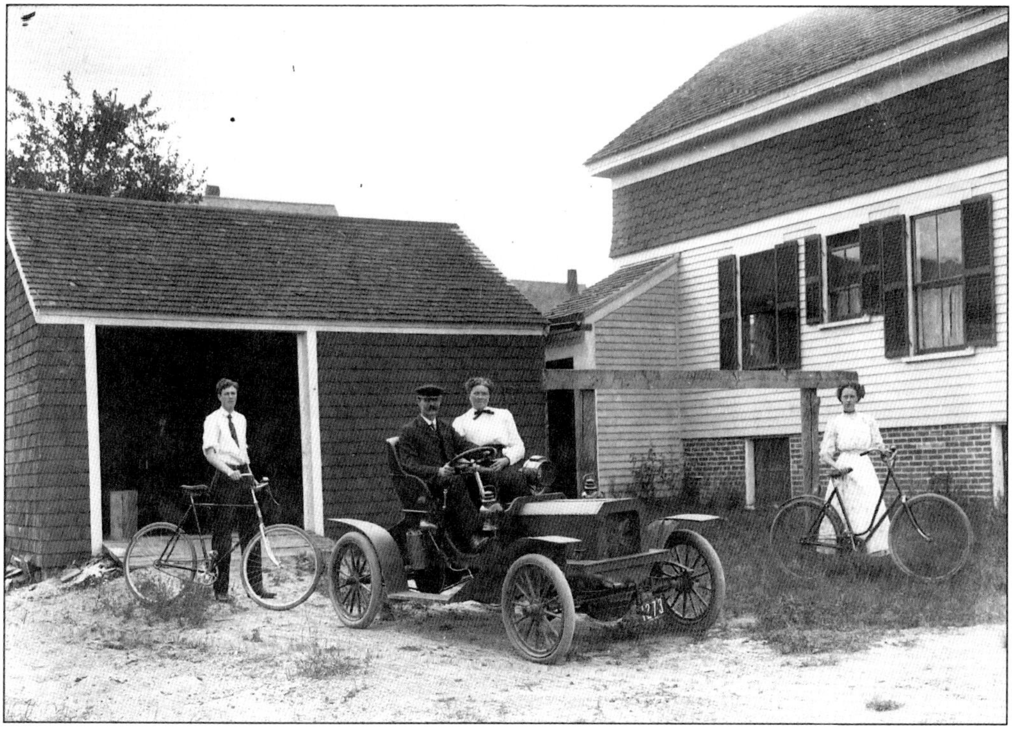

THE CORSONS OF WINTER STREET IN 1910. Ralph Corson and his sister Blanche pose with their bicycles. Fred and Julia, their parents, are in the family car, which Fred had modified. Father and son were both inventors.

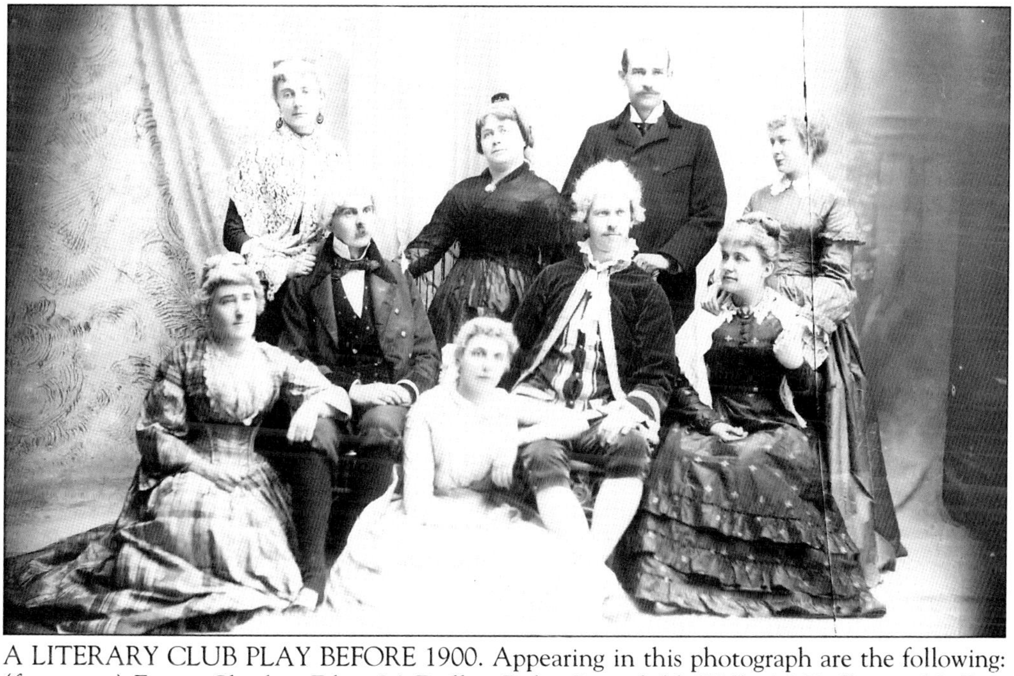

A LITERARY CLUB PLAY BEFORE 1900. Appearing in this photograph are the following: (front row) Emma Chesley, Edgar McDuffee, Delia Greenfield, Willis McDuffee, and Lillian Plummer; (back row) Ella Cochrane, Myrtie Hoyt, Reverend J.M. Adams, and Mary Glidden.

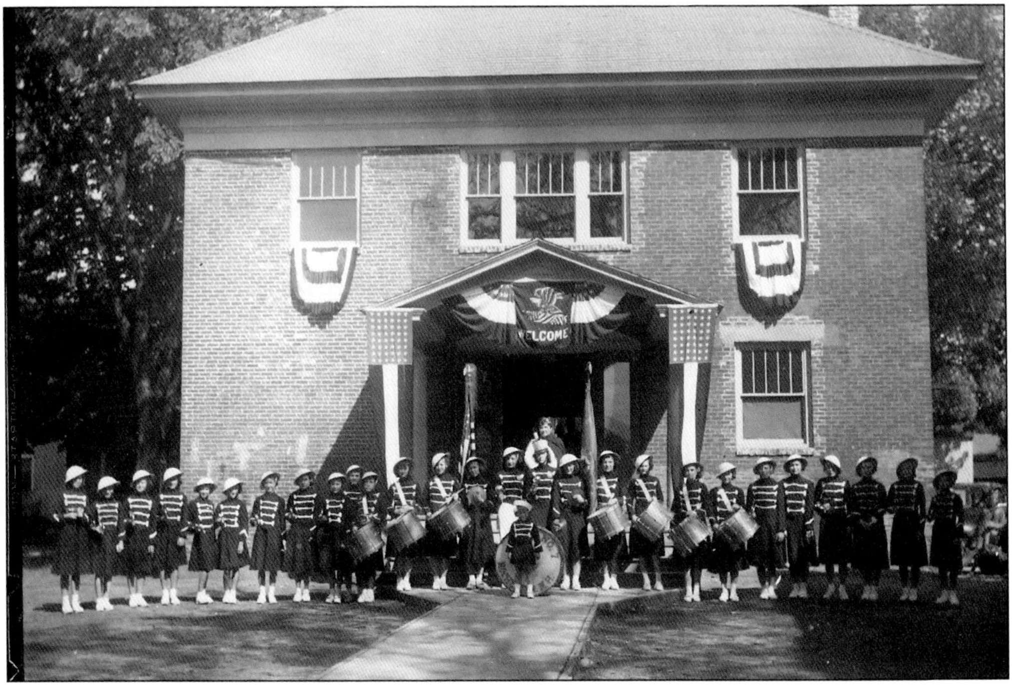

A DRUM AND BUGLE CORPS. A girls' marching group sponsored by the American Legion, Post #7, was organized in the late 1930s and remained active for several years.

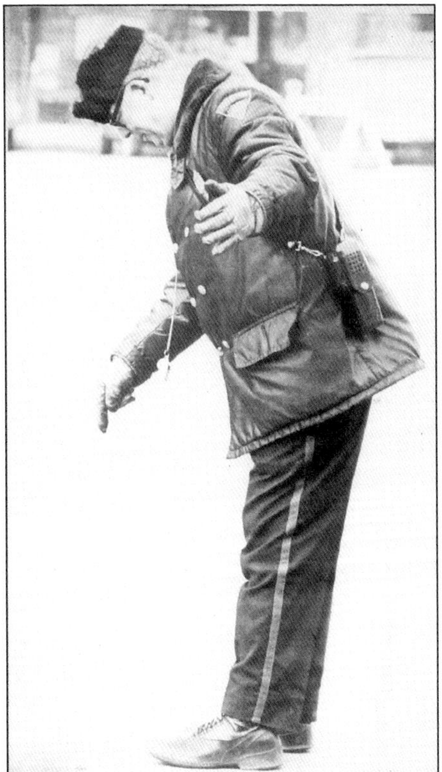

WILLIS "RED" HAYES. Red Hayes, who retired in 1973, was a popular police officer in Rochester for thirty-two years. He died in 1986.

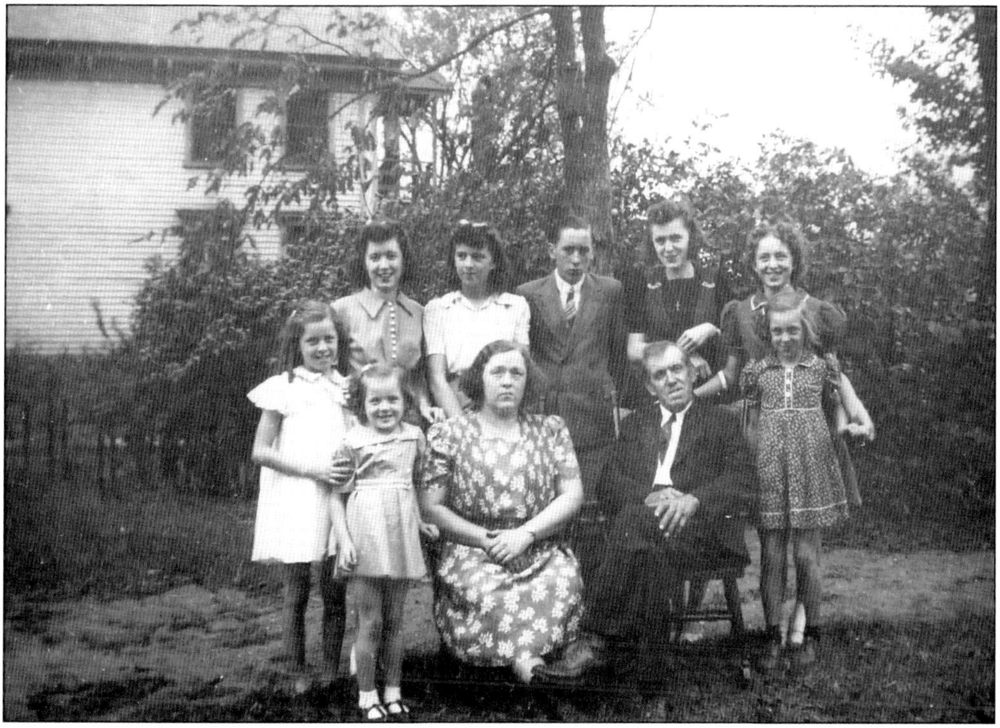

THE AUTHOR'S FAMILY. This is the family of Ernest and Valea Horne (seated center) in 1941. Clockwise, the children are Lorraine, Barbara, Florence, Violet, Ernest Jr., Edythe, Beatrice, and Shirley.

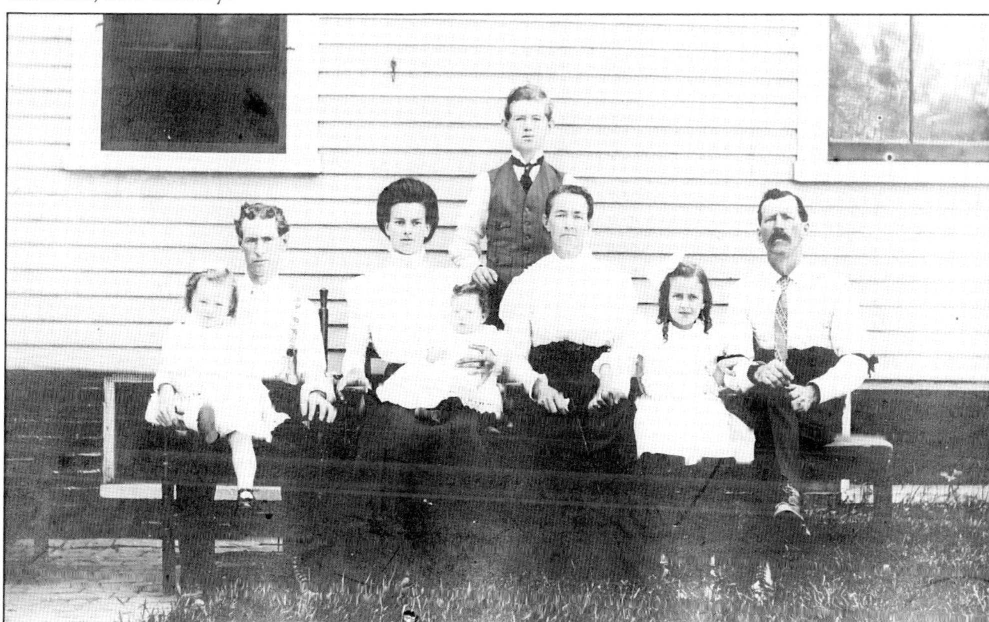

THE LESSARD FAMILY, c. 1907. Joseph Lessard is holding Louise, and Rosalie Lessard is holding Romeo. Also pictured are Georgiana Lessard, Exila Lessard, and Pierre Lessard. Narcisse Lessard is standing.

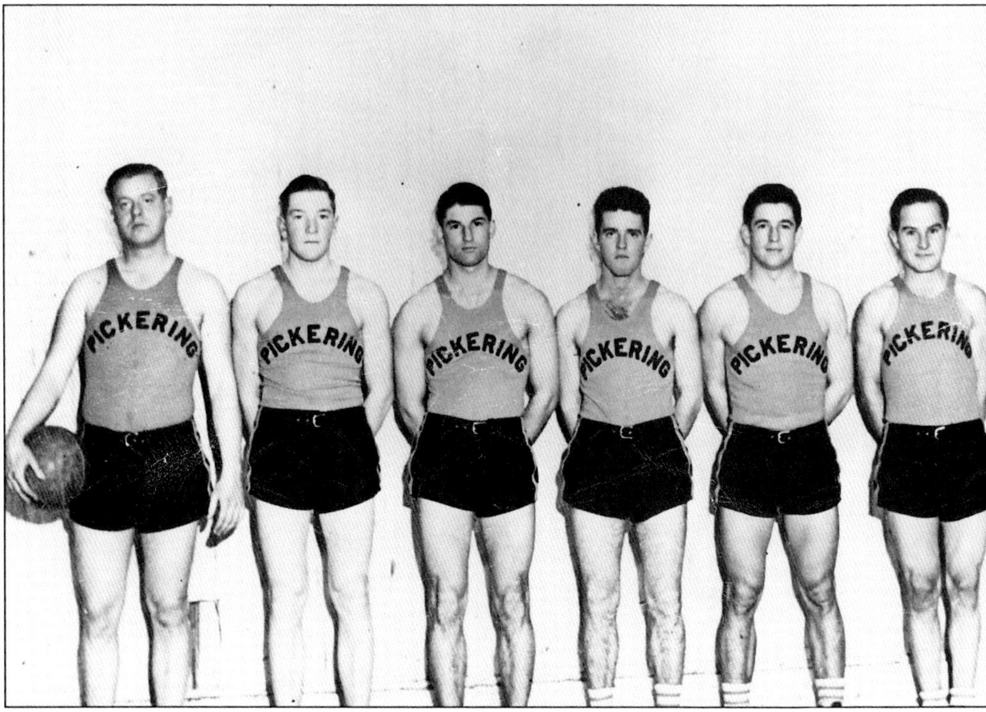

PICKERING A.C. IN 1930. Pictured are John Spiers, Pete Witherall, George Young, Joe Springfield, Bill Young, and Roger Roulx.

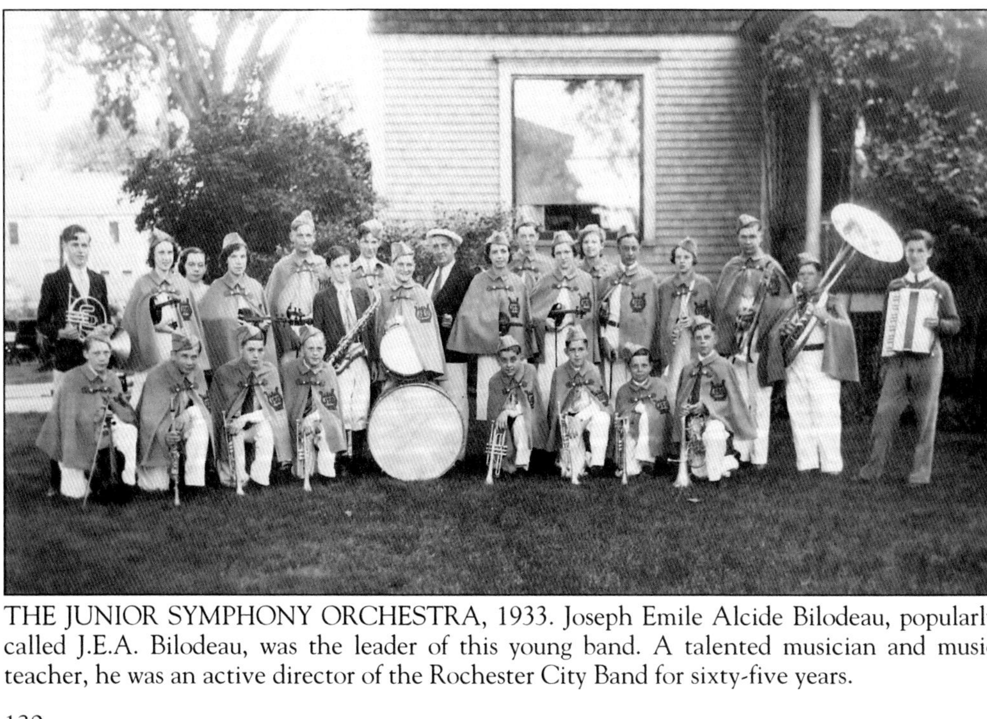

THE JUNIOR SYMPHONY ORCHESTRA, 1933. Joseph Emile Alcide Bilodeau, popularly called J.E.A. Bilodeau, was the leader of this young band. A talented musician and music teacher, he was an active director of the Rochester City Band for sixty-five years.

Eleven

Hotels and Restaurants

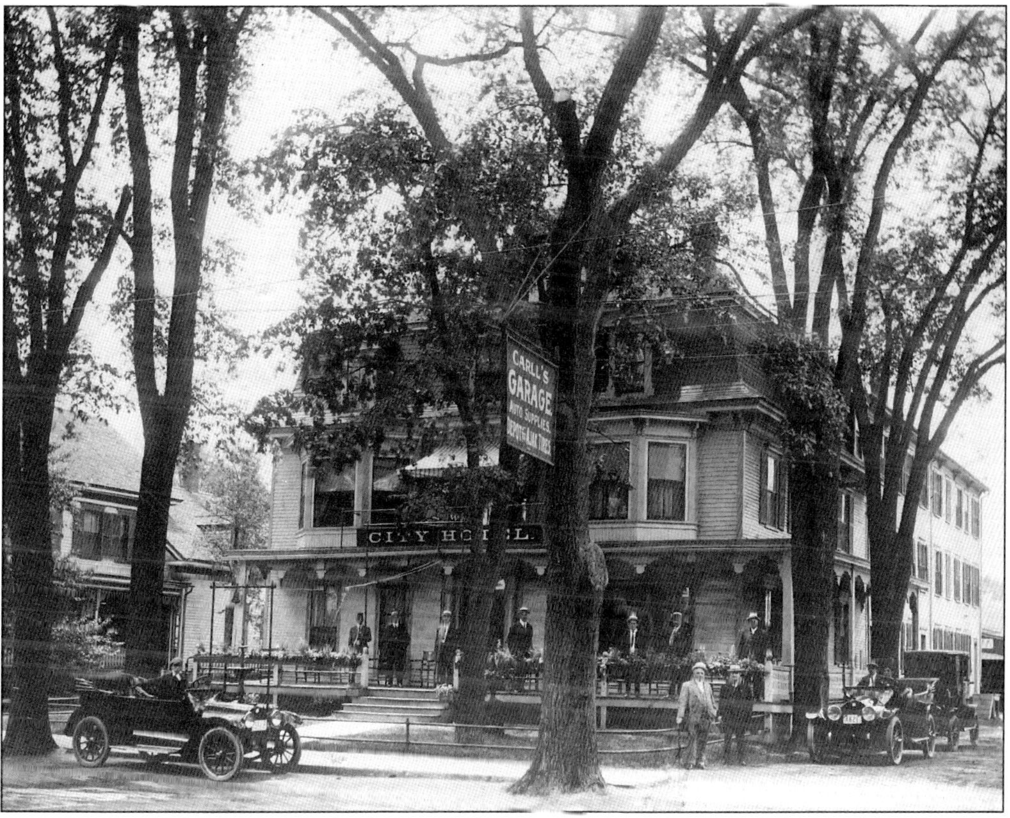

CITY HOTEL. This house was built in 1799 by Captain Samuel Storer and was sold to Jeremiah Woodman in 1806. Silas Wentworth purchased the Woodman estate in 1867 and turned the house into a hotel named the Mansion House. The hotel at 47 South Main Street had many name changes, but it is probably best remembered as the City Hotel. It was last known as the Hotel Hampshire when it closed and was razed in 1964.

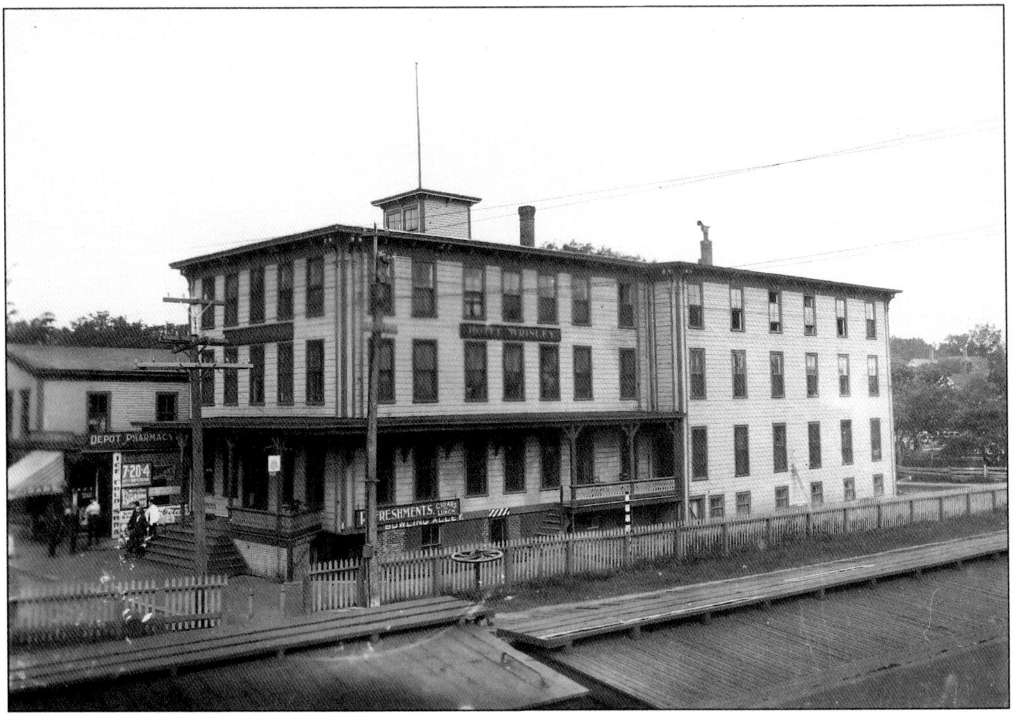

HOTEL WRISLEY. Mrs. Levi Roberts, a widow, opened this forty-four-bedroom hotel near the railroad station on December 5, 1881. After three years she sold the hotel to Bueduc & Thurston. Five years later, Thurston sold out to Bueduc.

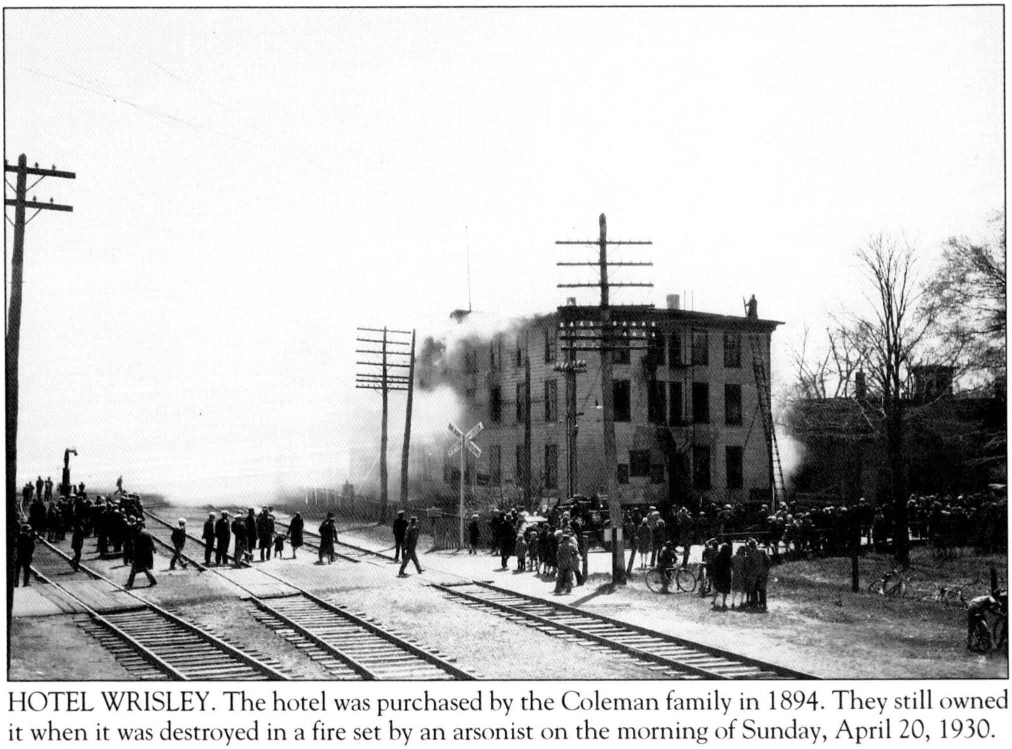

HOTEL WRISLEY. The hotel was purchased by the Coleman family in 1894. They still owned it when it was destroyed in a fire set by an arsonist on the morning of Sunday, April 20, 1930.

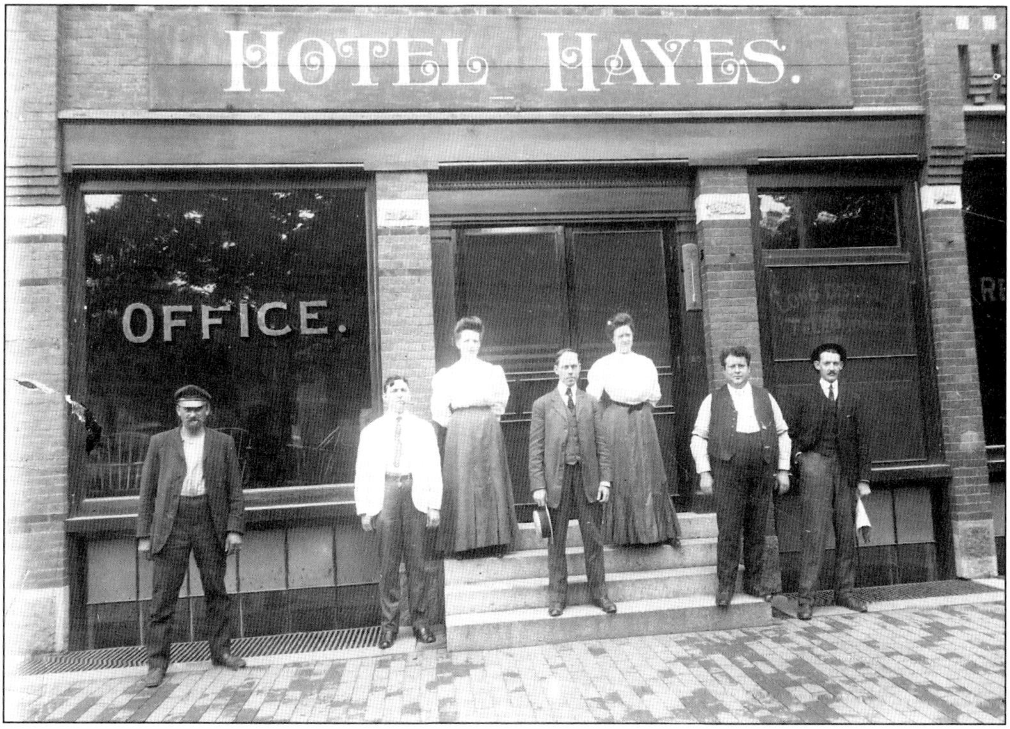

THE HOTEL HAYES. The Hotel Hayes on Portland Street was originally named Cascade House. The proprietor, Albert A. Hayes, later named it for himself. In 1932 it was called Hotel Rochester. It burned in 1972.

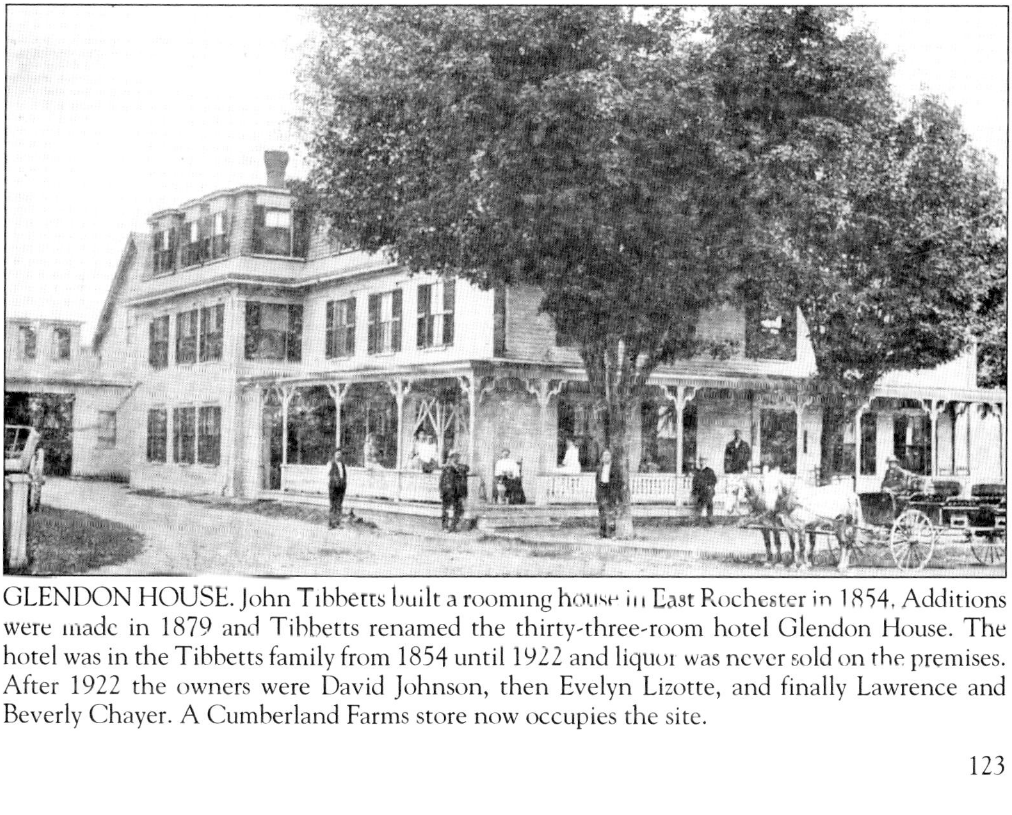

GLENDON HOUSE. John Tibbetts built a rooming house in East Rochester in 1854. Additions were made in 1879 and Tibbetts renamed the thirty-three-room hotel Glendon House. The hotel was in the Tibbetts family from 1854 until 1922 and liquor was never sold on the premises. After 1922 the owners were David Johnson, then Evelyn Lizotte, and finally Lawrence and Beverly Chayer. A Cumberland Farms store now occupies the site.

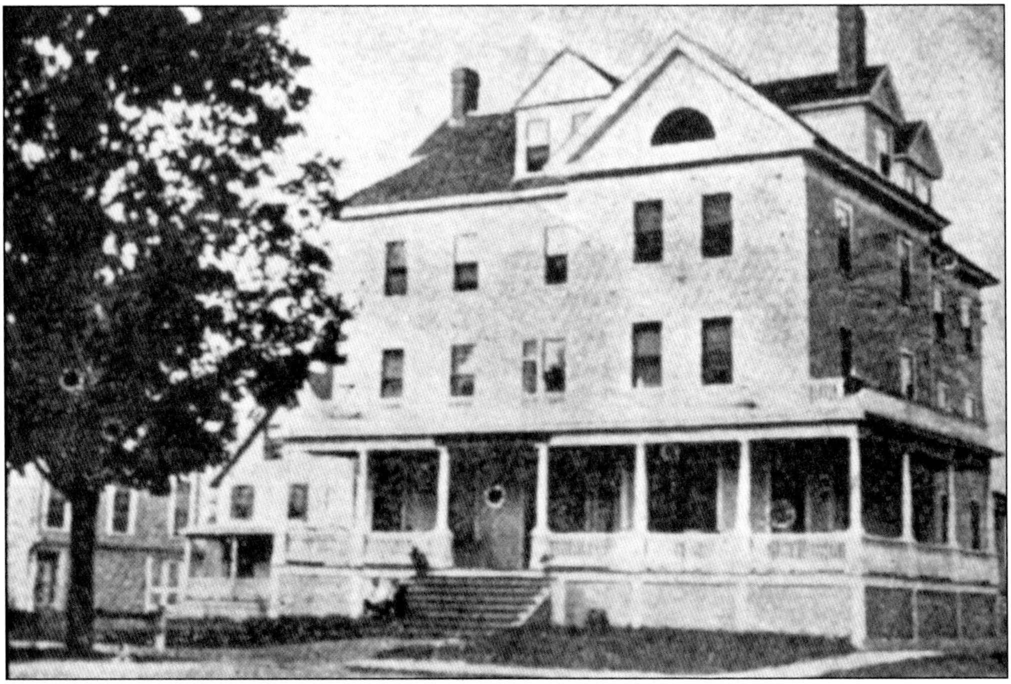

THE BRADFORD INN. This inn in Gonic replaced a smaller rooming house. The proprietors, Charles G. Durgin and Winslow L. Page, had the house moved in 1898 and in October of that year this three-and-a-half-story building was opened for business. In 1905 the sixty-three-room hotel had forty regular boarders in addition to transients.

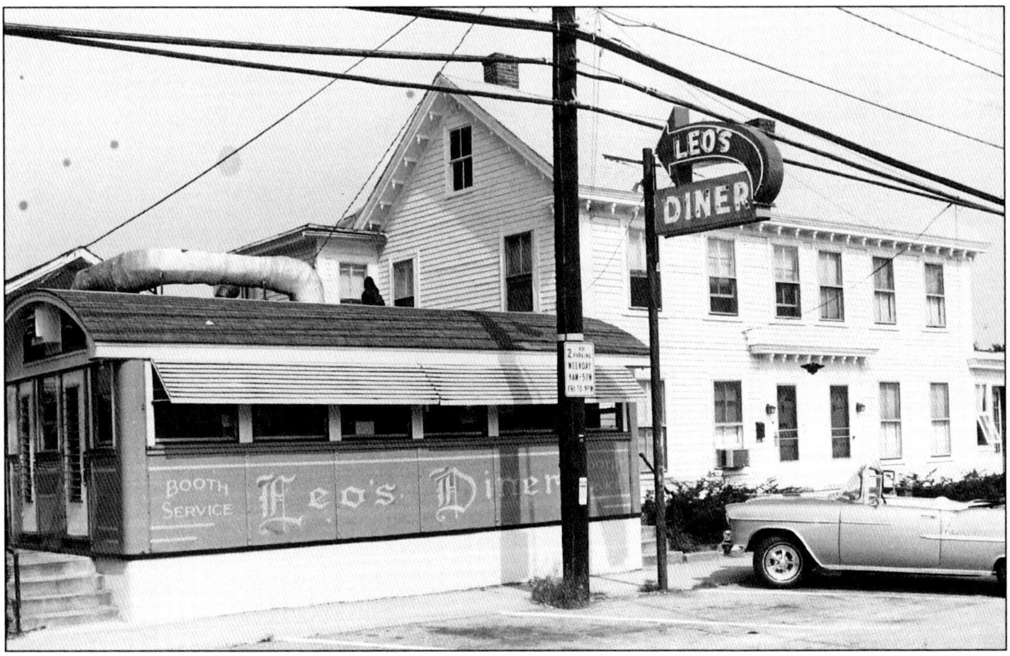

LEO'S DINER. This diner at 114 South Main Street was purchased by Leo and Edith Denault in 1946. In 1965 they sold it to her son, William Clark, and his wife Lorraine. When Clark died in 1985 the popular diner closed. In 1988 it was sold and moved to Salem.

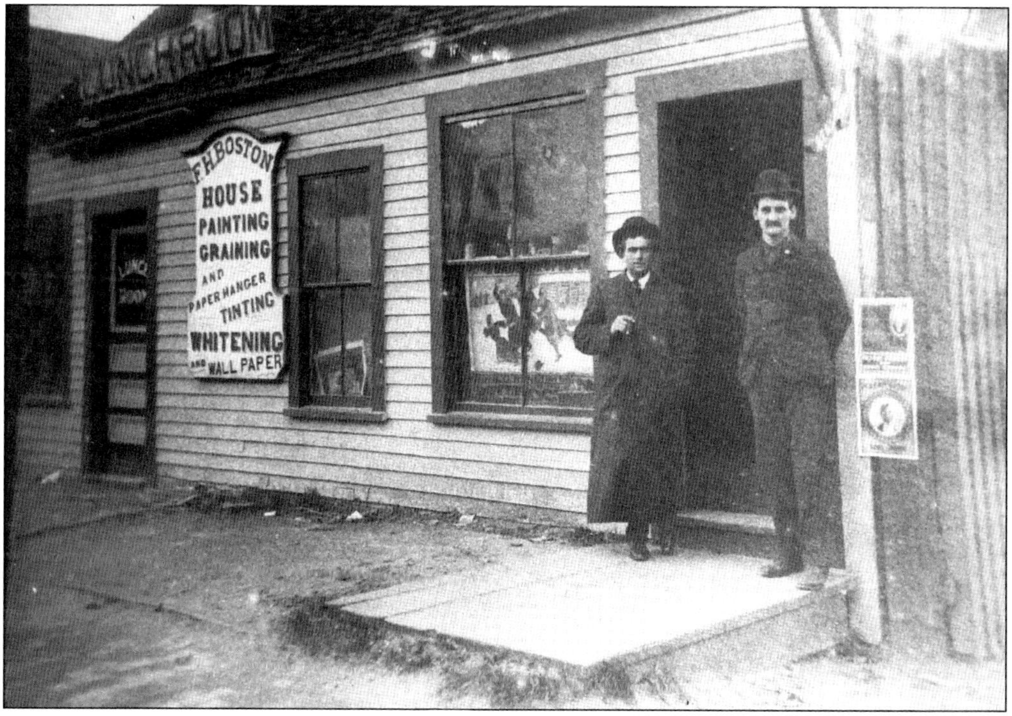

PERREAULT'S LUNCH ROOM. This restaurant at 44 North Main Street was owned by John Perreault in 1910.

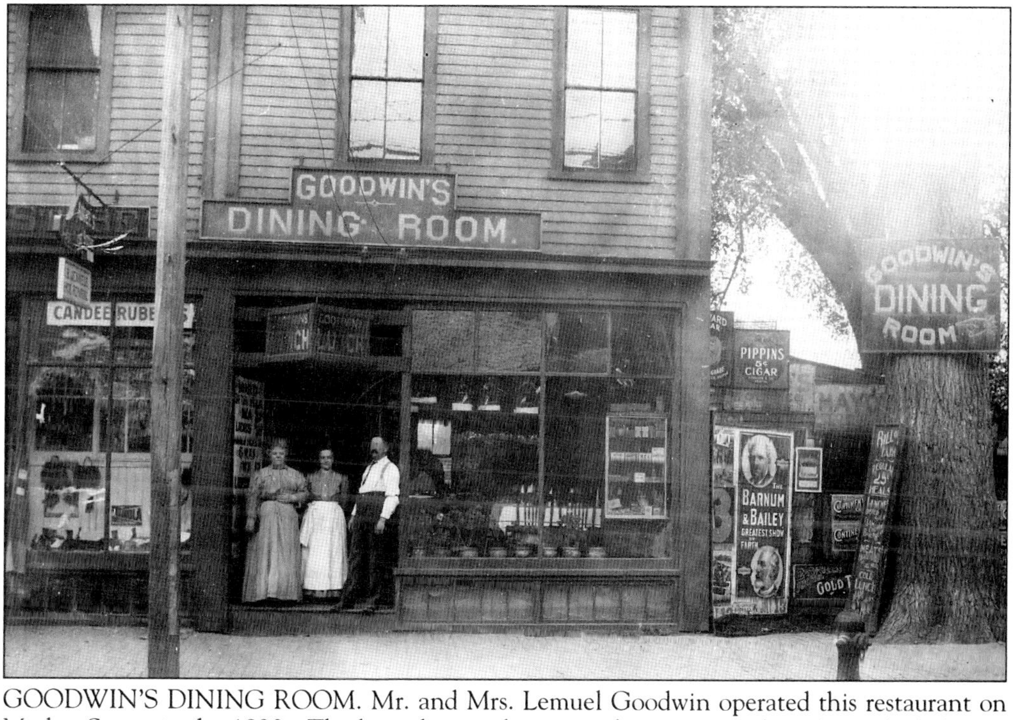

GOODWIN'S DINING ROOM. Mr. and Mrs. Lemuel Goodwin operated this restaurant on Market Street in the 1890s. The busy dining place served approximately 125 people daily and advertised meals for as low as 25¢.

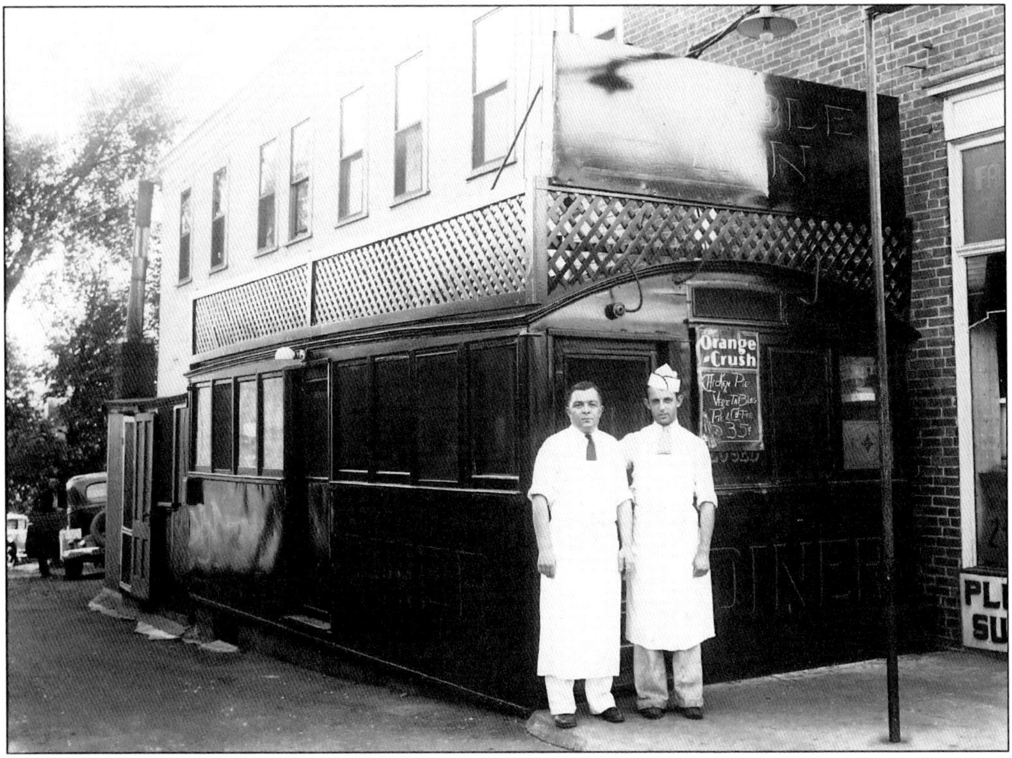

THE TUMBLE INN. This lunch cart was at 36 North Main Street in 1928. Charles Andrews was proprietor and Emilio Gagne was a cook. It was moved when the Snow Block was built in the early 1930s.

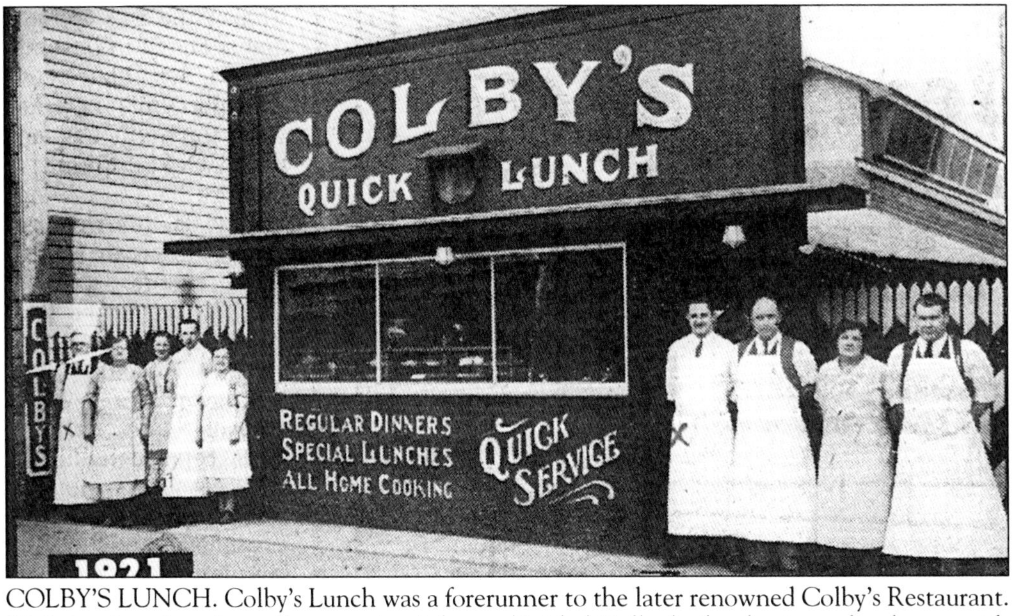

COLBY'S LUNCH. Colby's Lunch was a forerunner to the later renowned Colby's Restaurant. With hard work and excellent service, John and Mabel Colby built a business that began with a popcorn stand.

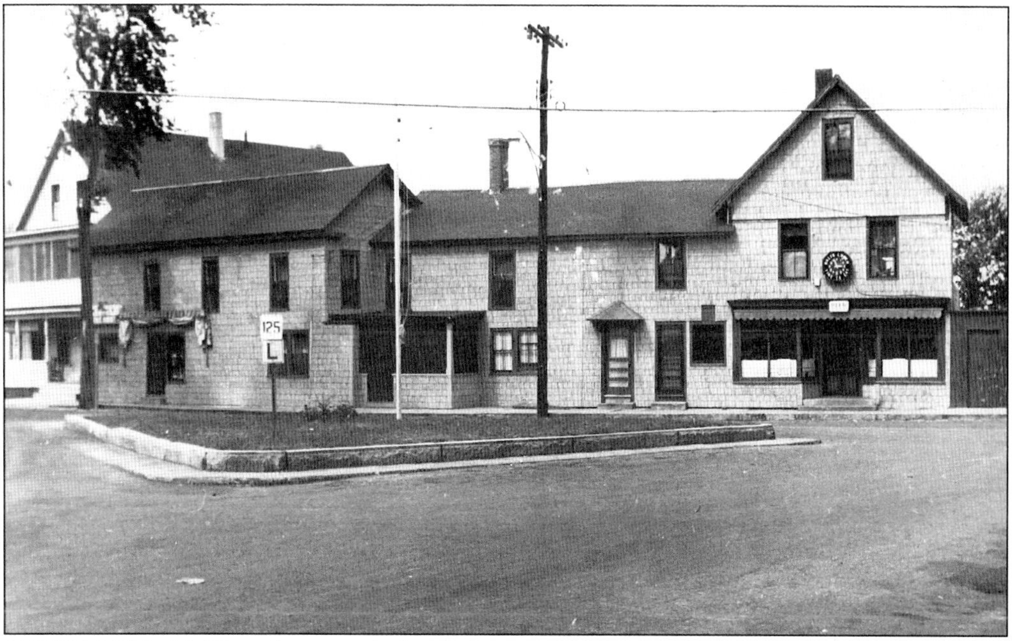

BUZZ'S LUNCH. This photograph shows Gonic Square, *c.* 1941. Roulx Market is on the left and on the right is Buzz's Lunch, owned by Robert and Henrietta Gagnon.

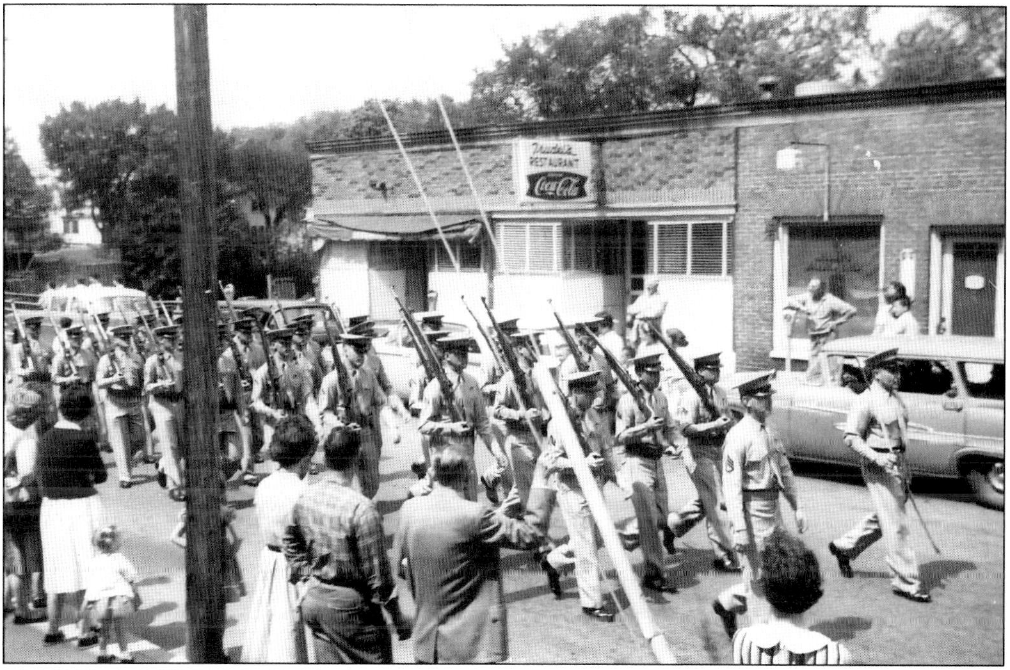

TRUDEL'S RESTAURANT. A parade on May 30, 1964, passes Trudel's Restaurant at 5 Bridge Street. Albert Trudel was proprietor.

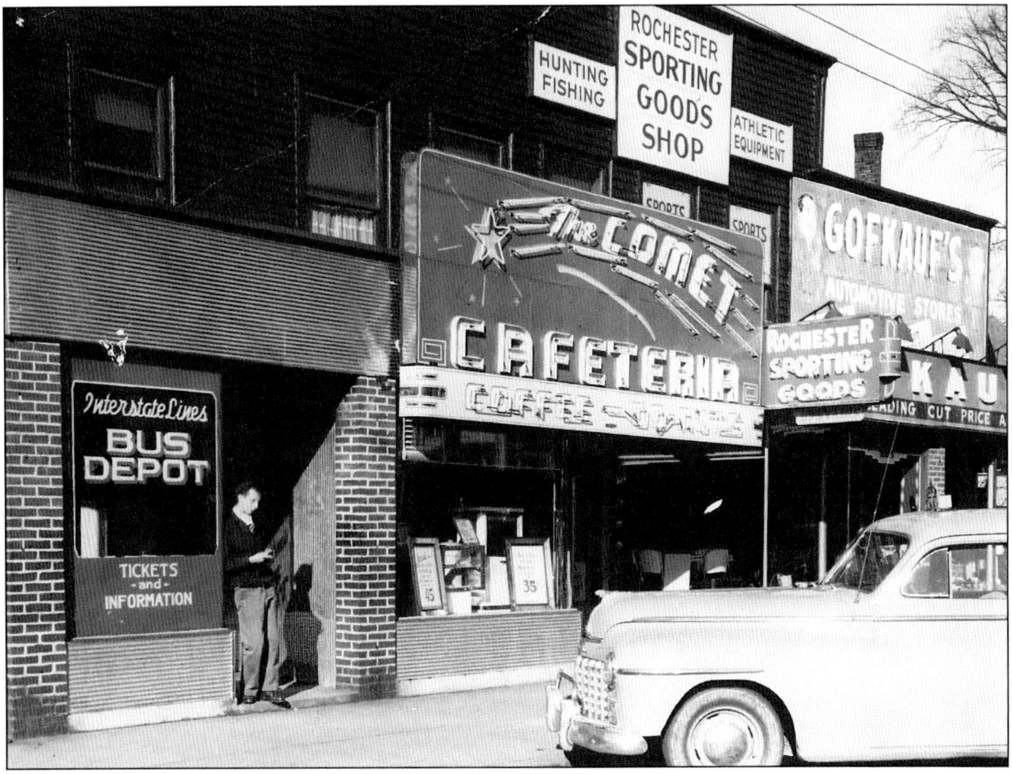

COMET CAFETERIA. The Comet Cafeteria on Wakefield Street was a popular gathering place in the 1940s and 1950s.

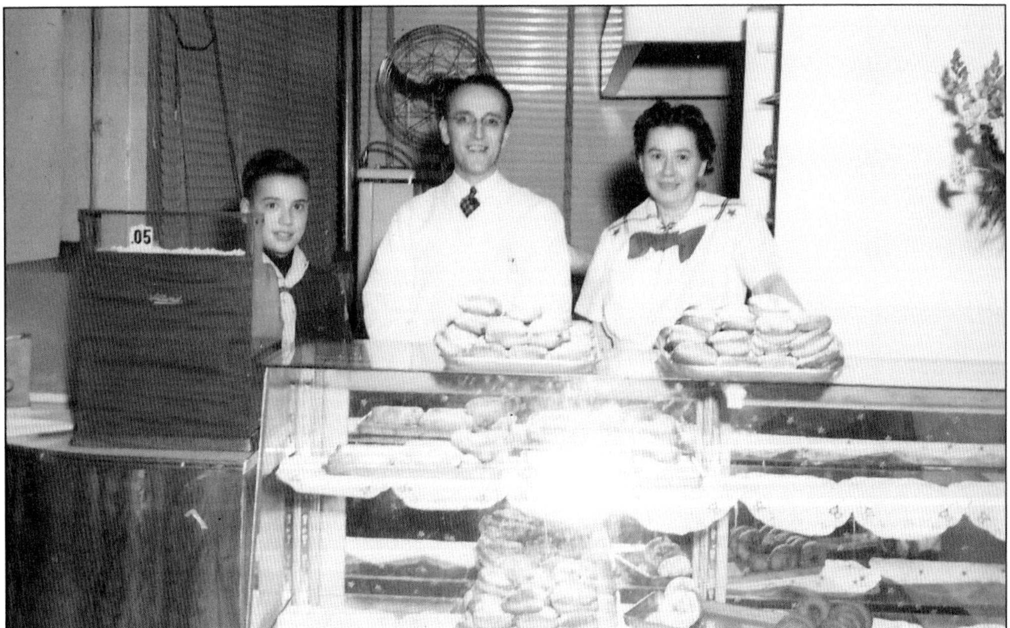

INSIDE THE CAFETERIA. Paul Hamel is shown here with his parents, Victor and Violette Hamel, the proprietors of the Comet Cafeteria.